The Psych 101 Series

James C. Kaufman, PhD, Series Editor
Director, Learning Research Institute
California State University at San Bernardino

Alan S. Kaufman, PhD, is Clinical Professor of Psychology at the Yale University School of Medicine, Child Study Center. Kaufman earned an AB degree from the University of Pennsylvania in 1965; an MA in Educational Psychology from Columbia University in 1967; and a PhD from Columbia University in 1970 (under Robert L. Thorndike in Psychology: Measurement, Research, and Evaluation). While Assistant Director at The Psychological Corporation from 1968 to 1974, Kaufman worked closely with David Wechsler on the revision of the Wechsler Intelligence Scale for Children (WISC) and supervised the standardization of the revised version—the WISC-R. He also collaborated with Dorothea McCarthy in the development and standardization of the McCarthy Scales of Children's Abilities. From the mid-1970s to the present, Kaufman has held several university positions prior to his current professorship at Yale, most notably at the University of Georgia (1974–1979) and the University of Alabama (1984–1995). Kaufman's texts, including *Intelligent Testing With the WISC-R* (1979), *Assessing Adolescent and Adult Intelligence* (1990), and *Intelligent Testing With the WISC-III* (1994), have been widely used for the interpretation of Wechsler's scales for children, adolescents, and adults. In 2009 he coauthored *Essentials of WAIS-IV Assessment* (with Liz Lichtenberger) and the second edition of *Essentials of WISC-IV Assessment* (with Dawn Flanagan). Kaufman's tests, developed with his wife Nadeen—most notably the 1983 Kaufman Assessment Battery for Children (K-ABC) and its 2004 revision (KABC-II)—have been widely used throughout the world to measure children's intelligence. Kaufman is a Fellow of four divisions of the American Psychological Association (APA) and of the Association for Psychological Science (APS) and is a recipient of the Mensa Education and Research Foundation Award for Excellence (1989) and the Mid-South Educational Research Association Outstanding Research Award (1988 and 1993). In 1997, he received the APA's prestigious Senior Scientist Award from Division 16 (School Psychology), and in 2005 he delivered the Legends in School Psychology Annual Address to the National Association of School Psychologists (NASP).

IQ Testing 101

Alan S. Kaufman, PhD

SPRINGER PUBLISHING COMPANY

Springer Publishing Company, LLC
11 West 42nd Street
New York, NY 10036
www.springerpub.com

Acquisitions Editor: Philip Laughlin
Project Manager: Mark Frazier
Cover design: Mimi Flow
Composition: Apex CoVantage, LLC

Ebook ISBN: 978-0-8261-2236-0

09 10 11 / 5 4 3 2 1

Library of Congress Cataloging-in-Publication Data

Kaufman, Alan S., 1944–
IQ testing 101 / Alan S. Kaufman.
p. cm.
Includes bibliographical references and index.
ISBN 978-0-8261-0629-2 (alk. paper)
1. Intelligence tests. I. Title. II. Title: IQ testing one hundred one.
III. Title: IQ testing one hundred and one.
BF431.K387 2009
153.9'3—dc22 2009014901

Printed in the United States of America by Hamilton Printing

To James Corey Kaufman
A bright, shining light as a child
Who has grown into a remarkable Renaissance Man

He is a gifted playwright, professor, researcher, author,
and mentor

He not only possesses enormous creativity,
but his ongoing innovative research on creativity has
revolutionized the field

He is my colleague and best friend, and, to me,
he will always be
Jamie

Contents

Acknowledgments

I am extremely grateful to three psychologists, Dr. Ron Dumont, Dr. Darielle Greenberg, and Dr. John Willis, who read an earlier draft of the entire manuscript and who made dynamic contributions to *IQ Testing 101* with their incisive edits, their suggestions, their corrections, and their challenging questions. Their contributions were exceptional and highly valued, as was that of Dr. Linda Silverman, who provided historical insights into Guilford's theory and read carefully the sections on intelligence theories. I am also thankful to Ms. Cynthia Driscoll, an attorney with a specialty in lead litigation, for her helpful comments on the section about the effects of blood lead on children's IQs.

An enormous debt of gratitude is due to Pearson Assessments—especially to Mr. William Schryver, Dr. Larry Weiss, Dr. Mark Daniel, Dr. Susan Raiford, Dr. Aurelio Prifitera, and Dr. Carol Watson—for allowing me to include figures, numerous illustrative test items, and quotations from a variety of tests and products that they publish. The sample items helped bring to life the nature of the tasks that compose the individually administered clinical IQ tests designed for children and adults. The quotations contributed greatly to the portion of chapter 9 devoted to the assessment of specific learning disabilities. All Flanagan, Kaufman, Kaufman, and Lichtenberger (2008) quotations that appear in chapter 9 are from a videotaped training program devoted to the "Best Practices" for identifying children with SLD: *Agora: The Marketplace of Ideas. Best Practices: Applying Response to Intervention (RTI) and Comprehensive Assessment for the Identification of Specific Learning Disabilities* [DVD]. Copyright © 2008 by NCS Pearson, Inc. Reproduced with permission. All rights reserved.

Dr. Daniel also kindly provided me with data from the KABC-II to permit comparison of IQs earned by children on different tests and on separate scales within a test. I am also thankful to Dr. Emily Krohn and Dr. Robert Lamp for allowing me access to their data on young children tested twice on two different IQ tests to help demonstrate that IQs differ across tests and across time. I am grateful to John Wiley & Sons for giving me permission to include figures and quotations from various of their publications (I am especially grateful to Ms. Peggy Alexander of John Wiley & Sons), and to Drs. Dawn Flanagan, Jack Naglieri, and John Willis for providing me with slides of their figures. And I gratefully acknowledge the Publications Department of the National Association of School Psychologists (NASP) for allowing me to liberally use and adapt quotes from articles, based on my invited Legends of School Psychology address, that appeared in the *NASP Communiqué* in 2005 (I am especially grateful to Mr. Chris Goode and Dr. John Desrochers of the Publications Department). I am also thankful to Consulting Measurement Group, Inc., especially to Dr. Jason Cole and Ms. Jessica Lee of that organization, for developing many of the figures that appear in this book.

I would like to thank Philip Laughlin of Springer Publishing for inviting me to write this book, for giving me feedback on the manuscript, and for his unflagging support every step of the way to its publication.

Finally, I want to thank my family for their love and support throughout this project, and for their contributions to the content of the book (many of my family members are psychologists)—my wife and scholarly colleague, Dr. Nadeen L. Kaufman (the love of my life ever since we were teenagers); my children, Dr. Jennie L. Singer (a clinical psychologist and professor of criminal justice) and Dr. James C. Kaufman (to whom I am also grateful for inviting me to write a book for the Psychology 101 series that he edits, and for his valuable insights and assistance with this project); and my adult granddaughters, Ms. Nicole Hendrix and Ms. Catherine Singleton.

1

Why Would Anyone Want to Read a Book About IQ Testing?

It will be less painful if I just come right out and admit it: I develop IQ tests. I've been doing it for over 30 years and I even have a partner in crime—my wife, Nadeen. We have been successful. Our Kaufman Assessment Battery for Children or K-ABC (Kaufman & Kaufman, 1983) and its revision, the KABC-II (Kaufman & Kaufman, 2004a) have been translated into many languages and are used in schools and clinics around the world. We've also had glitches. Our Kaufman Adolescent and Adult Intelligence Test (KAIT; Kaufman & Kaufman, 1993), sadly, has been all but ignored in the United States. But neither success nor failure makes it easier telling people what we do.

When someone asks us about our jobs, we try to get away with a terse "psychologist" or "psychology professor," but most want more information (probably because they're afraid we've already begun to psychoanalyze them). Sometimes we have the courage to say, "We write IQ tests," and just gear up for the range of emotions that awaits us—anything from curiosity to admiration to disgust. We'd like to answer the "What do you do for a living" question with the smug confidence of Faye Dunaway in the 1967 movie classic *Bonnie and Clyde* when she announces, "We rob banks," but our words always come out as a timid apology.

Try not to hold my job against me and try to refrain from the knee-jerk response that IQ tests are unfair, maybe even dangerous, and require the label: WARNING—MAY BE HAZARDOUS TO YOUR CHILD'S HEALTH!! That's myth, not reality. IQ tests had a difficult birth in England and France more than a century ago, had an accelerated childhood in the United States during World War I, and have experienced the turmoil of adolescence ever since. But they have improved, and aren't simply one-dimensional villains. Maybe you'd like to put the IQ test in the place where you think it is best suited (and perhaps flush it). You would not be in bad company. In fact, in 1922, in a series of six essays that appeared in the magazine *New Republic,* Walter Lippmann, an influential political commentator and journalist, skewered one of the early incarnations of intelligence testing—the army intelligence tests (Block & Dworkin, 1976).

But before you adopt the extremist position that IQ tests can do no good, first learn about these tests and the mysterious IQs they yield, and then make an informed decision. You may still think the world can easily do without them, but you may come away with more insight about your own intelligence and what's likely to happen to your mental abilities as you approach old age. At the least, you'll have a better idea why some people think the tests are of little or no value; or maybe you'll even start to like them, warts and all, and reach a grudging acceptance of how they can actually benefit society. I hope so. That is one of the reasons why I wrote this book.

But it's not the only reason. IQ is a prevalent concept within society and is part of the vernacular of professionals and laypersons alike. U.S. culture is steeped in the IQ tradition, and one is apt to hear the question "What's your IQ?" when overhearing the casual conversation of adolescents or adults or simply watching a TV sitcom. IQ is often used to mean nothing more than "background knowledge," as in magazine quizzes intended to test your "Professional Football IQ" or "Classic Movies IQ."

"I FOUND OUT MY IQ"

"My IQ's 144; what's yours?" someone might ask. "I saw it on my transcript." "Just 121," you reply, trying to hide your blend of embarrassment and envy. And fury that you could possibly be dumber than the cabbagehead with proof positive that she's smarter than you.

Though people often criticize IQ tests, and may call them biased or invalid, the IQ test still possesses an aura of mystery and fear when it comes to your own IQ. "I peeked at my school record," or "I overheard my mom and dad talking when they thought I was sleeping," or "My therapist told me," or "I saw it on the vocational counselor's desk when she looked away," or "I just took an IQ test on the Internet." There's always some secrecy involved, and a little ingenuity on the part of those who desperately want affirmation of what they already know (that they're brilliant). And there's the accompanying panic that they will score lower than anyone in the history of the world.

Some people believe in the magical IQ, the single number that sums up a person's mental ability, a number that is imprinted perhaps somewhere inside the skull or in a cranial crease, immutable and eternal. Well, it's a crock, a common misconception. There's no such thing as a person's IQ. It varies. Change the IQ test and you change the IQ. Change the examiner, the day of the test, the person's mood, or the examiner's alertness, and you change the IQ. Test the person 12 times and you might get a dozen different IQs.

Much of the lore around IQ and the tests that measure IQ is steeped in misconceptions or half-truths. Some people have a stimulus-response reaction ("IQ tests? They're biased."), but most have no real conception of what an IQ test looks like or what it measures. A simple aim of this book, on a nuts-and-bolts level, is to present a commonsense approach to what IQ is and what it is not, and to the nature of IQ tests. A deeper goal is to clear up misconceptions about IQ and IQ tests and to educate readers about this controversial topic that belongs not just to psychologists or educators but to all of society. The bottom line? To excite readers about a topic that has inspired and thrilled me for more than 40 years, and to offer answers to such real-life questions as "Do we get smarter or dumber as we get older?" "Is IQ genetic?" "What is a learning disability?" and "Will a little bit of lead in our preschool children's blood lower their IQs forever (and maybe turn them into delinquents)?"

INDIVIDUALLY ADMINISTERED VERSUS GROUP-ADMINISTERED IQ TESTS

You've all taken IQ tests, or at least think you have. In school, maybe, or when applying for a job, or some other time you're not quite sure of. You've sat in your chair next to dozens of others taking the same test. You've stared at the string of inane multiple-choice items, most ending with "All of the Above" or "None of the Above" or even "A and C, but not B." The most dreaded items always include one answer you absolutely know is right. But just before you blacken in the box for Response A, you notice that the next-to-last choice is tempting ("Both A and C are correct"), while the last choice instantly moistens your armpits ("A is always correct, B is sometimes correct, and C is partially correct during tornadoes or earthquakes").

Most people think of IQ tests as multiple-choice affairs that require as much skill as Pin the Tail on the Donkey. They're not.

Some IQ tests are given to groups and are composed of questions with four or five choices, but these are not the IQ tests that are used for the clinical evaluation of children, adolescents, or adults who are referred for diverse reasons, such as possible brain damage, emotional disturbance, giftedness, or learning disabilities. Neither are the kinds of IQ tests you can take on your computer, by clicking on a Web site that promises to present you with your IQ in a matter of minutes. (Those IQ tests are practically worthless in every way, which will become evident as you read the next few chapters.)

Wechsler's tests (such as the WISC and WAIS), the Stanford-Binet, the Kaufman tests, and the Woodcock-Johnson tests (all discussed in the chapters that follow) are *individual* tests, administered one-on-one by an expert in clinical assessment. These are the kinds of IQ tests that form the focus of this book. The particular IQ tests just listed, and a handful of others, are the tests that are used to help make real-life decisions: Is an elderly man competent to manage his own affairs? Does a 9-year-old girl have a specific learning disability? Is a nurse who poisoned 20 patients mentally ill, brain damaged, or at least a little quirky? Is Daryl Atkins, a convicted murderer, smart enough to be executed for his crime?

I'm not finding fault with group IQ tests. It's simply that group IQ tests, the kind most of us are familiar with, are quite different from individual IQ tests. Even people who have heard of Wechsler's tests have a preconception that they are paper-and-pencil tests, and I want to break that association. Try to start thinking of IQ tests as personal experiences, where the examiner has met you and calls you by name, not as a no-win encounter between you and a computer-scored answer sheet. In fact, most individual IQ tests require little, if any, reading and writing.

I've seen misconceptions in unlikely places, such as the *Sporting News,* that jokingly proposed to settle an IQ dispute between a basketball coach and a player by having the two men "placed in glass-enclosed booths and scribble furiously as they plow through the Wechsler Adult Intelligence Scale" ("Keeping Score," 1988).

What are individual tests of intelligence *really* like? What kinds of open-ended questions are included in the verbal and nonverbal portions of IQ tests? If you let your imagination and anxiety run wild, you might conjure up the following kinds of "IQ" items:

Verbal Intelligence

- Describe the history of the Papacy from its origins to the present day, concentrating especially (but not exclusively) on its social, political, economic, religious, and philosophical impact on civilization. Be brief, concise, and specific.
- Take a position for or against truth. Prove the validity of your position.
- Develop a realistic plan for refinancing the national debt. Trace the possible effects of your plan in the following areas: cubism, the Donatist controversy, the 1969 World Series, and the wave theory of light.

Nonverbal Intelligence

- You have been provided with a razor blade, a piece of gauze, and a bottle of vodka. Remove your appendix. Do not suture until your work has been inspected. You have 20 minutes.
- Write a piano concerto. Orchestrate and perform it with flute and drum. You will find a piano under your seat.
- The disassembled parts of a high-powered rifle are in a box in your desk. In 10 minutes, a hungry Bengal tiger will be admitted to your room. Begin!

But these test questions, which I've borrowed from a highly creative but anonymous source from a generation ago, appear as IQ items only in our nightmares. The open-ended questions in individually administered IQ tests are challenging but not outlandish, as will become clear in the next two chapters, which deal with the history and development of the array of exceptional IQ tests on today's testing scene.

When I first learned to give IQ tests back in 1967 during my clinical training at Columbia University, I was eager to try out this new toy. And it is a toy. The test kits for individually administered clinical IQ tests are filled with concrete, toy-like materials like blocks and pictures and puzzles and verbal games.

So I was eager to play with my new toy. I administered the IQ tests to more children and adults than I was required to, because my neighbors in Baldwin, New York, seemed so interested in what I was doing and I was caught up in the power I felt when I walked into someone's home holding my Wechsler Intelligence Scale for Children (WISC) kit in its maroon carrying case. One Saturday morning, I spent nearly two hours testing Tommy, an athletic child of about 8. When we were done, we walked upstairs from the basement of his house. My mind was somewhere in space, as I was planning my afternoon's work of scoring Tommy's test protocol, obtaining his IQs, and preparing the feedback conference that I had promised each neighbor.

Tommy's parents greeted me at the top of the stairs, looking visibly shaken, perhaps grief-stricken. Neither parent was able to speak, and Tommy's mother seemed to be fighting back tears, when she was finally able to blurt out: "We can't take the suspense any longer. Will he get into Harvard or not?!?" Well, no IQ tests are *that* valid.

VALIDITY AND RELIABILITY OF IQ TESTS

IQ tests predict pretty well, but not with pinpoint accuracy, not in isolation, and not 10 years down the road. And IQ tests sometimes yield high scores for people who act dumb; no one denies that. *The Book of Lists #3* (Wallace, Wallechinsky, & Wallace, 1983, p. 409) tells us that a 29-year-old Florida woman named Tina had an IQ of 189. She became obsessed that she was dying from stomach cancer, the illness that had killed her mother, and vowed to cleanse her body. Her method: eating no food for days at a time, but drinking as much as four gallons of water a day. The result: Tina actually drowned herself from the inside out, overwhelming her kidneys and lungs with fluid. Not too bright for a genius.

IQ tests make mistakes, but they have been shown to be valid for over a century. They correlate substantially with children's achievement in school (Naglieri & Bornstein, 2003), and they have "high validity predicting performance ratings and training success in all jobs" (Hunter, 1986, p. 359), especially complex jobs such as those of managers, clerks, and salespersons (Ghiselli, 1966, 1973). IQs are much higher, on average, for highly educated adults than for those with only a few years of formal schooling, and that is true whether one is evaluating language ability (related to schooling) or the ability to solve novel problems that are not taught in school (see chapter 4).

But, rather like the best opinion polls, IQ tests (even the most accurate and reliable tests) contain errors of measurement, and different tests yield different IQs for the same person; so do different examiners; and so do different IQ scales within the same test. I cover all of these issues in chapter 5 ("The IQ Construct, Part 2: How Accurate Are IQ Tests?"). In that chapter, I let you in on some trade secrets to make sure that you abandon, once and for all, the idea that a person has a single IQ. Actually, I take the risk in chapter 5 that maybe you'll stop reading the book and toss it in the waste basket because the darned IQ is too wishy-washy to be anything but worthless.

It's not. But I can't try to package the IQ as a magical elixir and disguise it as an unblemished tool used by pure scientists in a sterile laboratory. It's not that either. In chapter 2 on the history of IQ tests, the answer to the question posed in the title ("Who Invented the IQ Test?") is a Frenchman by the name of Alfred Binet. But he did more than invent the first IQ test. He taught us that to measure something as complex as human intelligence, you must be able to live with a margin of error. If Binet was able to accept error when he invented the test, then I think we ought to be able to tolerate imperfection more than a century later, when IQ tests have been improved and refined beyond Binet's imagination (chapter 3). I'm hoping you will agree.

IQ TESTS AND CONTROVERSY

I have been on the firing line of IQ controversy since 1968 when I worked for the test publisher that created the leading IQ tests in the world—Wechsler's tests. I worked directly with Dr. David Wechsler in the early 1970s, helping him develop the revision of the Wechsler Intelligence Scale for Children—the WISC-R (Wechsler, 1974). My book, *Intelligent Testing With the WISC-R* (Kaufman, 1979b), presented a psychometric and clinical method of profile analysis that "had a profound effect on intelligence test interpretation" (Kamphaus, Winsor, Rowe, & Kim, 2005, p. 28). I knew the title would be misspelled in most reference lists as "intelligence testing" (the title was misspelled in my contract with the book publisher, John Wiley & Sons). But I loved the term *intelligent testing*—which was coined by one of my mentors, Alexander Wesman (1968)—because in my experiences as test developer, researcher, and trainer of school and clinical psychologists, I had seen so much *stupid* testing. In fact, the interpretive approach that I termed the intelligent testing philosophy has been the source of past and current controversy by critics who don't think it's so smart at all (e.g., McDermott, Fantuzzo, Glutting, Watkins, & Baggaley, 1992; Watkins & Canivez, 2004). So, too, has been the theory-based test that my wife and I developed in 1983, the K-ABC, which took a new perspective on how intelligence should be measured and which greatly reduced IQ differences among ethnic groups. Approaches that deviate from the traditional produce emotional responses, and I have always had one foot firmly planted in the hotbed of controversy (see Miller & Reynolds, 1984, for the full flavor of the emotional controversies surrounding the K-ABC).

Even now, apart from my role as IQ test developer, I am in the midst of IQ controversies. I have published articles during the last half-dozen years that have been frankly critical of the research studies that have implicated low blood lead level and other toxins as the cause of serious neuropsychiatric deficits, much to the anger of the researchers who have used their findings to change public policy and to generate huge amounts of federal funding (Cicchetti, Kaufman, & Sparrow, 2004a, 2004b; Kaufman, 2001a, 2001b). I have also published articles on the provocative new legislation ("IDEA 2004") on revised guidelines for learning disabilities assessment and have incurred the wrath of those who insist that we should "Just say no" to the use of IQ tests for identifying and diagnosing children with learning disabilities (Hale, Naglieri, Kaufman, & Kavale, 2004; Kavale, Kaufman, Naglieri, & Hale, 2005).

I don't mind being at the center of these controversies. Actually, I must admit that I rather enjoy it. I believe in the value of IQ tests if they are used appropriately and are intended to help children and adults. I am aware, however, that many people use and interpret IQ tests stupidly. Stupid testing, for example, occurs when a boy with an IQ of 132 is called *intellectually gifted* and accepted into an accelerated class, while one scoring 127 is left to feel like a loser. Dumb testing is labeling an adolescent girl with an IQ of 64 as having an *intellectual disability*—the same girl who comes home every day after school to prepare dinner for the family and help supervise her eight siblings while Mom and Dad are at work. (Intellectual disability is a new, official, politically correct term for mental retardation. But it's defined the same way, so it doesn't change anything.)

The only ways that I know of to combat the stupidity is to improve the measurement of IQ, challenge traditional approaches, and put myself in the line of fire. That, I believe, is the best way to reach out and effect change. And that is one of the reasons I wrote *IQ Testing 101*. I'd like to reach out to students, professionals, and anyone in society with an interest in IQ and help shape them into intelligent testers (even if figuratively and not literally) who understand what IQ tests are and how they can be used as instruments of help rather than pain.

EXCITING IQ RESEARCH

But it is not only controversies that are at the root of *IQ Testing 101*. I also want to share the results of the exciting research on aging and IQ that I have been conducting for the past 20 years with my colleagues (Kaufman, 2001c; Kaufman, Reynolds, & McLean, 1989), including the fascinating study recently published on the growth and decline in reading, writing, math, and IQ from young adulthood to old age (Kaufman, Johnson, & Liu, 2008). And I want readers to understand the *Flynn Effect*, the notion that our American society gets smarter at the constant rate of 3 IQ points per decade (Flynn, 1987, 2007)—an optimistic-sounding result until one realizes that the United States trails nearly all other developed nations in IQ gain. This array of studies tells us where we are heading, as individuals who are aging and as a society. When buttressed with the chapters on the history of IQ testing and the meaning of IQ, the several chapters on current IQ controversies, and a final chapter on where I believe the field of IQ testing is heading, this book presents snapshots of the past, present, and future of the fascinating field of IQ testing.

THERE'S REALLY NO SUCH THING AS IQ TESTING

I need to end this introduction with a small disclaimer. This book is called *IQ Testing 101* and I will be using the term *IQ testing* from start to finish. But there is really no longer an IQ, much less an IQ test. IQs are, literally, Intelligence Quotients, but the so-called IQ tests haven't yielded actual quotients for a few generations, as discussed in more detail in chapter 4.

Originally, IQ was thought of as a ratio of Mental Age (MA) divided by Chronological Age (CA) and multiplied by 100. Mental age was the age at which a person was functioning intellectually according to the test. So if a person of any age scores as well as the average child of 8 on an intelligence test, then that person's MA = 8 years. For an 8-year-old, an MA of 8 yields an IQ of 100. At age 6, MA = 8 corresponds to an IQ of 133 (great performance), and at age 16, the IQ of 50 is not so good. The idea was clever, but it didn't work too well, because one year's growth in mental ability or height has very different meanings across the age range—it corresponds to a great deal of growth from age 3 to 4, for example, but not so much from age 16 to 17. And what do you do with adults who are 25 or 40 or 80 years old? The whole notion of the ratio IQ falls apart.

So back in 1939, David Wechsler (more about him later) got rid of the quotient and replaced it with standard scores, a terrific statistic. But he continued to call the overall scores IQs. The Stanford-Binet replaced the traditional quotient with standard scores in 1962, begrudgingly following Wechsler's lead. But like Wechsler (1939), Terman and Merrill (1960) retained the anachronistic term IQ for the Stanford-Binet. Wechsler's (2003, 2008) scales still yield Full Scale IQs, but the Binet gave up the term in its fourth edition, replacing it with the euphemistic Standard Age Score Composite (Thorndike, Hagen, & Sattler, 1986). And a plethora of labels abound for other tests, such as the Mental Processing Composite, General Cognitive Index, General Conceptual Ability, Broad Cognitive Ability Composite, Fluid-Crystallized Index, and on and on.

The IQ as a ratio or quotient is long gone, and the IQ test label should be a thing of the past. Today's tests are referred to as cognitive ability tests, mental processing tests, or tests of multiple cognitive abilities by the professionals who develop the tests and by those who interpret them. But "IQ test" remains in the public's vernacular and is alive and well in the professional community as well. So I will be using the terms IQ and IQ test throughout, even though I know quite well that neither label is technically correct. But they do communicate. And they are much quicker to write and say than "Broad Cognitive Ability Composite" or "standard-score-yielding-multiple-cognitive-abilities test."

THE VALUE OF IQ TEST DEVELOPERS

I'll end this chapter with an anecdote I told a few years ago at an invited address at the National Association of School Psychologists (NASP) convention in Atlanta, a talk that was reprinted in the *NASP Communiqué* (Kaufman, 2005a, 2005b).

When the K-ABC was first published in 1983, there was a lot of media coverage, which made us think that maybe we were important or, at least, doing something important. One morning, just before we had to fly to Philadelphia for a TV interview, we were at the University of California campus in San Diego, about to be interviewed for a Canadian radio show called *Quirks and Quarks*. They had invited three different groups of researchers to be interviewed. The interviewer knew nothing about the research topics, and, just before the program started, asked the first group of researchers what they did. A male professor of astronomy said, "We are physicists and astronomers and we feel that we have come up with a theory that makes the big bang theory obsolete. We think that we truly know how the world got started." The interviewer found that very interesting and asked the next group. A female professor at the UCSD medical school said, "We're working on cancer research and finally, last week, we think we have this breakthrough, a cure for six kinds of cancer." The interviewer was impressed and then looked at us and asked, "What do you two do?" I said in a small whisper, "We write tests." He said, "Sorry, could you speak up?" I said a little louder, "We write IQ tests." His jaw dropped and he said in a too-loud voice, "IQ tests! Why are they important?" And Nadeen and I looked at each other and we said in one voice, "We have no idea." In our field it helps to keep perspective and maintain a sense of humor.[1]

---

1. Copyright 2005 by the National Association of School Psychologists. Bethesda, MD. Adapted with the permission of the publisher. www.nasponline.org

2

History, Part 1: Who Invented the IQ Test?

In June 1763, the whole Mozart family embarked on a grand concert tour of Europe that lasted more than 3 years. While in London, 8-year-old Wolfgang appeared at court before King George III, and had his "IQ" tested by the philosopher Daines Barrington, who gave a report to the Royal Society. Mozart also wrote his first symphonies at age 8 (Gregson, 1989).

IQ TESTS FROM LONG AGO

So even Mozart was referred for evaluation, tested, and perhaps diagnosed as gifted. Or maybe as having a disorder like Tourette's syndrome, as has been hypothesized by Simkin (1992) based on Mozart's tics and frequent obscenities. Mozart even had a case report written about him before case reports were invented. What IQ test was he given? The Barrington-Binet? The Philosopher's Intelligence Scale for Students, Artists, and New Talents (PISS-ANT)? Did Wolfgang's father, Leopold, complain that the test was biased, and accuse Barrington of failing to uncover the boy's true creative potential? Undoubtedly. But, most importantly, intelligence tests were alive and well in the mid-1700s.

China in 2200 BC

Actually, mental tests predate Mozart by about 4,000 years (Dubois, 1970). The emperor of China, around 2200 BC, allegedly gave proficiency tests to his officials every third year, a practice that continued for quite some time. About 1,000 years later, when the Chan dynasty got started, formal ability tests were required for candidates for office—a policy that might have some interesting ramifications if incorporated into the current political scene. There's even a biblical reference to mental examinations (Judges 12:4–6), a one-item test ("Pronounce the word shibboleth") given by the Gileadites to identify the fleeing Ephraimites hiding among them (Wainer, 1990). Dr. Robert Williams, a leading spokesperson against IQ tests in the 1970s, when anti-IQ sentiments were rampant, accused tests of silently mugging the African American community and of committing Black intellectual genocide (Williams, 1974a, 1974b). But never have the results of a test had harsher consequences than the biblical exam. Talk about genocide (or high-stakes testing!): The bodies of the 42,000 who mispronounced the word and flunked the test polluted the Jordan River (Wainer, 1990)!

Modern IQ testing, though, has more recent roots. Proficiency testing had its origin in early China. So did the use of standardized testing procedures—that is, giving the tests under the same controlled conditions each time, and using objective methods of scoring the items. But IQ tests as we know them today, as well as concepts about giftedness and intellectual disabilities or retardation, stem from 19th-century Europe. Fittingly, breakthroughs came from the study of the two IQ extremes, since only a radical would have suggested that "normal" people (you and I) differed in their intelligence.

Early Pioneers From France

France provided the early pioneers, men who worked with individuals with intellectual disabilities. Jean Esquirol (1828, 1838) distinguished between mental retardation (intellectual disabilities) and mental illness, unlumping idiocy from madness (Kaufman, 1983). He began testing "feeble-minded" as well as "demented" people, focusing on their language and speech patterns (a bulls-eye, in terms of current tests) and on physical measurements such as the shape of the skull (a blind alley). He even had crude notions of the mental age concept, declaring that idiots could never acquire the knowledge learned by others of the same age. Esquirol got a bit carried away with his discoveries, though, and gave us more than just the first modern mental test. He also gave examiners of his day the first opportunity for test abuse: a system for labeling individuals with intellectual disabilities. When someone calls you an idiot or an imbecile, think of Esquirol. He formed a retardation hierarchy, with moron at the top. If someone calls you a moron, you might inquire, "high-grade or low-grade?" Or you might get back at your nemesis by calling him an imbecile. But the ultimate insult is to shout "idiot," Esquirol's bottom rung.

When current classification systems use such terms as profound, severe, moderate, or mild mental retardation, they are just using euphemisms for Esquirol's original terms. I despise such systems—I hate seeing IQs used to label, classify, and weed out—but I must admit that moderate mental retardation (or the new, politically correct term, intellectual disability), has a better ring to it than moron. Not that long ago I came upon a case report describing the medical and psychological evaluation of "Charlie," aged 35, institutionalized since age 20, who had been making recent progress. My eyes froze when I read the physician's statement: "Charlie, an imbecile, has been advancing so well that he has a chance to become a low-grade moron." Way to go, Charlie! If you ever improve so much that you learn how to read, and you pick up that doctor's report, you'll become clinically depressed and may need Prozac or Celexa.

Joining Esquirol as an innovator was Edouard Seguin, who, in the mid-1800s, tested individuals with mental retardation (OK, I know I said I would use the new term, intellectual disability, even though I don't understand why it is more politically correct than mental retardation. The old and the new terms sound equally offensive to me. But I'll try to avoid the outdated labels.) Seguin used methods that were nonverbal (as opposed to Esquirol's verbal tests) and oriented toward sensation and motor activity (Kaufman, 1983). Seguin provides an interesting link between the 18th and 20th centuries. He adopted the methods developed by a young French medical student, Jean Marc Gaspard Itard, just before the turn of the 19th century. Itard had some success applying his novel teaching approach to educating Victor, a so-called feral child of about 12, who was found wandering the woods near Saint-Sernin-sur-Rance in 1797 (he was called "the wild boy of Aveyron"). In turn, Seguin (1866/1907) was the inspiration for Maria Montessori. Seguin's form board is still used by some psychologists. And many of his methods and materials live today in Montessori schools everywhere, schools that feature sense education and learning through activity (Montessori, 1912/1964; Orem, 1966).

Both Esquirol and Seguin were influential in changing attitudes toward people with intellectual disability and mental illness, and in reducing the neglect, torture, and ridicule heaped on them. Seguin (1866/1907) was especially optimistic about improving the intelligence of children and adults with intellectual disabilities, and he developed comprehensive treatment programs. Esquirol seemed more content to identify and label those with intellectual disabilities. But both contributed to their more humane treatment, and both had profound impacts on the field of testing. Seguin influenced not only Montessori but future pioneers in testing who stressed nonverbal intelligence and coordination; Esquirol's followers emphasized language tests. Together, their methods are embodied to this day in the most popular intelligence tests used throughout the world, Wechsler's series of scales ranging in age from preschool to elderly adulthood.

England's Contribution: Sir Francis the Great

Seguin's approach was evident in the slightly later work of Sir Francis Galton, half-cousin to Charles Darwin and a man not given to modesty. The multitalented Galton—he earned awards for his explorations of southern Africa, invented instruments for charting the weather, and translated his half-cousin's ideas about evolution into the study of genetics and mental measurements (Cohen & Swerdlik, 1999)—was impressed with his own intellect and that of his relatives. Although he started with the measurement of sweet peas, he switched to people to understand genes and men of genius. The peas were undoubtedly better behaved and without the complexity of people, but he wanted to see whether his pea-inspired statistical discoveries applied to individual differences in humans.

Sir Francis's choice was fortuitous. Forget the genetics. Forget his fascist-like desire to improve the human species through eugenics. He started with a keen interest in genius but became the first scientist to actively study individual differences in the ordinary man, not just in those at the tail ends of the normal curve. He had no toleration for errors in his measurements, perhaps a residue of his work with plants, perhaps part of his desire to make his psychological investigation as pure a science as biology or physics. So he developed mental tests that were a series of objective measurements of such sensory abilities as keenness of sight, color discrimination, and pitch discrimination; sensory-motor abilities such as reaction time and steadiness of hand; and motor abilities, including strength of squeeze and strength of pull (Cohen & Swerdlik, 1999).

That's not intelligence, you say? No, it's not. We've become fairly sophisticated, and we take for granted what took scientists years to discover about mental ability. Galton's (1869, 1883) theory of intelligence was simplistic: People take in information through their senses, so those with better developed senses ought to be more intelligent. His approach was similar to Seguin's with severely low-functioning people, but what worked with the low end of the spectrum just didn't extend to the average or bright. In effect, Galton made a perfect landing at the wrong airport. The trouble is, no one knew it, and his fame and methodology spread far and wide.

IQ Hits America

What began with Galton's own Anthropometric Laboratory at the World's Fair in London in 1884 wound up populating Europe (most notably Wilhelm Wundt's experimental psychology laboratory in Leipzig) and stretching to the United States. James McKeen Cattell, who earned a PhD with Wundt in Germany and worked with Galton ("the greatest man I have known") in England (Roback, 1961), established a Galton-like mental test laboratory in 1890 at the University of Pennsylvania (Cattell, in fact, coined the term *mental test*). Cattell (1890) moved his laboratory to Columbia University in New York City the next year, and IQ testing in the United States was born. Following Galton's approach, Cattell developed 50 tests of sensory capacity, discrimination, and reaction time; his goal was to select superior individuals for responsible positions. Whereas Galton (1869) was obsessed with the role of heredity in intelligence, Cattell (1915) emphasized the vital role played by environmental opportunity (Silverman, 2009).

People came from near and far to pay 3 or 4 pence to be measured at Galton's Anthropometric Laboratory. When the World's Fair ended in 1885, Galton moved his lab to a science museum in South Kensington for 6 years. In all, more than 9,000 people were given Galton's so-called intelligence test, ranging in age from 5 to 80 (Dubois, 1970). To the world, Galton's definition of intelligence was intelligence. The scholarly French voices of Alfred Binet and his colleagues dissented, but no one listened. Galton's tests were scientific, objective, reliable, consistent, accurate, accepted. And, by proclamation and faith, they were valid.

As irony would have it, one of Galton's statistical discoveries became his undoing. He cleverly devised statistics that demonstrated relationships between two variables, forerunners to the coefficient of correlation that was perfected shortly thereafter by his friend and biographer, mathematician Karl Pearson. Now that a statistic was available to show how two things relate, it was possible to validate Galton's tests. Studies conducted around the turn of the century at Cattell's Columbia laboratory and at Titchener's Cornell laboratory (Titchener was Wundt's disciple) showed that Galton's so-called intelligence test was misnamed. American versions of Galton's sensory-motor tests correlated at close to zero with meaningful criteria of intelligence, such as grade-point average in college (Sharp, 1898–1899; Wissler, 1901). Despite the further irony that the research causing Galton's downfall was severely flawed, his tests were through. Finished. He made the world aware of the existence of individual differences, and he developed what was really the first modern intelligence test, but his time in the limelight had run its course.

THE INNOVATIONS OF ALFRED BINET

Even though the Columbia and Cornell research soured people on testing, period, the Frenchman Binet persevered—although his tests, too, were criticized in the Cornell study as unreliable. During the 1890s, Binet began to develop mental tasks with his colleagues Victor Henri and Theodore Simon. Except that his tests were complex, measuring memory, judgment, reasoning, and social comprehension. Unlike the largely nonverbal measures in the Galton-Cattell system, Binet followed Esquirol's lead and focused on language abilities (Binet & Henri, 1895; Binet & Simon, 1905).

To Binet, the concept of measuring something so complex as intellectual ability with simple sensory and motor tests bordered on the absurd. And he made another decision, one that was not too popular with pure scientists: that the measurement of intelligence—unlike the measurement of height, weight, reaction time, or strength of pull—had to include a certain amount of error. This acceptance of some degree of error in the measuring process, taboo to hard-core scientists, may have been Binet's greatest contribution. But give an assist to the great 19th-century English philosopher, John Stuart Mill, whom Binet (1903) considered to be his "only teacher of psychology" (p. 68). Mill (1875) claimed, "The science of human nature . . . falls far short of the standard of exactness now realized in Astronomy" (p. 432). It's too bad that many people today do not understand this basic tenet. These people are found in state departments of education, in university admissions offices, in local school districts identifying gifted students, and in countless other corners of the world. They are well-meaning people who routinely apply simple formulas and rigid IQ cut-off points to make complex decisions, key decisions that affect the futures of children and young adults. They never learned Mill's simple truth, a simple truth that enabled Binet and Simon to publish the first real test of intelligence in 1905.

The road to publication was not easy. Binet and his colleagues developed task after task that measured high-level thinking, starting about 1890, but to no avail. Binet even started a journal in 1895, *L'Année Psychologique,* in order to have his own forum. But aside from Herman Ebbinghaus and a few other German scholars who embraced some of Binet's views, the world remained enamored with Galton. Not until the minister of public instruction in Paris beckoned in 1904 did Binet get a chance to show that his tests were valid. The minister wanted to separate so-called retarded (intellectually disabled) children from normal children in the public schools. The new Binet-Simon scale—published only a year later and seemingly assembled in record time—did just that (Sattler, 2008). But the speed at which the test was developed was illusory. Binet and his colleagues had developed about 15 years worth of tasks that were gathering dust while waiting in the wings. Also, the goals of the minister, and even of Binet, were not noble. They were interested in weeding out the intellectually disabled so the normal student would not be slowed down; they had no special plan or program for those who flunked the Binet-Simon scale. But the minister solved his practical problems, and Binet finally found a publisher for his long-ignored series of mental tasks.

Binet sequenced tasks from easy to hard within the scale (a new approach) and had items such as taking candy out of a paper wrapper; comparing the length of two lines; defining the words *house* and *fork;* repeating from memory a 15-word sentence; constructing a sentence that uses the words *Paris, gutter,* and *fortune;* and distinguishing between abstract words such as *sad* and *bored.* He soon revised his test in 1908 and again in 1911, insightfully organizing the tasks into age level groupings (the 5-year-old tasks, for example, were the ones passed by about 60% to 90% of children at age 5). Binet and Simon also added levels geared to adults, introduced the concept of mental age, and provided more objective scoring rules (Sattler, 2008). The mental age concept allowed the test results to be converted to a meaningful score. If someone passed the 9-year-level tasks but failed the ones at the 10-year level, then that person had the intelligence of the typical 9-year-old—whether the person was 6, 9, or 30.

Binet had finally made it, as evidenced by the most sincere sort of flattery: imitation. Countries throughout the world began to develop and use Binet tests. Binet, personally, felt like a failure. His quest was to be given an elite professorship, but he lost out at both the Sorbonne and the Collège de France. His interests were scattered, ranging from hypnosis to somnambulism to palmistry to test development, preventing his creation of a "final work." He died in 1911, in his early 50s, just when his test was about to receive worldwide acclaim. He never realized his impact (Ellenberger, 1970).

But Alfred Binet is the answer to the question posed by the present chapter's title. He invented the intelligence test. Never mind that the critical columnist Walter Lippmann called Binet's tests "stunts" (Block & Dworkin, 1976). Forget the irony that though adaptations of his tests were popular worldwide, they were not used extensively in his native France until the early 1940s—and only then when a French social worker, who had spent much time in the United States, helped bring the *American* version of the Binet to France (Miller, 1962). No matter. Alfred Binet was the inventor of IQ tests.

Was his test really the first? No, that distinction could be claimed by an unknown Chinese emperor, by Esquirol, by Galton, undoubtedly by others. Binet's test was the first IQ test as we know it today. Many of his original tasks and test items are still included in contemporary intelligence tests, and will be administered, whether by computer or by psychologist, for decades to come. Every IQ test in existence has been impacted greatly by Binet's work and incorporates many of the same kinds of concepts and test questions that Binet came up with in the late 1800s.

Does he deserve to be credited with the discovery of IQ tests when others may have been there first? Did Columbus really discover America? Hadn't an inordinate number of Native Americans and perhaps even a few Vikings, Irish monks, and Iberian fishermen found it first?

Transporting Binet Across the Atlantic

Following the publication of the 1905 version of Binet's test, the race was on to see who would emerge victorious in the American-Binet sweepstakes. Translations of Binet's test abounded, and numerous aspirants tried to claim the prize. H. H. Goddard was first out of the gate, and the Goddard-Binet took a commanding lead (Goddard, 1908). Stanford's Lewis Terman lacked Goddard's boldness, and he published a "tentative" revision of the Binet-Simon in 1912 (Terman & Childs, 1912). Americans continued to use the Goddard-Binet or the Kuhlmann-Binet or some other Binet, while Terman took his time adapting, expanding, and revising Binet's scale and testing many American children with it. By the time he was done in 1916, the Stanford-Binet was born (Terman, 1916). (Sample items at each age level are shown in Table 2.1.) While many Binet imitators in Europe and the United States took Binet's items as the gospel, Terman took pains to do more than just translate. He made a test that was geared to American culture, and he did it with state-of-the-art methodology. He piggy-backed onto William Stern's clever concept of the Mental Quotient and introduced the Intelligence Quotient (Kaufman, 1983). Neither luck nor coincidence caused the Stanford-Binet to leave its competitors in the dust and become the American IQ test for another half-century.

Still, to Goddard and even to Terman, IQ tests were primarily for identifying the so-called feebleminded, for weeding out the unfit. Despite Galton's interest in men of genius, IQ tests in America were for the opposite end of the intelligence spectrum.

WORLD WAR I AND THE IQ

Necessity gave birth to invention in 1917 when the United States became involved in World War I. If the creative mind of Alfred Binet led to the first great innovation in IQ testing, then the practical recruitment issues of World War I, close on the heels of the various American Binets, led to the second. The United States needed a way to evaluate the mental abilities of hundreds of thousands of recruits and would-be officers in rapid-fire fashion, and it had to find a way to measure the burgeoning population of immigrants. The latter group often couldn't understand tests in English, much less pass them. Do you declare them mentally unfit for combat? That wouldn't be

TABLE 2.1 SAMPLE ITEMS ON LEWIS TERMAN'S 1916 STANFORD-BINET

Year III	Knowing one's sex ("Are you a little boy or a little girl?") Naming a pencil
Year IV	Copying a square Counting 4 pennies
Year V	Naming the colors red, yellow, blue, and green Selecting which of 2 faces is the "prettiest"
Year VI	Counting 13 pennies Knowing what to do if you're going some place and miss your train or car
Year VII	Repeating 5 digits Knowing the difference between a *fly* and a *butterfly*
Year VIII	Counting backwards from 20 to 1 Telling how *iron* and *silver* are alike
Year IX	Giving the date (day, month, and year) Using 3 words in a sentence (WORK, MONEY, MEN)
Year X	Explaining why we should judge people more on their actions than words Naming 60 different words in three minutes
Year XII	Defining abstract words such as *envy* Telling how a *book, teacher,* and *newspaper* are alike
Year XIV	Giving 3 main differences between a *president* and a *king* If a man's salary is $20 a week and he spends $14 a week, how long will it take him to save $300?
Average Adult	Explaining the difference between abstract terms such as *character* and *reputation* Repeating 6 digits reversed
Superior Adult	Repeating the main thought of passages that are read (on topics such as "the scientific value of intelligence tests") Figuring out how to bring back exactly 7 pints of water from a river using only a 3-pint vessel and a 5-pint vessel

Note. The 1916 Stanford-Binet included six tasks at each level (Year XII was an exception with eight), with most tasks composed of several items. These examples are actual test items. The 1937, 1960, and 1972 Binets were also organized by age level, included the same kinds of tasks, and even retained many items from Terman's original Binet. The 1986 and 2003 versions are substantially different tests.

too patriotic. And what do you do, during wartime, with this new breed of doctor, the PhD in psychology who can't even set a broken arm? The front line? Administrative work? IQ test development? In many cases the last mentioned, thanks to Robert Yerkes and the American Psychological Association (Kaufman & Lichtenberger, 2006).

- As a result of World War I efforts, Terman's student Arthur Otis (1919) spearheaded the development of a group-administered IQ test, kind of a multiple-choice Binet. A variant of Otis's test, the Army Alpha, was administered to thousands of men drafted into the armed forces and hundreds of officers. The eighth edition of Otis's (1919) group ability test, the Otis-Lennon School Ability Test (OLSAT 8), lives today and is still widely administered to groups of students in the United States to measure their IQs, for example, in New York City to help identify gifted children.
- Nonverbal scales of intelligence—not just Galton-like sensory and motor tests, but problem-solving tasks—were created to test anyone who couldn't speak English or was suspected of malingering. Many nonverbal ("Performance") scales in use today, including several subtests in Wechsler's popular IQ tests, have their antecedents in the Army Mental Tests (Yoakum & Yerkes, 1920).
- IQ tests were found to be valuable for adults, not just children, and for bright people as well as those who are not so bright. Although the army tests were used to identify those not smart enough to serve, they also gained respect as tools for selecting officers and placing men in different types of service.
- IQ tests were validated on huge samples (nearly two million) and some of the results were intriguing. The tests were scored A to D–, with the percentage scoring A supporting their validity: 7% of recruits, 16% of corporals, 24% of sergeants, and 64% of majors. The best evidence of validity, though, was the Peter Principle in action. Second lieutenants (59% A) outperformed their direct superiors, first lieutenants (52%) and

captains (53%), while those with ranks higher than major did not do as well as majors (Kaufman & Lichtenberger, 2006).

Whenever examiners administer tests, whether group or individual, they must use exactly the same words with each person or group tested to maintain *standardized* procedures. My favorite set of test directions comes from the Army Alpha (E. refers to the examiner):

> In giving the following directions E. should speak rather slowly, distinctly, and with proper emphasis. *He should expect and demand perfect order and prompt response to commands.*
>
> When everything is ready E. proceeds as follows: "Attention! The purpose of this examination is to see how well you can remember, think, and carry out what you are told to do. We are not looking for crazy people. The aim is to help find out what you are best fitted to do in the Army. The grade you make in this examination will be put on your qualification card and will also go to your company commander. But just relax!" (Yoakum & Yerkes, 1920, p. 53)

Actually, I added "But just relax," but everything else is word-for-word, including the italics about expecting and demanding perfect order and prompt responding. How every psychologist who has given a clinical IQ test or every teacher who has given a group IQ test would have loved to have that kind of control!

Ultimately, the army test results led to wild misinterpretation of the data, controversy, cries of racism, and public debates about the value of IQ tests and the social implications of the test scores (Cronbach, 1975). The average person in the White draft was deemed to have a mental age of 13, just above the level commonly associated with a moron, and ethnic groups from southern and eastern Europe were deemed inferior in intellect by a psychologist who mostly ignored the fact that the data pertained to recent immigrants. And Lewis Terman engaged in a widely publicized, heated, and very sarcastic debate with famed columnist Walter Lippmann that was more emotion based than issue based—establishing the blueprint for IQ debates during each successive generation (Block & Dworkin, 1976).

THE GENIUS OF DAVID WECHSLER

While Terman and Lippmann argued during the early 1920s about whether IQ was innate and whether early experiences could enhance intelligence, David Wechsler was starting his career as a clinical psychologist. While psychologists (an epithet to Lippmann) began to worship IQ tests and the scores they yielded, Wechsler began to think of the tests in a new way—as clinical instruments, as windows to the child's or adult's personality. And in the 1930s, while the professional community was firm in its belief that you can't challenge the Binet approach to IQ (in much the same way the previous generation told Binet to stop wasting his time trying to unseat Galton), the chief psychologist at Bellevue Hospital in New York City was developing the Wechsler-Bellevue Intelligence Scale (Wechsler, 1939).

His innovation was not in his selection of tasks; he borrowed from Binet and from the army tests, and he did so with pride. Why not choose from among the best, most carefully developed and validated tasks anywhere? He took subtests (sometimes even exact items) from the Stanford-Binet and the Army Alpha group test and created his Verbal Scale. But he believed that verbal intelligence was only a part of IQ. He also assembled a Performance Scale from the nonverbal, visual-motor subtests that were developed during the world war to evaluate people who couldn't speak English very well or whose motivation to succeed was in doubt. His greatest source of subtests was from the individually administered Performance Scale Examination, the test of last resort in the army, but he also took tasks liberally from the Army Beta (a nonverbal group test). A person who flunked the verbal Army Alpha was given the Army Beta. A two-time loser was given the individual exam. So Wechsler chose for his Performance Scale a collection of tasks that was designed "to prove conclusively that a man was weakminded and not merely indifferent or malingering" (Yoakum & Yerkes, 1920, p. 10).

Test publishers were leery. How can tests developed for the low end of the ability spectrum be used to test normal people's intelligence? Why, they asked, would a psychologist spend 3 minutes having someone solve a picture puzzle when that same person could be asked to define 10 words in that same time? Nonverbal tests were fine for foreigners, for new immigrants, but not for "us." The postwar psychological community reverted to the belief that IQ tests were primarily useful for predicting children's school success, and they were further critical of Wechsler for developing a test primarily for adolescents and adults.

But Wechsler persisted. He was a visionary in realizing that people with poor verbal intelligence may be exceptional in their nonverbal ability, and vice versa. His notions of intelligence predated later neurological findings about the left and right hemispheres of the brain. Probably Wechsler was influenced by his older brother, Israel, a leading neurologist of the day, but mostly he was guided by his uncanny clinical sense, an intuitive understanding of people's thinking that I experienced firsthand in the early 1970s when he served as my mentor.

Like Alfred Binet, Wechsler met with frustration and couldn't find a publisher willing to subsidize his bold venture. So he did it himself. With several of his psychologist friends, Wechsler tested nearly 2,000 children, adolescents, and adults in Coney Island, Brooklyn, New York. The sample didn't represent the whole country, and it was far too urban. But it was still quite good, because Wechsler knew from his own research that socioeconomic status was the key to getting a good "norms" sample. If you want to find out how well Americans aged 7 to 70 do on an IQ test, then test people at each age who form a mini-U.S. sample on such variables as education and occupation. If the U.S. Census in the 1930s says that 5% of adults in the United States are college graduates, then make sure that 5% of the adults tested in the norms sample have graduated from college. But when the census called for farmers, farm managers, or farm laborers to be included in the norms group, Wechsler couldn't find any farmers in Brooklyn. So he tested barbers. He had done some research, and found that barbers and farmers performed about the same, on average, on his Wechsler-Bellevue test. His sample may have had too many barbers, too many people who were raised on Nathan's hotdogs and fries in Coney Island, and not enough midwesterners. But for the 1930s, his methods were darned clever.

Once Wechsler had spent the time and money to norm his own test, he had no problem finding a willing publisher in The Psychological Corporation, a company that James McKeen Cattell helped found shortly after World War I. The original Wechsler-Bellevue (Wechsler, 1939) now has great-great-grandchildren with names such as the Wechsler Intelligence Scale for Children—Fourth Edition (WISC-IV) and the Wechsler Adult Intelligence Scale—Fourth Edition (WAIS-IV) (Wechsler, 2003, 2008). Figure 2.1 illustrates the 11 subtests he chose for the Wechsler-Bellevue, tasks that continue to populate Wechsler's scales to the present day. The original subtests dominated Wechsler's scales through the 1990s, but the most recent editions of them have included novel tasks (see chapter 3).

The similarity of Wechsler's original set of subtests to the tasks used to evaluate recruits, soldiers, and officers during World War I is striking. The Army Beta included a page filled with pictures—each missing an important part (Pictorial Completion)—and the soldiers had to draw in the missing part (such as a mouth on a face or an ear on a rabbit). The Beta also included a clerical speed-and-accuracy test (Digit-Symbol) that required the soldiers to rapidly copy symbols that were paired with numbers (Yoakum & Yerkes, 1920). These tasks became, respectively, Wechsler's Picture Completion and Digit Symbol subtests (Digit Symbol is called Coding on WISC-IV and WAIS-IV) (see Figure 2.1). The Performance Scale Examination included a two-item picture puzzle test called Manikin and Feature Profile; these two picture puzzle items were later included on Wechsler's Object Assembly subtest; it had a cube construction test that was a variant of Block Design;

Wechsler Adult Intelligence Scale (WAIS) Sample Items

Test	Description	Example
Verbal Scale		
Information	Taps general range of information	On which continent is France?
Comprehension	Tests understanding of social conventions and ability to evaluate past experience	Why do people need birth certificates?
Arithmetic	Tests arithmetic reasoning through verbal problems	How many hours will it take to drive 150 miles at 50 miles per hour?
Similarities	Asks in what way certain objects or concepts are similar; measures abstract thinking	How are a calculator and a typewriter alike?
Digit span	Tests attention and rote memory by orally presenting series of digits to be repeated forward or backward	Repeat the following numbers backward: 2 4 3 5 1 8 6
Vocabulary	Tests ability to define increasingly difficult words	What does repudiate mean?
Performance scale		
Digit symbol	Tests speed of learning through timed coding tasks in which numbers must be associated with marks of various shapes	Shown: Fill in: 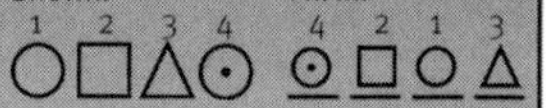
Picture completion	Tests visual alertness and visual memory through presentation of an incompletely drawn figure; the missing part must be discovered and named	Tell me what is missing: 
Block design	Tests ability to perceive and analyze patterns presenting designs that must be copied with blocks	Assemble blocks to match this design: 
Picture arrangement	Tests understanding of social situations through a series of comic-strip-type pictures that must be arranged in the right sequence to tell a story	Put this picture in the right order: 
Object assembly	Tests ability to deal with part/whole relationships by presenting puzzle pieces that must be assembled to form a complete object	Assemble the pieces into a complete object: 

FIGURE 2.1 Sample items for 11 traditional Wechsler subtests, for children and adults, which first appeared in the 1939 Wechsler-Bellevue Intelligence Scale.

Note. Digit Symbol is also known as Coding. From *Wechsler Adult Intelligence Scale—Third Edition (WAIS-III)*, 1997, San Antonio, TX: The Psychological Corporation.

like the Army Beta, it included the Digit Symbol Test; and it included a Picture Arrangement test (Yoakum & Yerkes, 1920).

The following are actual Army Alpha items (correct responses are listed first for Tests 3 and 8) (Yoakum & Yerkes, 1920):

Test 2—Arithmetical Problems

If you save $7 a month for 4 months, how much will you save? (Answer = $28)

If you buy two packages of tobacco at 7 cents each and a pipe for 65 cents, how much change should you get from a two-dollar bill? (Answer = $1.21)

Test 3—Practical Judgment

Why do soldiers wear wrist watches rather than pocket watches? *Because*

- They are handier
- They keep better time
- They are harder to break

Why judge a man by what he does rather than by what he says? *Because*

- What a man does shows what he really is
- It is wrong to tell a lie
- A deaf man cannot hear what is said

Test 8—Information

Carrie Nation is known as a: suffragist singer temperance agitator nurse

The tendon of Achilles is in the: heel head shoulder abdomen

Direct adaptations of these three Army Alpha tests became staples of Wechsler's Verbal Scale for children, adolescents, and adults—Arithmetic, Comprehension, and Information (see Figure 2.1).

Wechsler's tests weren't instant hits because of a fierce loyalty to the Stanford-Binet that lasted into the 1950s and early

1960s. But Wechsler chipped away at the monopoly, and overtook the Binet during the 1960s as the learning disabilities movement and the emergent field of neuropsychology gained popularity. Psychologists and educators were no longer content with a single IQ. They wanted a profile of scores to help identify the strengths and weaknesses that are known to characterize children with specific learning disabilities or SLDs (although even this long-held belief is now a hotly debated topic; see chapter 9). Wechsler's 10+ subtests provided the profile of scores that the one-score Binet lacked. And Wechsler's separate Verbal IQ and Performance IQ helped identify bright children with SLDs who had language difficulties (high Performance IQ) or visual-perceptual problems (high Verbal IQ). The Stanford-Binet offered just one IQ, and the test was so verbally oriented that people with exceptional nonverbal intelligence were unfairly penalized. My colleague John Willis (personal communication, October 9, 2008) has a hypothesis as to why the original Stanford-Binet was so oriented toward verbal ability: "I have heard that Terman was a klutz and struggled with the brass instruments of the psychology laboratory in graduate school. Perhaps his high verbal and weak performance abilities influenced his selection of tests."

Ultimately, Wechsler triumphed over the Binet because he tried harder. He never stopped improving his tests or using the most advanced statistical techniques. When I was an assistant director at The Psychological Corporation in the early 1970s and helped Dr. Wechsler develop the Wechsler Intelligence Scale for Children—Revised (WISC-R; Wechsler, 1974), he was in his mid-70s and as active and involved in his tests as ever. He showed me notebooks filled with new items, including comic strips he had cut out from newspapers to adapt for nonverbal test items. With his own tool kit, he had constructed a variety of wooden dolls and formboards, always in search of new ways of measuring mental ability.

Dr. Wechsler (I never called him David) was the most important influence in my professional life. I told the following story as part of an invited address I gave in Atlanta (Kaufman, 2005a, 2005b).

David Wechsler was my main mentor in psychology. Robert Thorndike was my major professor at Columbia, but he was so intimidating and private that I barely spoke to him during my entire graduate student career. But Dr. Wechsler was my true mentor. Sometimes you can have a mentor and not even realize it, and that undoubtedly characterizes my early relationship with Dr. Wechsler—I perceived him sometimes as an antagonist with whom I was required to engage in weekly battles about the revision of the WISC. But when we weren't battling (i.e., me trying to explain to him why this or that WISC item just HAD to be deleted from the revised WISC, and him glaring at me like I didn't have a clue about clinical assessment), I could recognize his aura. He was a wonderful human being and I loved listening to him talk. I loved the stories he would tell about being greeted at the airport by the King of Romania on a recent trip, about 70 years after he had to flee Romania to avoid religious persecution.

When I started at the University of Georgia in 1974, I told my first classes of school psychology graduate students that I had worked with Dr. Wechsler on the WISC-R. They were somewhat impressed, I think. I told them that I was sure I could arrange a telephone interview with him, and they were excited. But he refused a phone interview, and I can just imagine what the students were thinking—maybe that I was some sort of pathological liar, and I liked telling people that I worked with David Wechsler, but that I probably never even met the man. Then, out of the blue, Dr. Wechsler wrote me and offered to come and visit with my students at the University of Georgia. He arrived on April 21, 1975, which I remember because it was both my 31st birthday and our daughter Jennie's 9th birthday. First, Dr. Wechsler met with the group of 16 students in my IQ assessment course; then, in the afternoon, he addressed a crowd of about 500 students and faculty. He was articulate, funny, charming, and self-confident. I believe that the students and faculty really enjoyed his lecture and that my small group of students relished the intimacy of asking the great man questions about assessment. That night he and Ruth came to dinner with us and we thought, finally, we can just relax. It had been an emotional day for me, especially having to introduce him to the large audience. I thought, "Let's just eat and enjoy this great meal and not talk about psychology." But Dr. Wechsler would not stop asking us questions. He knew that he wasn't very good at Block Design anymore, and that he wasn't about to earn bonus points on visual-motor tests, not even on his own WAIS Performance Scale (see chapter 8 on aging research). We were sitting at a table at our favorite Athens restaurant, but Dr. Wechsler wouldn't even let us go up to get our salads. He was developing a test that, had it ever been published, would have had the greatest acronym ever—the WISE—or the Wechsler Intelligence Scale for the Elderly. He wanted to know what we thought intelligence was in adults that made it distinct from intelligence in children. We started talking about neurological and cognitive development. We talked about our feelings about using childlike tasks, such as Object Assembly, to measure adults on the WAIS. It is embarrassing to have a bright, articulate adult put together a cut-up elephant really quickly, when, in fact, that adult's main reason for being assessed is to decide whether to go to law school or medical school. Dr. Wechsler was taking notes all over his napkin and all I could think of was that I wanted to eat some steak and salad.[1]

Wechsler always had his eye on the future, which is one reason he was so successful. The Stanford-Binet started to plunge in popularity when professionals demanded a profile of abilities instead of just a global IQ. In addition to three IQs, Wechsler offered separate scores on 10 or more specific subtests; the Stanford-Binet, until its fourth edition (Thorndike et al., 1986), persisted in offering just a single IQ. The Binet, now in its fifth edition, is a sophisticated, well-made test (Roid, 2003), but once

1. Copyright 2005 by the National Association of School Psychologists. Bethesda, MD. Adapted with the permission of the publisher. www.nasponline.org

the Wechsler scales took over the throne from the Stanford-Binet in the 1960s, the Binet remained in the rearview mirror. Terman originally succeeded when other Binet pretenders failed because he was so meticulous and ahead of his time. As irony would have it, Terman's Stanford-Binet lost favor when revisions of the battery after his death in 1956 proved to be shortsighted and geared to expediency.

Despite the profound impact that Wechsler achieved by developing IQ tests, an even bigger part of his legacy concerns how he transformed the very nature of IQ testing. I discussed this topic in the invited address I mentioned above (Kaufman, 2005a, 2005b).

I enjoyed Wechsler the man, but Wechsler the clinical psychologist was even more impressive. He was an innovator whose impact cannot be measured by his test batteries alone. When he emerged on the assessment scene in the 1930s he was trying to contend with a field that was already well established. The Stanford-Binet was a one-score test, general intelligence was the only construct worth measuring, and a psychometric approach to interpretation was the only method that was valued. Quinn McNemar wrote the book on the interpretation of the 1937 Stanford-Binet (McNemar, 1942), and he was a statistician who had no clinical inclinations. McNemar and Terman set the tone of IQ assessment, and that tone was decidedly psychometric, focusing on reliability, standard errors of measurement, validity, group differences—and the concept of global, overall, general, or total intelligence, or mental energy, that Charles Spearman (1904) nicknamed *g*.

Then came David Wechsler, the consummate clinician. Wechsler was also a *g* theorist, believing in the reality and importance of Spearman's global or aggregate intelligence. But the fact that his theoretical background was no different from Terman's or McNemar's did not stop him from transforming the entire field of IQ interpretation from *psychometric measurement* to *clinical assessment*. He believed that a person's scores on the 10 or 12 subtests were largely a function of *g*, but that when profile fluctuations occurred they were likely a function of differences in personality, temperament, motivation, perseverance, and so forth (what Wechsler, 1950, referred to as the "conative" aspects of assessment). He considered IQ testing part of personality assessment and believed that people's specific responses, as well as the fluctuations in their test profiles, provided a window to their personality. He lifted IQ testing out of its psychometric bedrock and planted it in fertile clinical ground. The field of IQ assessment has never been the same since. I'm not saying that psychometric properties and statistical interpretation of test data are not important, but I'm saying that David Wechsler was making a more important statement. He changed the perspective to focus on the whole person, not just on cognition in isolation. He was a clinician, and he was saying that we can get much more information from an individually administered test than just IQ. He was asking the field of assessment, What were the goals of testing? What can we do with the test profiles in a dynamic, clinical way? These were questions that had been asked before. The first practical application of Alfred Binet's IQ tests, with all of his genius, was not to help the children who scored low—it was to get them out of the classroom so the "normal" children would not be slowed down. Wechsler's approach was to use these tests to make a difference in people's lives, to help understand mental illness and brain damage and psychopathic behavior, and to see beyond the scores.[2]

THEORY ENTERS THE IQ TESTING REALM

Virtually all of the innovations that occurred from the time of Binet through the decade of the 1970s concerning the *development* of IQ tests were based on clinical, psychometric (statistical), and practical considerations. Theories of intelligence and

2. Copyright 2005 by the National Association of School Psychologists. Bethesda, MD. Adapted with the permission of the publisher. www.nasponline.org

learning abounded from the early 1900s, but they remained inexplicably insulated from the field of IQ test construction. Finally, in the 1970s, theories entered the field of IQ testing—not regarding test development (that would wait until the 1980s), but concerning the *interpretation* of test scores on the traditional Wechsler and Binet scales. The importance of theory for test interpretation dominated the 1970s; its role in test development dominated the 1980s and continues to dominate through the first decade of the 21st century. In this chapter, I will enter the realm of theory by examining its meaning for Alfred Binet and David Wechsler and how it affected the way test scores on their tests were interpreted. In the next chapter, I'll focus on the great breakthrough in the theory-IQ test relationship, namely, the construction of tests from a distinctly theoretical foundation. Let's start with what theory meant to Binet and Wechsler.

Alfred Binet and Theory

Binet was driven to a large extent by practical and statistical concerns. He wanted to solve an early 20th-century Parisian societal problem by identifying, and weeding out, those children who couldn't keep pace with so-called normal students. He cleverly organized mental tasks into age levels but used simple statistics—not theory or research on child development—to determine whether a task was a 7-year task or a 10-year task. And if he had too many tasks at one age level and too few at another, he could easily switch tasks around by modifying the scoring system. The average 4-year-old child, for example, might be able to name 3 out of 5 pictures on a page. But if he needed that task to be classified at Age 3 instead, he would simply change the scoring criteria to require only 2 of the 5 to be named correctly; or if he needed a mental task for Age 5 he would raise the bar to 4 out of 5 right for credit. Nonetheless, Binet chose tasks according to an *implicit* theory of intelligence. "According to Binet and Simon, intelligent thought is composed of three distinct elements: direction, adaptation, and criticism.... Because of his emphasis on test development, Binet has often been accused of being atheoretical.... To the contrary, he and Simon conceived of intelligence in ways that were theoretically sophisticated and that resembled in content much of the most recent thinking regarding cognitive processing" (Sternberg, J. C. Kaufman, & Grigorenko, 2008).

David Wechsler and Theory

Not surprisingly, Dr. Wechsler told me more than once, "First and foremost, IQ tests are clinical instruments." For example, based on the answer to "What should you do if a 2-year-old kicks you in the shin?" (this is an adapted version of the actual wording), Wechsler believed he could identify the following:

- Dependency ("Tell my mom");
- Aggression ("Knock the crap out of her");
- Loose thinking ("Little boys, little toys... Fighting and biting");
- Regression or immaturity ("Cry");
- Fearfulness ("Run away");
- Passivity ("I'd just let him kick me"); or
- Socially appropriate restraint ("Just walk away").

This type of clinical interpretation of verbal responses has never been validated by research and is from an earlier generation, a time when some clinical psychologists (not Wechsler) were knee-deep in psychodynamic interpretation of verbal responses and profile fluctuations on Wechsler's Verbal and Performance IQs and separate subtests. They took the interpretation of Wechsler's subtests and scales to an extreme of personality-disorder-hyperbole. Consider the interpretations given to truly innocuous verbal responses to the Comprehension item on the old WAIS, "Why should we keep away from bad company?" (see Table 2.2). As a graduate student, I administered the WAIS to prisoners. Can you imagine the trepidation when you have to ask a convicted murderer in a federal penitentiary why he ought to avoid bad company? Thankfully that item was eliminated from revisions of the WAIS.

TABLE 2.2 MEANINGS ATTRIBUTED TO ADULTS' VERBAL RESPONSES TO THE OLD WAIS ITEM, "WHY SHOULD WE KEEP AWAY FROM BAD COMPANY?"

Response	Possible Meaning
"They hurt people"	Phobic
"I prefer bad company"	Negative, provocative
"They're bad"	Naïve, retarded
"I don't want to think about it"	Hysterical, repressive
"I don't think we necessarily should, some chance we can straighten them out"	Obsessive, righteous
"Who knows what bad company is?"	Pseudo-sophisticated

Note. From *Clinical Interpretation of the Wechsler Adult Intelligence Scale,* by I. L. Zimmerman and J. M. Woo-Sam, 1973, p. 65, New York: Grune & Stratton.

But the silliness of interpreting simple responses to simple questions as evidence of phobia, repression, or obsessiveness pales in comparison to the psychodynamic interpretations assigned to profiles on Wechsler's IQ tests by researchers and clinicians influenced by theory, but by *psychoanalytic theories of personality* rather than by cognitive theories of intelligence (Allison, Blatt, & Zimet, 1968; Mayman, Schafer, & Rapaport, 1951; Rapaport, Gill, & Schafer, 1945–1946). Some illustrations are shown in Table 2.3. It is never wise to interpret differences between subtest scaled scores, because the errors of measurement are too large to allow any kind of interpretation—much less inferring that a difference between Digit Symbol and Digit Span is conceivably related to depression, hypomania, or excessive anxiety; or that high Comprehension and low Information reflects a hysteric reaction. And the interpretations of Verbal versus Performance IQs are not only contrary to common sense but to data. An 8- to 10-point difference may mean *obsessive-compulsive* tendencies? The *average* child or adult has a *10-point* difference between his or her Verbal and Performance IQs. A difference of

TABLE 2.3 PSYCHODYNAMIC INTERPRETATION OF WECHSLER TEST PROFILES

Rapaport, Gill, and Schafer (1945–1946); Mayman, Schafer, and Rapaport (1951)

- Misses easy Comprehension items = *schizophrenia or psychotic depression*
- Adequate Comprehension with low Information = *hysteric reaction*
- High Picture Completion = *possible paranoid trend*

Allison, Blatt, and Zimet (1968)

- *Digit Symbol Versus Digit Span*

"High Digit Symbol with Low Digit Span suggests a person 'who seems to be controlling strong and pressing anxiety by excessive activity' (p. 32).

"When we find the reverse pattern, a High Digit Span and a low Digit Symbol, we are usually confronted with an essentially depressed person who is attempting to ward off recognition of depressive affect perhaps in a hypomanic way, usually via denial, but not necessarily through activity and acting out behavior" (p. 32).

- *Verbal-Performance IQ Discrepancies*

"An eight to ten point difference between Verbal and Performance IQs . . . indicates only a highly verbal subject with possible obsessive-compulsive tendencies. When the Verbal IQ begins to have a marked imbalance over the Performance IQ (by greater than 15 points), more serious pathological trends may be considered" (p. 34).

"A Performance IQ greater than a Verbal IQ in individuals of at least average intelligence is atypical. Three major diagnostic trends, all of which have acting out as a primary feature, are suggested by such a pattern: hysteric, narcissistic, and psychopathic character disorders" (p. 35).

Note. From *Assessing Adolescent and Adult Intelligence*, 3rd ed., by A. S. Kaufman and E O. Lichtenberger, 2006, New York: Wiley. Copyright © 2006, by John Wiley & Sons. Quoted with permission.

15 or more points may mean *serious pathological trends*? About 25% of normal children and about 20% of normal adults have discrepancies that large (Kaufman, 1979b; The Psychological Corporation, 1997, Appendix D). Verbal IQ and Performance IQ are no longer offered in the latest versions of Wechsler's scales,

but that has not stopped the overinterpretation of small fluctuations among a person's test scores. Psychologists have long tended to grossly underestimate the normal variation among subtest scores and many continue to do so despite the publication of contradictory data from the WISC-R (Kaufman, 1976) and the subsequent inclusion of such data in test manuals (e.g., Wechsler, 1991, Appendix B).

However laughable these assertions seem by today's standards—which are guided by cognitive theories and neuropsychologically based approaches to interpretation—Wechsler's emphasis that IQ tests are valuable as *clinical* instruments remains true. Most professionals will agree that watching a person assemble a puzzle or arrange mixed-up pictures tells a good clinician much about that individual's impulsivity, planning ability, frustration tolerance, distractibility, anxiety, decision-making capacity, reflectiveness, and the like.

Wechsler always insisted that he could diagnose an adult's personality based on his or her answer to the question, "What is the population of the United States?" He was such a wonderful clinician that I never doubted that *he* personally could do it. But I always doubted that he was very impressed with the diversity of theories of intelligence, learning, and development that proliferated between the 1930s when the Wechsler-Bellevue was published and the early 1980s when the WAIS-R (Wechsler, 1981) was published shortly before his death. And I didn't understand it. How was it possible that a pioneer in IQ testing, David Wechsler, did not believe that theories were relevant to the construction of intelligence tests? Up to the early 1980s, how was it feasible that IQ tests were almost impervious to decades of research devoted to cognitive and neuropsychological theories that tried to understand how children learn and solve problems and how mental abilities develop from infancy through old age? It made no sense. Wechsler (1958, 1975) clearly had his own theory of intelligence, a well-organized theory that boiled down to a person's overall capacity to understand and cope with his or her environment. But he did not use his theory to guide the construction of his tests.

Spearman's *g* or General Intelligence Theory

It is not that theories of intelligence were totally ignored. Charles Spearman's (1904) *g* or general-factor theory, often credited as being the first theory of intelligence (Silverman, 2009), posits that intelligence is largely a single global ability. Spearman's (1904) ground-breaking theory focused on *g* but also included smaller, specific factors, labeled *s*. However, IQ tests tended to emphasize *g* and ignore *s*. L. L. Thurstone (1938) was an outspoken opponent of Spearman's *g* theory who went well beyond Spearman's narrow definition of *s* by developing a theory of seven primary mental abilities—verbal comprehension (V), word fluency (W), number (N), spatial ability (S), associative memory (M), perceptual speed (P), and reasoning (R) or induction (I). The group-administered Primary Mental Abilities Test (Thurstone & Thurstone, 1949) was popular and was the instrument used by Schaie (1996) in his classic studies of aging and intelligence (see chapter 8). But Thurstone's influence on individually administered IQ tests, either their interpretation or their development, was trivial until the mid-1980s when his notion of primary mental abilities formed part of the foundation of the fourth edition of the Stanford-Binet (Thorndike et al., 1986).

Yet for more than three-quarters of a century, Spearman's *g* theory was the only one that mattered for clinical assessment of intelligence. Indeed, Spearman's *g* was at the root of Terman's adaptation of Binet's test in the United States, providing the foundation for offering only a single score, the global IQ, and was at the core of Wechsler's belief system about intelligence.

Spearman (1927) set out to isolate intelligence from the contaminating influences of learning, emotion, and temperament (Silverman, 2009). Building his research on Pearson's new methods of correlation, Spearman gave proof that measures of different mental abilities correlated substantially with each other. He postulated that those positive correlations indicated that there must be a general function common to all abilities, which became widely known as "the Spearman *g*." He further theorized that mental tasks varied in the degree to which they measured *g*, with complicated mental activities containing the "most" *g*. In a nutshell, tests of analytical reasoning ability captured the essence of *g*.

But Spearman's *g* was not linked only to the Binet. Even though Wechsler offered three IQs—Verbal, Performance, and Full Scale—he did not consider these IQs to reflect different kinds of intelligence, as he explained in the WISC-R test manual (Wechsler, 1974). First, he said, "Intelligence is the overall capacity of an individual to understand and cope with the world around him" (p. 5). (Clearly political correctness and gender equity were not alive and well in 1974.) Wechsler's strong belief in *g* theory seems incompatible with his decision to organize his tests into Verbal and Performance scales and not only to provide examiners with three IQs but to offer a profile of a person's abilities on 10 to 12 tests. However, he sidestepped this apparent contradiction by stating that "Intelligence can manifest itself in many forms, and an intelligence scale, to be effective as well as fair, must utilize as many different languages (tests) as possible. It is for this reason that the *WISC-R* emphasizes the importance of probing intelligence in as many different ways as possible; . . . It does so also because it assumes . . . that intelligence is best regarded not as a single unique trait but as a composite or global entity" (Wechsler, 1974, pp. 5–6).

I found out firsthand just how much Dr. Wechsler admired Spearman's theory during his April 1975 visit to Athens, Georgia, that I mentioned earlier. I had just introduced him to the large audience of students and professors when he began his speech by saying, "As I'm sure Alan has emphasized over and over to his students, nothing is more important than *g* for understanding intelligence. Global ability is *the* ability that underlies my IQ tests." In fact, I had taught my students the exact opposite—that nothing is *less* important than *g* because it assumes that you can summarize a person's intelligence with a single number. What is important to me? The separate cognitive abilities that make up a person's intellect, because they permit an understanding of an individual's strong and weak areas of intelligence. The next day, when I met with my students, I had some explaining to do.

Despite Dr. Wechsler's reluctance to embrace the multiple-ability models, these "anti-*g*" theories had been gaining in popularity for at least a decade prior to his visit to Georgia. The relevance of theory for IQ tests began to be talked about in the 1960s and 1970s, especially regarding the *interpretation* of IQ tests. But, as I said earlier and will expand upon in chapter 3, theories were not acted on until the 1980s when they formed the blueprint for the *development* of new clinical tests of intelligence. It is not that Spearman's theory had outlived its usefulness. To some research psychologists, most notably Arthur Jensen (1998), Spearman's *g* remained the theory of choice. And to psychologists who study gifted assessment, *g* is of paramount importance. As Silverman (2009) notes, "Abstract reasoning and general intelligence (g) are synonymous. Giftedness is high abstract reasoning. . . . Therefore, g could as easily stand for giftedness as for general intelligence (p. 966).

Intelligent Testing and *g*

I don't dispute the empirical studies that support the value of *g* for understanding intelligence from a theoretical perspective or the fact that some excellent professionals assign key roles to *g* in identifying children for gifted programs. But I do not believe that *g* theory is useful for the bulk of children who are referred for psychological evaluation for such reasons as possible intellectual disabilities, learning disabilities, attention-deficit hyperactivity disorder (ADHD), autistic-spectrum disorders, emotional disturbance, behavior disorders, and the like. For those children, the emphasis on *g* is often a dead end, as I emphasized and elaborated upon in *Intelligent Testing With the WISC-R* (Kaufman, 1979b), a book that found a wide audience. The essence of the intelligent testing message was to apply theory to the interpretation of children's WISC-R test scores, even though Wechsler did not develop his tests from theory, and to elevate the notion of multiple abilities (not *g*) to the forefront of test interpretation. Only then would clinicians have a crisp idea of a person's *profile* of abilities—areas of decided strength and clear-cut weakness—an approach that had far more implications for helping children than a simple global ability score that did little more than mask the peaks and valleys in the test profile. Implicit in this method was the ability to identify strong and weak areas for everyone, even people who earned very high or very low IQs (thus, average performance on some tasks would be a decided strength for a person with an intellectual disability, but a weakness for a gifted child or adult). This general approach of identifying *relative* strengths and weaknesses is known as *ipsative* (as opposed to *normative*, which compares everyone to the so-called average person). The intelligent testing approach has sometimes been praised: "Further evidence of the influence of measurement science on intelligence test interpretation and the problems associated with profile analysis can be found in an influential book by Kaufman (1979b)" (Kamphaus et al., 2005, p. 29). Also: "Kaufman's prominent 'intelligent' approach to Wechsler intelligence test interpretation is at the core of our teaching, writing, research, and practice" (Flanagan, McGrew, & Ortiz, 2000, p. xviii). However, the "intelligent" method has occasionally been sentenced to death (McDermott et al., 1992): "Perhaps most popular among contemporary practices is the method of ipsative ability assessment advocated by Kaufman (1979b)... a common element in university curricula for preparing professional psychologists" (p. 506). "Such approaches essentially violate primary principles guiding valid test interpretation" (p. 523).

But ipsative assessment was only one aspect of the intelligent testing philosophy. The crux of the approach was a virulent anti-*g* theory message: "Global scores are deemphasized, flexibility and insight on the part of the examiner are demanded, and the test is perceived as a dynamic helping agent rather than as an instrument for placement, labeling, or other types of academic oppression" (Kaufman, 1979b, p. 1). To accomplish these goals, innovative and well-researched theories of multiple cognitive abilities had to leave the ivory tower of the laboratory and enter the real world of intelligence testing in schools and clinics.

When multiple-ability theories finally crashed the IQ party, the most prominent were (a) Guilford's (1967) structure-of-intellect model; (b) brain-based approaches (Luria, 1966; Sperry, 1968) that emphasized two styles of information processing, sometimes referred to as *sequential* and *simultaneous*; and (c) the Cattell-Horn theory of fluid intelligence (*Gf*) and crystallized intelligence (*Gc*), referred to as *Gf-Gc* theory, where *Gc* reflects the knowledge a person acquires from school and culture and *Gf* denotes a person's ability to solve novel problems (Horn & Cattell, 1966).

I will discuss Guilford's theory in this chapter because its main claim to IQ fame was as a model for interpreting the Stanford-Binet and Wechsler subtests; also because the huge number of intelligences it posited was the polar opposite of Spearman's *g* theory. But Guilford's model never formed the basis for a clinical, individually administered IQ test. In chapter 3, I will focus on neuropsychological processing theories and on the Cattell-Horn-Carroll (CHC) theory of cognitive abilities (the current version of *Gf-Gc* theory), because these two approaches changed the face of IQ testing.

Guilford's Structure-of-Intellect Model

Joy P. Guilford's structure-of-intellect (SOI) theory was the first to make a dent in the IQ armor when Mary Meeker (1969), a devotee of Guilford's theory, interpreted Terman and Merrill's (1960) Form L-M of the Stanford-Binet in terms of this theoretical perspective. (Though named Joy, Guilford was a man; there was no room in the world of theory for women at that time—there was barely room in doctoral programs.) Guilford defined intelligence in terms of three dimensions: (a) the *operations* or intellectual processes needed to solve a problem (such as *memory* or *evaluation*), (b) the *content* of the problem, that is, the nature of the stimuli (such as *semantic* or *symbolic*), and (c) the *products*, namely how the stimuli are organized (as in *units* and *systems*).

SOI was the "in" theory for psychologists and educators for about two decades until *Gf-Gc* theory took over the reins in the mid-1980s. It was so big that some universities taught complete courses devoted to the SOI model. Indeed, Dr. Linda Silverman, a leading expert in gifted assessment, sent me an interesting e-mail documenting the long-ago popularity of Guilford's theory: "In the late 1970s and early 1980s, many school districts throughout the United States employed the SOI Learning Abilities Test by Mary Meeker as part of their identification processes for selecting gifted students. It was particularly popular in school districts in Colorado. In response, the University of Denver offered a course on SOI theory, and later added a second, more advanced course on this subject" (L. K. Silverman, personal communication, July 10, 2008). The three-pronged theory became imprinted on a generation of education and psychology students in the form of a cube whose three dimensions were operations, contents, and products. The cube that depicted Guilford's SOI theory was reproduced ad nauseam in Psychology 101 and Educational Psychology 101 texts even after it began to go out of fashion, probably because the idea that intelligence can be expressed in so many different ways was an optimistic, fascinating notion for a nation that was virtually spoon-fed on Spearman's *g* theory and global IQ.

Based on the SOI's three dimensions, any mental task can be categorized into one or more of 120 different cells (implying that there are 120 types of intelligence, that is, 5 operations × 4 contents × 6 products). Meeker (1975) identified the SOI cell (or, in most cases, cells) measured by each Wechsler Verbal and Performance subtest. So, for example, Vocabulary measures cognition of semantic units (CMU). This Verbal subtest, which requires individuals to define a list of words spoken by the examiner, requires the comprehension (cognition) of words (semantic) presented one at a time (units). The SOI model made particular inroads in the field of gifted assessment, in part because the plethora of intelligences the theory posited had the potential to mirror the diverse aspects of a gifted student's brilliance, and gave educators a way of classifying each gifted child's areas of strength. But even more importantly, Guilford's theory paid more than lip service to the forgotten part of intellectual assessment—creativity. And though the SOI name for creativity was the obscure term *divergent-production,* its inclusion in the model made it a natural fit for the field of giftedness that grew up alongside the field of creativity (Torrance, 1962). The polar opposite of divergent-production is convergent-production, which rewards the one and only one correct answer to a problem. By contrast, divergent-production gives high fives to unusual or original responses and to other aspects of creative thinking (for a thorough treatment of Guilford's definition of divergent-production and Paul Torrance's [1974] measurement of it, see J. C. Kaufman, 2009; see also J. C. Kaufman, Plucker, & Baer, 2008).

As mentioned, Meeker developed a test based on Guilford's theory (Meeker, Mestyanek, Shadduck, & Meeker, 1975); she also developed a remediation program designed to improve children's abilities when they earned a low score on a "pure" SOI ability (Meeker & Shadduck, 1973). Add to the equation Paul Torrance's (1974, 2008) insightful translation of divergent-production to a test of creativity, and all the ingredients were in place for Guilford's theory to dominate not just gifted education but the theory-hungry field of intellectual assessment. Torrance's popular test made it possible to measure Guilford's notion of creativity both verbally and nonverbally, a direct parallel to Wechsler's division of IQ. And Meeker's work made it possible to individualize assessment and instruction for each child identified as gifted.

Yes, the ingredients for success were there, but ultimately the SOI model became a fad of the 1970s and early 1980s for the field of intellectual assessment. Why? Whole bunch of reasons. The theory clearly had the potential to mirror the diverse aspects of a gifted student's intellectual strengths and to individualize gifted curricula. But that potential was not realized. Although SOI theory did broaden the base for identifying gifted students, individualization was the exception rather than the rule.

The theory had strong advocates within the field of education. Linda Silverman (personal communication, July 8, 2008) pointed out in an e-mail to me that "Guilford's model was well received by educators, particularly those who decried the narrowness of some of the older conceptions of intelligence. The concept of a number of intelligences left room for everyone to be gifted in some way." But the SOI model didn't pass the litmus test of any would-be psychological theory—it was panned by the critics who counted. Among the most vocal were a veritable *Who's Who in the Psychology of Intelligence in the 1960s and 1970s*—John Carroll (1968), Lee Cronbach (1970), John Horn (Horn & Knapp, 1973, 1974), Lloyd Humphreys (1962), Philip Vernon (1979), and my major professor at Columbia University, Robert L. Thorndike (1963). These researchers claimed that there wasn't enough evidence to support the existence of the independent abilities that Guilford had described. Horn and Knapp (1973), for example, stated that "the factor analytic results that have been presented as evidence for the theory do not provide convincing support because they are based upon methods that permit very little opportunity to reject hypotheses" (p. 33). "The point is that such results provide only about the same support as can also be provided for arbitrary theories of a kind generated by grouping variables at random to represent factors" (p. 42). No minced words there.

So despite the support of educators, the disdain expressed by the dominant psychologists of the era helped doom the popularity of Guilford's SOI model. And apart from the methodological and conceptual criticisms of the crème de la crème of psychologists, the SOI model ultimately presented too many obstacles to practitioners in the field. For one thing, the categories were often obscure and did not make sense in a practical or meaningful way. For example, Wechsler's Object Assembly (rapidly putting together cut-up picture puzzles) measures cognition of a figural system (CFS), cognition of figural transformations (CFT), and evaluation of figural relations (EFR). That is more than a mouthful. It is confusing. It is overwhelming. It is impractical. If a person gets a low score on Object Assembly, how do we know which of those three abilities is the weakness? Or maybe it is none of the three, but the problem is that the person simply was reflective, had a problem with visual acuity or visual perception, or otherwise had difficulty putting the puzzles together quickly?

Guilford's SOI model would not be the theory that would turn IQ testing into a theory-based profession. On the most basic level, it suffered from a problem similar to the one that afflicted Spearman's *g* theory. If one ability was too few to build a theory on, then 120 was just as clearly too many. And Guilford did not stop at 120. He kept refining the theory, adding to its complexity. He decided that one figural content was not enough, so he split it into figural-auditory and figural-visual (Guilford, 1975). Nor was a single memory operation adequate, so he subdivided it into memory recording (long-term) and memory retention (short-term) (Guilford, 1988). The revised and expanded SOI model now included 180 types of intelligence!

What was the right number? Clearly not 1 and just as clearly not 120 or 180. For a while, it seemed like 2 was the answer when Raymond Cattell's doctoral student, John Horn, revived Cattell's (1941) almost-forgotten notions of fluid and crystallized intelligence and began to popularize *Gf-Gc* theory (Horn & Cattell, 1966). Matarazzo (1972) applied *Gf-Gc* theory to Wechsler's scales, pointing out that Wechsler had unwittingly developed an intelligence test that corresponded to the Horn-Cattell theoretical notions of fluid intelligence or *Gf* (Performance IQ) and crystallized intelligence or *Gc* (Verbal IQ). But two general abilities were hardly more than one and didn't move the field of IQ testing forward. The Horn-Cattell *Gf-Gc* dichotomy provided a theoretical rationale for Wechsler's Verbal and Performance IQs (one that would ultimately prove to be bogus; Woodcock, 1990), but from a clinician's standpoint, so what? What was different?

Well, a lot was different. Horn's (1968, 1985) expansion of *Gf-Gc* theory to include an array of abilities, not just two, rose to prominence. And clinical tests of intelligence began to spring up in the 1980s, built directly on theoretical foundations. The next chapter in the history of IQ tests is also the next chapter of this book: "At Long Last—Theory Meets Practice."

3

History, Part 2: At Long Last—Theory Meets Practice

Theory was alive and well in psychological laboratories throughout the world from the early years of the 20th century (Spearman, 1904), and so were IQ tests (Binet & Simon, 1905). But apart from a few attempts to apply theory directly to the interpretation of IQ tests, or to the development of group-administered IQ tests (Meeker et al., 1975; Thurstone & Thurstone, 1949), the decade of the 1970s ended with theory failing to make a dent in the construction of a clinically based IQ test.

In the 1980s, as Guilford's (1967) SOI theory was going out of favor, two important things occurred. First, neurological theories of mental processing, notably Sperry's (1968) ideas about cerebral specialization and Luria's (1966, 1973) notions of successive and simultaneous processing, formed the basis of a clinical test of intelligence, the Kaufman Assessment Battery for Children (K-ABC; Kaufman & Kaufman, 1983); and (2) Horn's (1985) expansion of *Gf-Gc* theory to include additional broad abilities, such as short-term memory (*Gsm*), visualization (*Gv*), and processing speed (*Gs*)—and its subsequent merger with Carroll's (1993) model to form Cattell-Horn-Carroll (CHC) theory—zoomed in popularity and soon formed the solid foundation for several IQ tests, most notably the Woodcock-Johnson—Revised (WJ-R; Woodcock & Johnson, 1989) and its sequel, the WJ III (Woodcock, McGrew, & Mather, 2001).

These two innovative pathways would radically change the face of IQ test development and IQ test interpretation, starting in the early 1980s and continuing to the present day. But before following these two roads that led to the present-day breed of theory-based IQ tests, two topics must be mentioned.

First, a final look at Guilford's impact is warranted, as articulated by Linda Silverman (personal communication, July 8, 2008): "In spite of the abounding criticism, the Structure-of-Intellect model has had an enormous influence on modern conceptions of intelligence. Even the most severe critics (e.g., Carroll, 1968; Horn & Knapp, 1973; Humphreys, 1962) have indicated that the model has provided a stimulus to creative test development and has provoked considerable re-evaluation of the nature of human abilities."

Second, the two main theoretical approaches featured in this chapter—neuropsychological processing and CHC—are two among many theories of intelligence. I am well aware that some of the most popular and ingenious theories, notably Sternberg's (1988b, 1999) triarchic theory of successful intelligence and Gardner's (1993) multiple-intelligence theory, are far more comprehensive and encompass many more abilities than the handful of theories that have formed the foundation of modern IQ tests. As Sternberg (1988b) has said for years, IQ tests measure only one of the three prongs of his theory—*analytic* abilities, but not *practical* intelligence or *creativity.* (He is correct.) From the perspective of Gardner's eight multiple intelligences, IQ tests assess only three: *linguistic, logical-mathematical,* and *spatial* (Chen and Gardner, 2005, give credit only for the first two, but IQ tests have measured spatial intelligence for 70 years). No question, though, IQ tests do not measure Gardner's other five intelligences, many of which are noncognitive: *musical, bodily-kinesthetic, naturalistic, interpersonal,* and *intrapersonal* (i.e., self-insight).

Two decades ago, Sternberg (1988a) said, "Intelligence tests of the present are anachronisms" (p. 8), and Gardner (1988) said, "The whole concept [of IQ tests] has to be challenged; in fact, it has to be replaced" (p. 4). More recently, Sternberg has softened his stance: "[N]ew intelligence tests developed during the past twenty years (including the fifth edition of the Stanford-Binet) have been built from theories of intelligence.... Indeed, it would be hard for a new or revised test *not* based on theory to be competitive" (Sternberg et al., 2008, p. 12). Gardner's current perspective is still hard-line: "We recognize that some current intelligence tests do measure more than two cognitive abilities...and that Carroll's work...measures up to eight different intellectual components...These intelligence tests are based on 'horizontal' theories of intelligence" (Chen & Gardner, 2005, p. 81). Never mind what Gardner means by *horizontal.* Suffice it to say that his theory is *vertical,* and, therefore, much better—though not every IQ expert agrees. Lloyd Humphries said, "Gardner has debased the meaning of intelligence by grouping everything but the kitchen sink under that rubric" (Cordes, 1986, p. 8). For a thorough treatment of Sternberg's, Gardner's, and other influential theories of intelligence, broadly defined and not limited to the lens of IQ testing, consult Flanagan and Harrison's (2005) comprehensive edited text or Plucker's (in press) *Intelligence 101*.

My own view? The existing IQ tests, simply by following their own theoretical approach to what intelligence is, are immediately wrong or invalid from boxloads of other, sometimes opposite, viewpoints. Develop an IQ test from one theory, and you instantly alienate and incur the wrath of a multitude of ivory-tower researchers who preach the righteousness of their own Word without understanding the constraints of the clinical assessment of IQ. I don't dispute the obvious fact that IQ tests measure only an aspect of intelligence. Formal testing may not even be the best way to measure some other aspects. Gardner wants to do away with contemporary IQ tests because they measure only a few of his eight intelligences. But what rational person would try to claim than an IQ test can, or should, try to measure *all* that is intelligence? That IQ tests can't measure the totality of intelligence is axiomatic. David Wechsler knew that quite well. His theory of intelligence—the overall capacity to understand and cope with one's environment (Wechsler, 1958, 1975)—was far more comprehensive than his measurement of it. How much time can a psychologist reasonably spend giving an IQ test to an adult or child referred for clinical evaluation? The answer, Wechsler knew, is usually an hour-and-a-half or two, tops. That is long enough to understand a person's strong abilities and weak abilities, general level of mental functioning, and learning style—but not long enough to explore every crevice in the person's brain.

About a half century ago, psychologists named Pinard and Laurendeau (1964) developed an intelligence test based on Jean Piaget's well-respected developmental theory of intelligence (e.g., Inhelder & Piaget, 1958), and they even standardized it on a large sample of Canadian children. Trouble is, the authors were a bit compulsive and developed a test with 27 long tasks that took about 14 hours to administer. The term *experimental mortality* is used figuratively in psychology to indicate those subjects who drop out of a research study because of lack of interest, illness, moving away, and so forth. I have a feeling that experimental mortality might have taken on a more literal meaning during the norming of that all-encompassing Piaget test! (The test itself died a quiet death.) I also suspect that near-death experiences (NDEs according to Connie Willis in her brilliant sci-fi novel *Passage*), which are now associated with tunnels of light and blissful peace, may take on a new meaning if Gardner enters the realm of clinical assessment of IQ with a test that reliably measures all eight of his intelligences.

NEUROPSYCHOLOGICAL THEORIES AND IQ TESTS

The clinical field of neuropsychology (Luria, 1966) and the laboratory research field of psychobiology (Sperry, 1968) have contributed much to the field of IQ testing, especially Luria's neuropsychological theory. But it was the fact that Sperry's brilliant work was ignored by IQ test developers in the 1970s that impelled me to register a strong complaint: "Individual intelligence testing has been remarkably resistant to change, despite advances in related fields such as psychology and neurology. . . . The item content and mental processes assessed by conventional intelligence tests have not changed very much since the turn of the century when Alfred Binet and his coworkers engaged in their pioneering test development research" (Kaufman, 1979a, p. 96). Happily, that complaint is no longer true.

Sperry's Split-Brain Research

In the late 1970s I was enamored with Roger Sperry's (1968) research on patients who had "split-brain" surgery and with the cerebral specialization theory that evolved from this research (Kaufman, 1979a). This radical surgery, which was sometimes given to patients with severe epilepsy, involved cutting the corpus callosum—a thick band of nerve fibers that runs across the top of the skull and connects the two hemispheres of the brain. Patients who had this surgery saw a lessening of their symptoms of epilepsy (sometimes violence), but the doctors and psychologists who evaluated them saw something else entirely: They saw people who seemed to have two separate brains. With the two hemispheres surgically separated, and the two halves of the brain no longer in regular communication, it was possible to test one hemisphere at a time using tachistoscopes and a little imagination. The results were astonishing. The same person would respond to the exact same test item differently depending on which half of the brain was being assessed. For example, one item showed a picture of a birthday cake on a plate and the person had to point to the picture that was most closely associated with the cake. When the left hemisphere was asked to respond, the person pointed to a knife and fork, which was a conceptual, functional, stimulus-response association. In contrast, the right hemisphere pointed to a cowboy hat, because the wide-brimmed hat looked like the cake on a plate.

Once the professionals recovered from the shock of watching a person give two different answers to the same question, the surgeons began to realize the full impact of the split-brain procedure and modified it to keep a few of the interhemispheric fibers intact. But before this insight was reached, there were already a number of children and adults who effectively had two brains. And they were studied, and studied again, by medical and psychological researchers (Bogen, 1969). Research revealed that the two hemispheres had different styles of solving problems (Levy & Trevarthen, 1976; Levy-Agresti & Sperry, 1968). The left brain was analytic, time oriented, and dependent on language, and it tended to think in a logical-sequential manner. In contrast, the right brain integrated many stimuli at once in a gestalt-holistic fashion, tended to be nonverbal and spatial, and processed information in a simultaneous format (hence, the right hemisphere selected the cowboy hat as the right answer because it *looked like* the cake on the plate).

I believed that cerebral specialization theory was a perfect foundation for an IQ test: "The time has come for individual intelligence tests, *the* construct of intelligence to many people, to be substantially modified in accordance with the implications of the vital and dynamic research relating to brain functioning....There can be little justification for being blind to the impact of split-brain research" (Kaufman, 1979a, p. 96).

Sequential Versus Simultaneous Processing

At first glance, Wechsler's armchair division of his subtests into Verbal and Performance scales seemed to mirror almost exactly what the hemispheres were specialized to do—the left was the verbal half of the brain and the right was the nonverbal. But that simple verbal-nonverbal distinction was known for years before Sperry's innovative research. Ralph Reitan (1955), who popularized the field of neuropsychology, had already conducted numerous studies of patients with known brain damage to a single hemisphere (e.g., adults who had a tumor in the left hemisphere or a stroke in the right hemisphere). He hypothesized that patients with left-brain damage should have a relatively low Verbal IQ whereas those with right-brain damage should have a low Performance IQ, and he conducted clinical research studies to try to prove his point (Reitan, 1955). However, that line of research never produced the promised fruits: In general, patients with right-hemisphere damage tended to earn Performance IQs that were lower than their Verbal IQs (V > P profiles), but left-damaged patients tended *not* to earn the opposite P > V profile (Kaufman & Lichtenberger, 2006, chapters 8 and 9).

Why did the research not fully support the prediction? That is where Sperry's innovative research came in. The original notion that equated the left hemisphere with verbal ability and the right hemisphere with nonverbal ability was a distinction that was based on the *content* of the test items—Did the questions involve verbal content (like Wechsler's Vocabulary subtest) or pictorial, figural content (like Wechsler's Block Design subtest)? At first the cerebral specialization researchers were also thinking content, but the more they evaluated split-brain patients, the more they focused on the *process* preferred by each hemisphere. The left half of the brain was analytical and sequential, which is useful for understanding language; but it was the *analytic-sequential processing style* that distinguished this half of the brain, not its capacity for language. By contrast, the right hemisphere favored a *simultaneous-holistic processing style*—again, this type of processing facilitated the handling of spatial, nonverbal stimuli, but the key was the process, not the content. The simplistic example of the birthday cake and the cowboy hat is helpful here. The content was held constant when each half of the brain was given the test (i.e., nonverbal, pictorial content)—but each hemisphere solved the problem differently because of its own distinctive style of processing information.

Ultimately, however, Sperry's cerebral specialization theory did not revolutionize the field of neurology or the field of IQ testing. Similar processing dichotomies had been springing up all over the broad field of psychology in the middle of the 20th century. The problem was that the field of psychology had become so specialized at that time that researchers in one area (e.g., psychobiology) didn't read journals in other areas (e.g., neuropsychology), and brain-related disciplines tended to ignore publications in the more traditional laboratory science journals (e.g., cognitive psychology). How else could one explain the psychobiologist Sperry's (1968) "discovery" that the right hemisphere was intelligent at nonverbal problem solving when the neuropsychologist Reitan (1955) had been conducting research on that very topic for years?

At the same time as Sperry was uncovering the mysteries of the right hemisphere's unique processing style, the great Russian neuropsychologist Alexander Luria was publishing his innovative clinical findings based on investigations of patients with damage to a single hemisphere—the left hemisphere. Luria (1966) was writing about two distinct mental processes: successive and simultaneous. And Luria's descriptions of these two fundamental processes were in lockstep with Sperry's distinction between left-brain (successive) and right-brain (simultaneous) processing. But Luria was not operating out of a left-right distinction (how could he, when he studied patients only with left-brain damage?). Instead, Luria described a *front-back* division of the brain. He considered successive processing to be primarily a function of the fronto-temporal regions of the brain, in contrast to the occipital-parietal localization (at the back of the skull) that accounts mainly for simultaneous syntheses. Luria had rotated the brain 90 degrees. Or maybe Sperry had rotated it 90 degrees. Did it matter? What was most important was that these two pioneers from different fields of neurology and different world views agreed that there were two basic, fundamental styles of solving problems and processing information that characterized human behavior.

And they were not alone in that belief. Outside of the brain sciences, researchers in cognitive psychology unearthed a processing dichotomy based on studies of visual search, attention, perception, detection, memory, and the like (e.g., Neisser, 1967). Only they referred to these two processes as *serial* and *parallel*. For example, Seller (1970) showed that the same type of stimuli (letters) could be processed either serially or in parallel depending on the demands of the task. When letters had to be matched based on physical identity, parallel processing was performed; in contrast, serial processing was a more efficient style that had to be used when the subjects could not rely on the physical properties of each letter to solve the problem. Many studies like Seller's established the existence of the two modes of information processing, but even more intriguing are the investigations by cognitive and other experimental psychologists who related the two processes to the left and right cerebral hemispheres. G. Cohen (1972), for example, extended Seller's work by showing the left hemisphere to be superior at matching names and the right hemisphere at matching shapes.

But the most consistent finding of the body of cognitive research was not the association of one type of processing to one hemisphere and a different type to the other half of the brain. The bottom line of all the research is that *process* hypotheses were supported far more often than *content* hypotheses. How the person goes about solving a problem was found to be more important than whether the questions involve handling verbal or pictorial or numerical stimuli.

Sequential or successive processing involves solving problems in a step-by-step fashion, placing a premium on the serial or time-related order of stimuli; in contrast, simultaneous processing demands a gestalt-like, frequently spatial, integration of stimuli to solve problems with maximum efficiency. We all tend to have our own preferred style of learning and problem solving. Suppose someone gives you a hand-drawn map so you can navigate a trip from his or her home to yours, a map that includes a snapshot of the entire trip from starting point to end point, including major roads and highways. Does the map make you feel happy and secure? If so, then you probably prefer a simultaneous-holistic processing approach to problem solving. You like a visual representation that shows the trip from start to finish—that is, the whole trip at a glance. But if the map strikes fear in your heart ("But where do I turn? Is it a right or left turn?"), then you are conceivably a sequential processor. You'd like to have a carefully spelled-out list of instructions: (1) Left at the third light (Spruce Street), (2) Right at the stop sign (Third Avenue), (3) Go about 1 mile and get onto Interstate 5 going north, and so forth. Simultaneous processors also have their moments of panic—like when they ask for directions at a toll booth and are told in rapid succession, "Take the second exit, then go about 4 blocks past the train station and turn right, then make a quick left onto a one-way street, and follow that with a sharp right at a T intersection; 2 or 3 miles ahead you'll see the shopping mall on the left, just past the post office."

And if you want the map *and* the written-out list of directions? Maybe you are insecure. Or maybe you are an integrated problem solver who relies on both sequential and simultaneous processing about equally. Or maybe you need to be given a comprehensive test to determine your best way of solving problems and processing information because who would trust a one-item test (i.e., using a map or not) in the first place? But one thing is true: People who give you directions are doing it the way *they* prefer to solve problems; they haven't got a clue about your preferred approach. Yet, suppose you know the other person's style of processing information and you are a teacher. Then you can adapt your teaching methods to the other's preferred processing style. And that is what Nadeen and I had in mind when we developed the K-ABC in the late 1970s and early 1980s.

The Kaufman Assessment Battery for Children (K-ABC)

As I reminisced during an invited address a few years ago (Kaufman, 2005a, 2005b):

I remember so clearly the day Nadeen and I came up with the ideas that would become the K-ABC. When we lived in Athens, Georgia, in the mid- to late-1970s, we frequently drove with our three kids to shopping malls in Atlanta for entertainment. One time we were going to see Luis from the television show *Sesame Street,* and while we were driving we were trying to plan our next project. We decided we were going to develop a test; on the entire 2-hour ride to Atlanta we were talking about Roger Sperry's cerebral specialization theory and the distinction between right and left hemisphere brain functioning. We were talking about cognitive styles, translations of test scores to educational remediation, nonverbal assessment, and fairness to ethnic minorities. We discussed the importance of developing interesting and novel tasks and the need to emphasize process instead of content. We were going to Atlanta in the first place, in part, because we felt guilty about not spending enough time with our kids and then we proceeded to ignore them the whole ride there! On the ride home we asked each other, "Who are we fooling? We will develop a test and nobody will publish it." So we decided to forget about that idea. Until the next day, a Monday, when we got a call from Dr. Gary Robertson, director of test development at American Guidance Service (AGS), a Minnesota test publisher. Gary asked whether Nadeen or I or both of us would like to develop a new test of intelligence. So being on the impulsive side of the impulsive-reflective cognitive style—at least at that moment—I blurted out, "Oh we developed an IQ test yesterday." It took a little bit of time to regain credibility with AGS, but that was the beginning of the K-ABC. Of course, if we had actually developed the precise test we had designed in the car, it would have taken about 24 hours to administer. Being idealists, we wanted to measure *everything* that we thought was important about children's mental ability and cognitive style. Being realists, we knew we had to be a bit more practical in what just *had* to be included in the K-ABC.[1]

Ultimately, we accomplished our most important goals: (a) to be rooted in theory; (b) to include new and interesting tasks; (c) to reduce IQ differences between White and African American children (the typical differences of about 15 points on Wechsler's scales were cut in half on the K-ABC); (d) to separate the ability to solve new problems (mental processing or "intelligence") from acquired knowledge and language skills ("achievement"), thereby providing a less language-based assessment of bilingual children's intelligence; and (e) to include "teaching items." These innovative teaching items ensured that children understood exactly what was expected of them for each task. Research had shown that young children have difficulty understanding basic concepts like "same" or "first" or "under" (Boehm, 1967). Similar concepts are commonly included in the directions spoken by the examiner when testing children on IQ tests (Kaufman, 1978). Because the tests are standardized, examiners aren't allowed to change the words of a question or an instruction. So we built in teaching items—an unscored sample item and the first two items of each subtest—enabling the examiner to feel confident that children understood the test directions. Examiners were told to teach the child, whenever necessary, by using different words, gestures, or a different language, including American Sign Language. These teaching items helped ensure that a low subtest score reflected low ability, not just bad communication between the examiner and child.

As we said in the test manual (Kaufman & Kaufman, 1983), "Intelligence, as measured by the K-ABC, is defined in terms of an individual's *style* of solving problems and processing information; this definition, which also stresses *level of skill* in each style

---

1. Copyright 2005 by the National Association of School Psychologists. Bethesda, MD. Adapted with the permission of the publisher. www.nasp online.org

of information processing, has a strong theoretical foundation in the domains of both neuropsychology and cognitive psychology" (p. 2). So we began by trying to develop an IQ test from Sperry's cerebral specialization theory but wound up building the K-ABC on a sequential-simultaneous foundation that spanned multiple theories and disciplines. We learned so much during the test development process, especially from our team of graduate students who went on to become international leaders in school psychology and assessment (Bruce Bracken, Jack Cummings, Patti Harrison, Randy Kamphaus, Jack Naglieri, and Cecil Reynolds). They helped us realize, ultimately, that the key was the distinction between the two processes, not the possible link-up between process and hemisphere. For children, especially, whose brains are "plastic," it is not really feasible to figure out whether Sperry's right-left or Luria's front-back distinction is more plausible. Moreover, the research on patients with brain damage is predominantly based on adults (Kaufman & Lichtenberger, 2006; Matarazzo, 1972), and the intact parts of a damaged brain might no longer function precisely as they did before the damage.

Word Order is an example of a K-ABC sequential processing subtest. The examiner says the names of objects (e.g., car—lamp—horn) and then the child has to point to pictures of the objects in the order in which they were named. For more difficult items, the child has to name pictures of colors before responding, an "interference task" that prevents rehearsal. Word Order, including the verbal interference task, is an adaptation of the clinical tests that Luria (1966) used to measure the higher brain functions of patients with brain damage.

Figure 3.1 depicts a K-ABC simultaneous processing subtest (Gestalt Closure). For this task, the child has to name the object or scene pictured in a partially completed inkblot drawing. This type of task was important to include in the K-ABC because "it has proved so valuable as an accepted prototype of simultaneous processing and right hemispheric functioning... [and] has produced approximately equal mean scores for [African Americans], Hopi Indians, and whites" (Kaufman & Kaufman, 1983, pp. 40–41).

What is this?
What is this?

FIGURE 3.1 Sample simultaneous processing items (similar to items on the K-ABC and KABC-II Gestalt Closure subtest).

Note. From *Kaufman Assessment Battery for Children, Second Edition (KABC-II)*, by A. S. Kaufman and N. L. Kaufman, 2004, Circle Pines, MN: American Guidance Service.

When the K-ABC was published, there was much media hype (TV interviews, radio interviews, radio call-in shows, cable TV features) for a couple of years, and controversy was rampant within the professional community as well. The media was interested primarily in the K-ABC's greatly reduced ethnic differences for African American, Hispanic, and Native American children. Psychologists and special educators debated the theoretical foundation of the K-ABC, the reasons underlying the reduced ethnic differences, and our decision to keep verbal tasks and measures of acquired knowledge (both staples of the Stanford-Binet and Wechsler IQs) out of the IQ scale. The *Journal of Special Education* published a special issue devoted to the K-ABC (Miller & Reynolds, 1984) in which the test was either praised or damned, depending on the perspective of the expert invited to contribute to the special issue. Ultimately, the key point was the theory on which the test was based, and there were wildly differing opinions. Raymond Dean, a leader in the field of school psychology who would later coauthor a neuropsychological battery, was complimentary, stating that "the K-ABC represents a theoretically consistent battery of tests that offers insights into children's cognitive processing beyond presently available measures of intelligence" (Dean, 1984, p. 251). Noted theorist Robert Sternberg disagreed, stating that the K-ABC "is based on an inadequate conception of intelligence, and as a result, it is not a good measure of intelligence" (Sternberg, 1984, p. 277). (My son James would eventually earn his PhD at Yale under Dr. Sternberg, who would prove to be a wonderful mentor for James as well as a collaborator on numerous books. And James would eventually edit the *Psychology 101* series.)

Despite our initial inspiration from Sperry's model and our clear statements in the test manual that our theoretical foundation was built on a research and theoretical base that encompassed both brain-related and cognitive perspectives, our test soon became known simply as a Luria-based test that addressed only a portion of Luria's neuropsychological model and was, therefore, incomplete. That criticism was not heard much in Europe and Asia, where adapted and translated versions of the K-ABC thrived and its sequential-simultaneous model (with language and factual items excluded from the IQ measure) was respected no less than Wechsler's traditional verbal-performance distinction. The K-ABC flourished, for example, in Germany (Melchers & Preuß, 1991), France (Voyazopolous, 1994), and Japan (Matsubara et al., 1994).

But in the United States, the K-ABC model of intelligence would come to be seen as an incomplete measure of Horn's (1989) broad abilities that focused too much on short-term memory (*Gsm*) and visual processing (*Gv*) and too little on fluid reasoning (*Gf*) and comprehension-knowledge (*Gc*) (Keith, 1985). Carroll (1993) concluded that most K-ABC mental processing tasks were the well-known ability factors of what he termed VZ (visualization), LD (language processing), and MS (memory span). The great theorist dismissed the K-ABC by stating: "With respect to factorial content, there is little if anything that is new in the K-ABC test" (Carroll, 1993, p. 703). I guess it's better than being ignored!

Nonetheless, the K-ABC served some useful functions from a historical perspective. It was the first *theory-based* individually administered, clinical IQ test, and it showed that the Wechsler-Binet monopoly could be challenged, opening the door for the spate of theory-based tests of cognitive processing and cognitive abilities that would follow it during the 1980s and that continue in the 21st century. It included truly novel IQ tasks, not the same old recycled verbal and nonverbal tasks that traced their lineage to Alfred Binet and American World War I psychologists. (In this regard, Dick Woodcock, 1978, was also a pioneer in developing innovative cognitive tasks for his Woodcock-Johnson Psycho-Educational Battery.) The K-ABC shifted the focus from content to process in the eyes of many clinicians, even those who continued to administer the content-based Wechsler scales. It showed that it was possible to greatly reduce ethnic differences in IQ when care was taken to ensure fairness. It included more than 40 research studies in the test manual to demonstrate that the test was valid, whereas previous test manuals barely provided validity evidence. And we encouraged our test publisher (then called AGS, now Pearson Assessments) to hire a school psychologist as project director (they hired Randy Kamphaus, now an eminent leader in the field of cognitive and behavioral assessment), in contrast to the statistical-mathematical experts who served as project directors for previous IQ tests. This latter change ensured that a scientist-practitioner, someone who actually administered clinical tests to children and adults, was in charge of test development, not someone who excelled as a scientist but lacked real-world experience.

Today, most of these K-ABC innovations have become standard practice in current tests, including revisions of the Wechsler and Stanford-Binet. Theory-based tests of exceptional quality abound. Teaching items and novel subtests are included in nearly every IQ test. The emphasis on processing characterizes all major IQ tests, including the WISC-IV and WAIS-IV, which now yield four process-based indexes instead of two content-based IQs (i.e., Verbal and Performance). And practitioner-scientists are the rule, not the exception, as project directors and executives of test publishers. The chief executives of the two test publishers we work with directly are a clinical neuropsychologist (Dr. Aurelio Prifitera of Pearson Assessments) and a clinical psychologist (Dr. Mireille Simon, of ECPA in Paris).

But the sequential-simultaneous theory on which the K-ABC was based did not stand the test of time, at least in the United States. From the perspective of neuropsychologists, the K-ABC was criticized as measuring only Block 2 of Luria's three-block model. As discussed in the next section, the K-ABC model has been superseded by a more complete representation of Luria's neuropsychological model.

Luria's Three-Block Neuropsychological Theory

Luria's (1970) goal as a neuropsychologist was to map out the brain's systems and functions responsible for complex behavioral processes, especially the high-level processes associated with the intake and integration of information and with problem-solving abilities. Luria perceived the brain's basic functions to be represented by three main blocks, or functional systems.

- Block 1 is responsible for arousal and attention.
- Block 2 uses successive (sequential) and simultaneous (holistic) processing to analyze, code, and store information.
- Block 3, associated with the frontal lobes of the brain, is responsible for planning, decision making, and what clinical neuropsychologists refer to as "executive functions."

Figure 3.2 summarizes the functions associated with each of Luria's three blocks. The arrows between adjacent blocks reflect Luria's emphasis that the *integration* of the three blocks is necessary to permit complex thinking.

Many empirical studies support Luria's (1970, 1973) clinical documentation of the three functional units (see, for example,

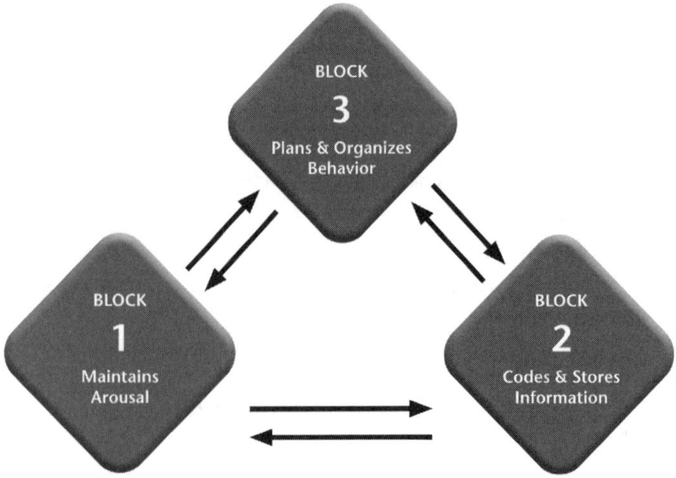

FIGURE 3.2 Luria's three blocks or functional units.
Note. From *Kaufman Assessment Battery for Children, Second Edition (KABC-II)*, by A. S. Kaufman and N. L. Kaufman, 2004, Circle Pines, MN: American Guidance Service. Copyright © 2004 by NCS Pearson, Inc. Reproduced with permission. All rights reserved.

Naglieri, 1999). Much neurological evidence supports the ages of 11 to 12 as crucial for the development of the prefrontal cortex, leading to the refinement of Block 3 executive functions, such as working memory, for making decisions, thinking abstractly, and solving complex problems (Golden, 1981). (Working memory is the mental scratchpad that allows us to hold onto information long enough to solve complex problems.)

Naglieri and Das's PASS Theory

Jack Naglieri and J. P. Das were instrumental in translating Luria's three blocks to the practice of cognitive assessment. Jack worked closely with Nadeen and me to develop the K-ABC, and J. P. studied with Luria in Russia. Together they developed the Luria-based PASS theory, which was an expansion of the K-ABC's sequential-simultaneous processing distinction. The **P** in PASS refers to Planning, the Block 3 function; the **A** denotes Block 1's Attention; and the two **S**'s refer to Luria's Block 2 coding processes, Successive and Simultaneous. They used PASS theory as the theoretical foundation of the Cognitive Assessment System (CAS; Naglieri & Das, 1997), a test for ages 5 to 17 years that has proved to be useful for developing educational interventions and treatment. Improving planning ability, for example, has been shown to lead to improvement in math achievement (Naglieri & Gottling, 1997; Naglieri & Johnson, 2000). In addition, groups of children with specific disorders such as ADHD or reading disabilities tend to display characteristic profiles on the CAS. Children with ADHD, for example, tend to perform considerably better on the Successive and Simultaneous scales than on Attention or Planning, whereas children with reading disorders tend to do worst on Successive Processing (Naglieri, 1999, Figure 6.3).

The two types of mental processing have already been defined. Let's look at the P and the A that make up the PASS model (Naglieri, 1999).

Planning is a mental process that requires a person to "develop a plan of action, evaluate the value of the method, monitor its effectiveness, revise or reject a previous plan as the task demands change, and control the impulse to act without careful consideration" (Naglieri, 1999, p. 13). This process is illustrated in Figure 3.3 by the CAS subtest Planned Codes, which requires the child to write a code (e.g., XO) under the appropriate letter (A, B, C, or D). The child's success is facilitated by the choice of an

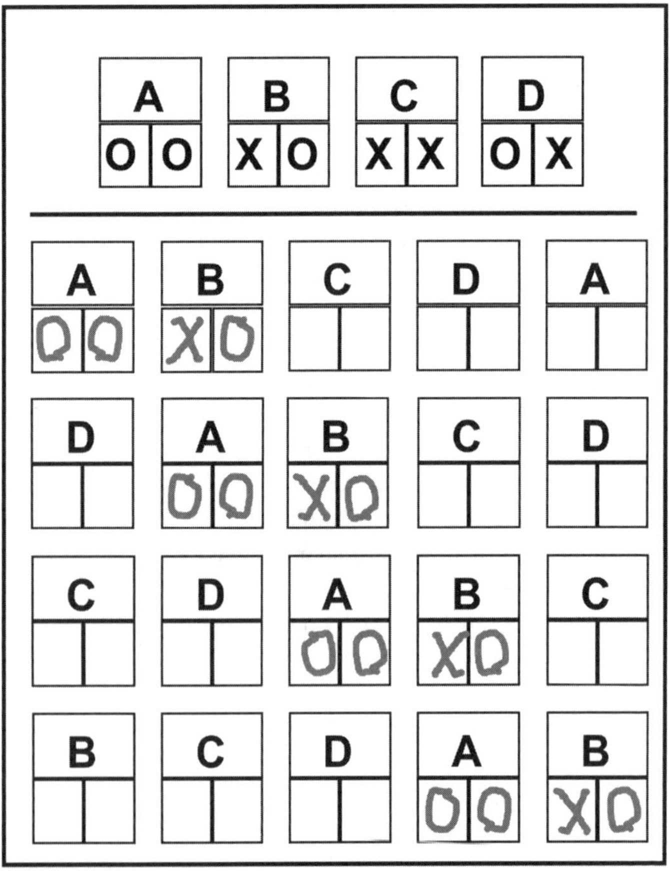

FIGURE 3.3 Example of a planning test item from the Cognitive Assessment System (CAS).

Note. From *Essentials of CAS Assessment* (p. 13, Figure 1.4) by J. A. Naglieri, 1999, New York: Wiley. Reproduced with permission.

effective strategy to permit very quick responding (e.g., doing all the A's first, then the B's, etc.). It is fascinating to realize that Binet was so far ahead of his peers such as Francis Galton and James McKeen Cattell when he theorized about intelligence, because he was talking about the Block 3 functions of the prefrontal cortex before anyone knew very much about these executive functions. Binet and Simon (1916/1973) considered intelligent thought to require *direction, adaptation,* and *criticism.* These aspects of intelligence form the essence of Luria's notion of planning ability: (a) direction "consists of knowing what has to be done and how to do it"; (b) adaptation "refers to the selection and monitoring of our strategy"; and (c) criticism "is our ability to criticize our own thoughts and actions... and to change our behavior in such a way as to improve our performance" (Sternberg et al., 2008, p. 10).

Attention is a mental process that requires a person to selectively focus on specific stimuli while inhibiting responses to competing stimuli. Figure 3.4 illustrates an Attention item from the CAS subtest Number Detection.

When we revised the K-ABC and developed the KABC-II (Kaufman & Kaufman, 2004a), for ages 3 to 18 years, we followed the lead of Naglieri and Das (1997) and expanded the neuropsychological theory underlying the KABC-II to include the Block 3 functions of planning ability, and we also added a learning scale to evaluate a child's ability to learn and retain new material

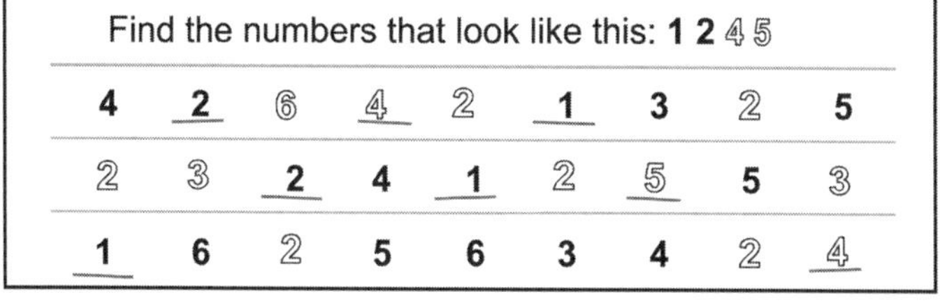

FIGURE 3.4 Example of an attention test item from the Cognitive Assessment System (CAS).

Note. From *Essentials of CAS Assessment* (p. 16, Figure 1.7) by J. A. Naglieri, 1999, New York: Wiley. Reproduced with permission.

during the assessment. Importantly, success on the learning tasks requires an integration of the three blocks. The KABC-II tasks demand Block 1's focused and selective attention, Block 2's coding and storage of auditory and visual stimuli, and Block 3's capacity to generate strategies to learn the material efficiently. Reitan (1988) said about Luria's theory that "integration of these systems constitutes the real key to understanding how the brain mediates complex behavior" (p. 333). To Luria (1970), "It is clear that every complex form of behavior depends on the joint operation of several faculties located in different zones of the brain" (p. 68).

Figure 3.5 shows sample items from a learning task that teaches the person a new language, namely, the word or concept

Stimulus:

Examiner: "Each of these drawings has a meaning (point to each rebus in turn)**. This means *bus*; this means *plane*; this means *the*; this means *and*."**

Stimulus:

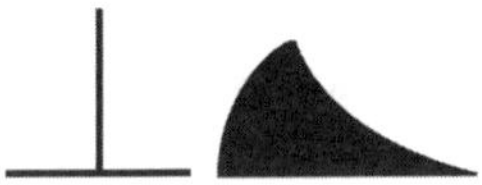

Examiner: "Read these drawings."

Answer: The plane. The plane and the bus.

FIGURE 3.5 Example of a learning subtest (Rebus Learning).
Note. From *Kaufman Adolescent and Adult Intelligence Test (KAIT)*, by A. S. Kaufman and N. L. Kaufman, 1993, Circle Pines, MN: American Guidance Service. Copyright © 1993 by NCS Pearson, Inc. Reproduced with permission. All rights reserved.

that corresponds to specific pictures and abstract symbols (rebuses). Then the person has to "read" both simple and complex sentences composed of these symbols. The figure illustrates Rebus Learning from the KAIT, which is very similar to the KABC-II Rebus subtest.

In developing the KABC-II we relied on a dual theoretical model—*both* Luria's three functional units or blocks *and* CHC theory. We believe that the two theories complement each other well, and that both theories have a great deal to offer for the measurement of intelligence. Which leads us to the next topic.

CATTELL-HORN-CARROLL (CHC) THEORY

Neuropsychological processing theories made their mark on IQ tests, but the theory that has most influenced today's intelligence tests is an amalgam of two related theories of cognitive abilities: Horn and Cattell's (1966) theory of fluid and crystallized intelligence and Carroll's (1993) three-stratum theory, known as the CHC (Cattell-Horn-Carroll) model. Let's take the original theories in sequence; Cattell-Horn's *Gf-Gc* theory (Horn & Cattell, 1966) had the first, dramatic impact on the interpretation of IQ tests, most notably Wechsler's scales, before Carroll's (1993) exhaustive research was even known by the field of IQ testing.

Cattell and Horn's *Gf-Gc* Theory

Some years after the elaboration of Spearman's (1904, 1927) influential *g* theory, Thurstone (1938) and other leading psychologists argued strongly against *g* and advocated theories that hypothesized group factors over and above Spearman's *g* and *s* (Jensen, 1998). Even the noted learning theorist Clark Hull wrote the book *Aptitude Testing* (Hull, 1928), which foreshadowed the shift in emphasis from *g* to multiple ability approaches (Thorndike et al., 1986). In contrast to the trend either to advocate *g* or to argue against *g* (by proposing a half-dozen or so multiple abilities), Raymond Cattell simply split *g* into two pieces. As Spearman's doctoral student, Cattell (1941, 1963) built upon his mentor's approach to intelligence. His new system embraced *g* but posited two types of *g* abilities, not just one:

- *Fluid intelligence (Gf),* the ability to solve novel problems by using reasoning; Cattell believed that *Gf* was largely a function of biological and neurological factors and was vulnerable to the effects of aging.
- *Crystallized intelligence (Gc),* a knowledge-based ability that Cattell considered to be extremely dependent on education and acculturation and largely resistant to the impact of aging.

Raven's (1938) abstract Progressive Matrices Test has always been used as the paradigm of fluid reasoning and was considered by Spearman to be the very best measure of *g* (Silverman, 2009). Raven's measure of abstract reasoning has been copied by many test developers, with adaptations appearing in recent versions of Wechsler's scales, the Stanford-Binet revisions, the Kaufman tests, and other batteries as well (e.g., Naglieri & Das, 1997; Woodcock et al., 2001). Figure 3.6 depicts an illustrative matrices item, which requires *Gf* to figure out the relationships among the abstract designs in the 3 × 3 matrix (this is a medium-difficulty example; see Figures 4.1 and 4.2 for easy and challenging items, respectively).

Figure 3.7 illustrates a Differential Ability Scales—Second Edition (DAS-II) task that uses numbers instead of designs to measure fluid reasoning (sequential and quantitative reasoning), and Figure 3.8 demonstrates KABC-II's Story Completion, which uses pictures to assess *Gf*.

The strategies needed to solve *Gf* items resemble Luria's notion of Block 3 planning and decision-making ability to a considerable extent, which is why the KABC-II scale for school-age children that measures high-level, complex, abstract reasoning is called Planning/*Gf*. In Story Completion, the child is shown a row of pictures that tells a story, but some of the pictures are

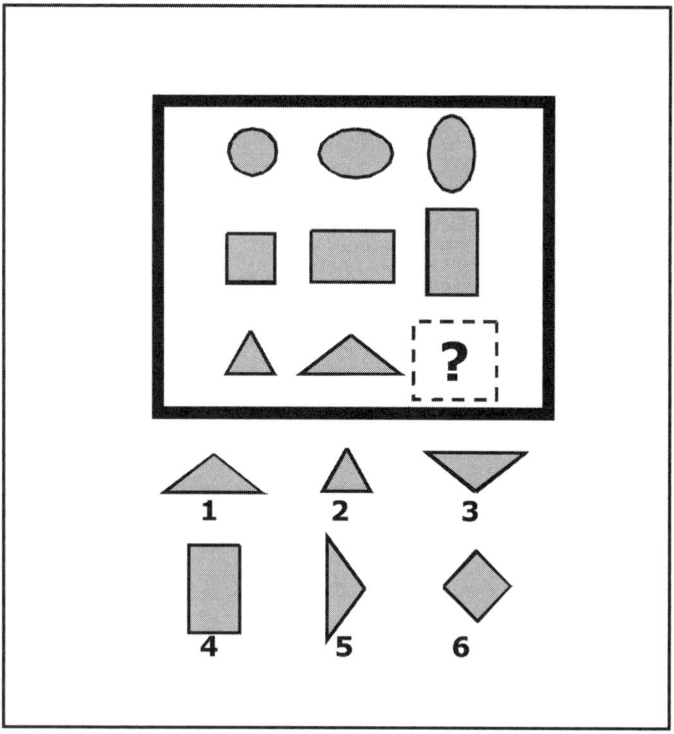

FIGURE 3.6 Example of a *Gf* matrices item (similar to items on a variety of matrices tests).

Note. The correct response is #5. From *Essentials of DAS-II Assessment,* by R. Dumont, J. O. Willis, and C. D. Elliott (p. 310, Figure 8.1), New York: Wiley. Reproduced with permission.

missing. The child has to complete the story by selecting pictures from an array of cards (see Figure 3.8). The *Gf* needed to select the appropriate pictures and insert them in their correct sequence in the story requires the Block 3 functions of developing a plan of action, generating hypotheses, making quick decisions, controlling impulses, and revising or rejecting previous plans as the task demands change.

Gc is measured by a variety of tasks, usually verbal. An example of a fairly pure *Gc* task is the Vocabulary subtest on the various

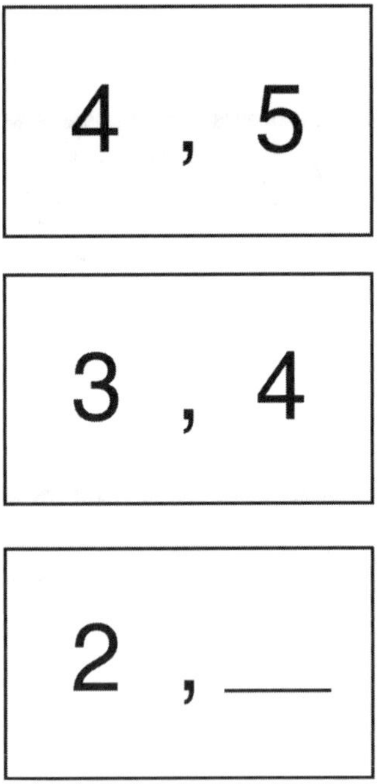

FIGURE 3.7 Example of a *Gf* subtest that uses numbers as stimuli (DAS-II Sequential and Quantitative Reasoning).
Note. Answer = 3. The child figures out how two pairs of numbers relate to each other and then applies the rule to discover the missing number in the incomplete pair. *Differential Ability Scales—Second Edition (DAS-II)*, by C. D. Elliott, 2007, San Antonio, TX: The Psychological Corporation.

editions of the Wechsler scales and Stanford-Binet ("What do we mean by *edifice*? What does *agitation* mean?"). But *Gc* tasks can also utilize pictorial stimuli, as illustrated by the KABC-II Expressive Vocabulary subtest (see Figure 3.9).

John Horn was Cattell's doctoral student. And just as Cattell expanded his mentor's theory of intelligence, so, too, did Horn. Horn and Cattell (1966, 1967) initially focused on the generation-old *Gf-Gc* dichotomy. But despite Cattell's (1963) devotion to *Gf* and *Gc*, Horn never really bought into the model. Almost from the beginning—indeed in his doctoral dissertation—Horn (1965)

FIGURE 3.8 Illustrative item for the Story Completion subtest (on the KABC-II Planning/*Gf* scale).

Notes. 1. Of the four pictures at the bottom, the first two on the left do not go with the story; they are distractors. The fourth picture from the left goes second in the story (showing the father letting go of the bike), and the remaining picture goes third in the story (showing the daughter riding by herself, just before the dog runs in front of her).

2. From *Kaufman Assessment Battery for Children, Second Edition (KABC-II)*, by A. S. Kaufman and N. L. Kaufman, 2004, Circle Pines, MN: American Guidance Service.

believed that the research supported more than just these two general abilities. He quickly identified four abilities in addition to *Gf* and *Gc* (Horn, 1965, 1968): short-term acquisition and retrieval (*Gsm*), long-term storage and retrieval (*Glr*), visual processing (*Gv*), and speed of processing (*Gs*).[2] That number would grow to 9 or 10 *broad abilities* by the mid-1990s (Horn, 1989; Horn & Noll, 1997).

The initial dichotomy had been expanded, but Horn did not consider any of the abilities to be more or less important than others. Although the theory continued to be called *Gf-Gc* theory, the 9 or 10 broad abilities were treated as equals, not as part of any type of hierarchy.

---

2. Different abbreviations and symbols have been used for various CHC abilities. The ones shown in parentheses are the ones currently used by most CHC theorists, not necessarily the original symbols.

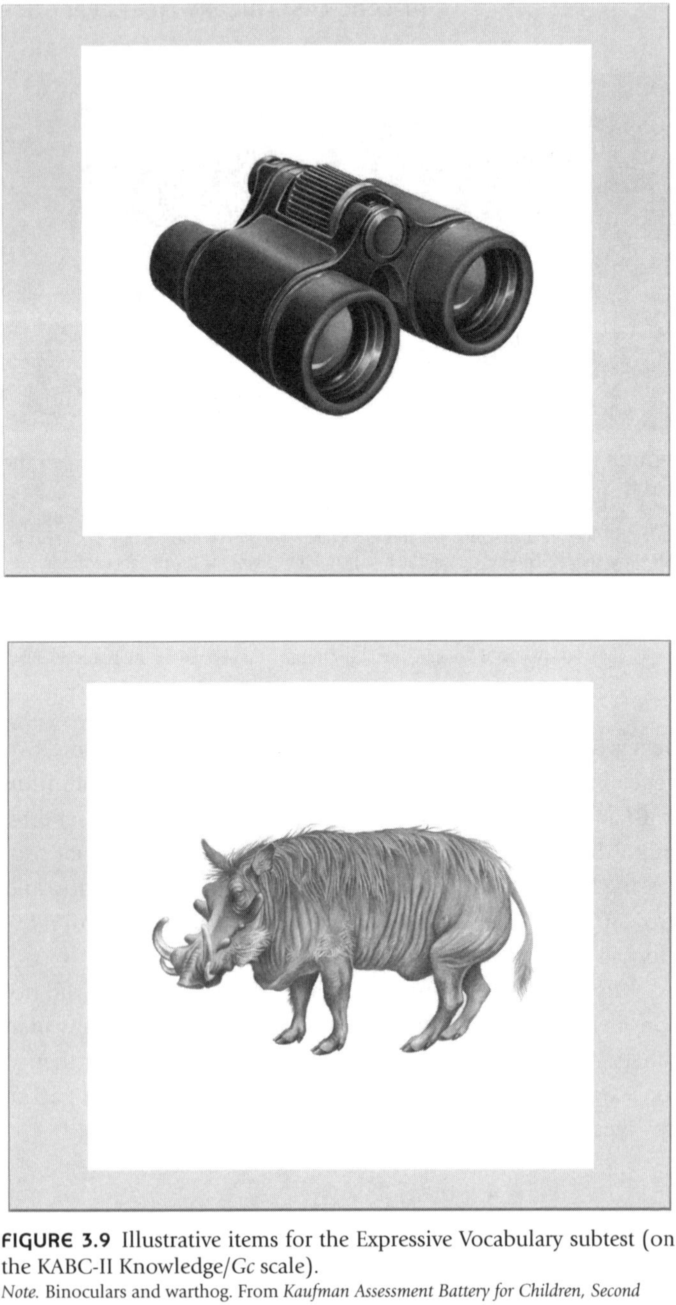

FIGURE 3.9 Illustrative items for the Expressive Vocabulary subtest (on the KABC-II Knowledge/*Gc* scale).

Note. Binoculars and warthog. From *Kaufman Assessment Battery for Children, Second Edition (KABC-II)*, by A. S. Kaufman and N. L. Kaufman, 2004, Circle Pines, MN: American Guidance Service. Copyright © 2004 by NCS Pearson, Inc. Reproduced with permission. All rights reserved.

John Carroll's Three-Stratum Theory

In contrast to Horn's egalitarian approach to cognitive abilities, John Carroll (1993, 1997) developed a hierarchical theory composed of three levels, or strata, of abilities:

- Stratum III (General), a Spearman-like *g*, which Carroll (1993, 1997) considered to be a valid and vital construct
- Stratum II (Broad), composed of 8 broad abilities that correspond closely to Horn's (1989) broad abilities and correspond roughly to Gardner's (1993) multiple intelligences (Carroll, 1997)
- Stratum I (Narrow), composed of about 70 fairly specific abilities, many of which indicate the person's "level of mastery, along a difficulty scale," "speed with which the individual performs tasks," or "rate of learning in learning and memory tasks" (Carroll, 1997, p. 124)

As my friend and colleague Mark Daniel (1997) said about Carroll's theory, "Never before has a psychometric-ability model been so firmly grounded in data" (p. 1043).

Horn's (1989) theory always focused on the broad abilities (Carroll's Stratum II), but Horn also discussed the more specific or narrow abilities as well. To Horn, Spearman's *g* (Stratum III of Carroll's model) had no place in any theory. It made him see red when other theorists defended it. Otherwise, the Carroll and Cattell-Horn theories were similar enough to warrant being merged into the new CHC theory.

The Merger of Theoretical Models to Form CHC Theory

The CHC model, the blend of the Cattell-Horn and Carroll theories, is a psychometric theory that rests on a large body of research accumulated over decades in literally thousands of empirical investigations. CHC owes a debt to Thurstone's (1938) pioneering primary mental abilities theory: "to a considerable extent, modern hierarchical theories derive from this theory" (Horn & Noll, 1997, p. 62).

Horn and Carroll agreed to merge their theories into a single model in the late 1990s, without fanfare, in a personal communication to Richard Woodcock in July 1999. But about a dozen years earlier, at a 1986 meeting in Dallas that included Horn, Carroll, and Woodcock, the intimate link between the Cattell-Horn theory and Carroll's comprehensive research was discovered. As Kevin McGrew (2005) recalled, "A collective 'Ah Ha!' engulfed the room as Carroll's WJ [Woodcock-Johnson] factor interpretation provided a meaningful link between the theoretical terminology of Horn and the concrete world of WJ tests" (p. 144). Though CHC theory would not be on the agenda for years to come, that 1986 meeting "was the flash point that resulted in *all* subsequent theory-to-practice bridging events leading to today's CHC theory and related assessment developments" (McGrew, 2005, p. 144).

CHC theory focuses on 10 broad abilities, which together define the range of the major human intellectual capacities, as determined by the research conducted by John Horn (1989) and his colleagues and by the intensive survey of literature assembled by John Carroll (1993). Each broad ability is subdivided into specific narrow abilities, which total about 70. The relationship between broad and narrow abilities is illustrated in Table 3.1 for crystallized intelligence (*Gc*) (Flanagan, Ortiz, & Alfonso, 2007, p. 281).

This table shows 12 narrow abilities—for example, listening ability, foreign language aptitude, and general science information—each measuring a different facet of *Gc;* taken together they demonstrate the depth and breadth of crystallized intelligence. Narrow abilities are important, but the linchpin of CHC theory is the array of broad abilities. It has never been clear whether Carroll's Stratum III (*g* or general ability) is part of CHC theory or not. The topic was rarely talked about while Horn and Carroll were alive because it was their one main bone of contention. To Carroll, *g* was a crucial and fundamental concept; to Horn it was

TABLE 3.1 DEFINITIONS OF CRYSTALLIZED INTELLIGENCE (*Gc*) NARROW STRATUM 1 ABILITIES

Stratum I (Narrow)	Definition
Crystallized Intelligence (Gc)	
Language development (LD)	General development, or the understanding of words, sentences, and paragraphs (*not* requiring reading), in spoken native language skills
Lexical knowledge (VL)	Extent of vocabulary that can be understood in terms of correct word meanings
Listening ability (LS)	Ability to listen to and comprehend oral communications
General (verbal) information (K0)	Range of general knowledge
Information about culture (K2)	Range of cultural knowledge (e.g., music, art)
General science information (K1)	Range of scientific knowledge (e.g., biology, physics, engineering, mechanics, electronics)
Geography achievement (A5)	Range of geographic knowledge
Communication ability (CM)	Ability to speak in "real-life" situations (e.g., lecture, group participation) in an adult-like manner
Oral production and fluency (OP)	Narrower or more specific oral communication skills than reflected by communication ability (CM)
Grammatical sensitivity (MY)	Knowledge or awareness of the grammatical features of the native language
Foreign language proficiency (KL)	Similar to language development (LD) but for a foreign language
Foreign language aptitude (LA)	Rate and ease of learning a new language

Note. From *Essentials of Cross-Battery Assessment*, 2nd ed. (p. 281, Table A2), by D. P. Flanagan, S. O. Ortiz, and V. C. Alfonso, 2007, New York: Wiley. Reproduced with permission.

anathema. So Stratum III has usually been ignored, and its role in CHC theory remains ambiguous (McGrew, 2005).

Regardless, broad abilities rule the roost, both from a theoretical perspective and for determining which scales constitute most of today's IQ tests. *Gf* and *Gc* have already been defined and illustrated. Here are capsules describing the remaining eight broad abilities.

Short-Term Memory (*Gsm*)

Gsm is a person's ability to take in and hold onto information, keep it in immediate awareness, and use it within a few seconds. "An example of *Gsm* is the ability to remember a telephone number long enough to dial it or the ability to retain a sequence of spoken directions long enough to complete the tasks specified in the directions" (Flanagan et al., 2007, p. 284). Word Order from the K-ABC and KABC-II (pointing to pictures named by the examiner in the order in which they were named), used earlier to illustrate sequential processing, is also a good example of a *Gsm* task. So too is Wechsler's Digit Span (Part 1—repeating numbers in the order in which they are spoken by the examiner; Part 2—repeating the numbers in the *reverse* order).

Processing Speed (*Gs*)

Gs is a person's ability "to fluently and automatically perform cognitive tasks, especially when under pressure to maintain focused attention and concentration" (Flanagan et al., 2007, p. 291). This Stratum II ability is illustrated by the Wechsler's Symbol Search subtest in Figure 3.10.

Auditory Processing (*Ga*)

Ga is a person's "ability to perceive, analyze, and synthesize patterns among auditory stimuli, and to discriminate subtle nuances in patterns of sound (e.g., complex musical structure) and speech when presented under distorted conditions" (Flanagan et al., 2007, p. 287). The WJ III measures *Ga* by several tasks, including incomplete words, for which the person hears a recording

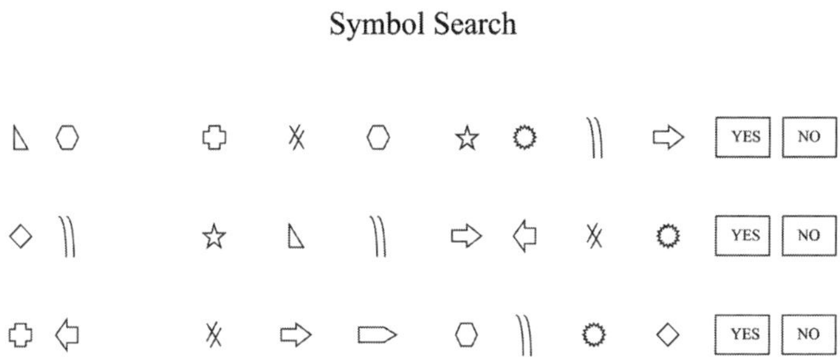

FIGURE 3.10 Illustration of a processing speed (*Gs*) subtest (Wechsler's Symbol Search).
Note. Symbol Search is a highly speeded task. The person has to look at the two symbols on the left side of each row and rapidly determine if either one of these target symbols appears in the array of symbols on the right. The person marks yes or no as quickly as possible. Of the three rows shown, only the third row is no. Simulated items similar to those in the Wechsler intelligence scales for adults and children.

of words missing one or more phonemes and has to identify the complete word (e.g., "__eanut __utter" for *peanut butter;* or "__edroo__" for *bedroom.*

Visual Processing (*Gv*)

Gv is a person's "ability to generate, perceive, analyze, synthesize, store, retrieve, manipulate, transform, and think with visual patterns and stimuli (Lohman, 1994)" (Flanagan et al., 2007, p. 286). *Gv* is essentially the same thing as simultaneous processing, which was illustrated in Figure 3.1 with the Gestalt Closure subtest. Whereas Gestalt Closure depends mostly on perception and synthesis, some *Gv* tasks require the ability to use short-term memory (see Figure 3.11, which illustrates KABC-II Face Recognition, designed for preschool children), and some require visual-spatial reasoning, such as the KABC-II Block Counting subtest (see Figure 3.12). For Block Counting, visualization is needed to "see" the picture of the pile of blocks as a three-dimensional structure and reasoning is needed to figure out how many blocks are hidden or partially hidden.

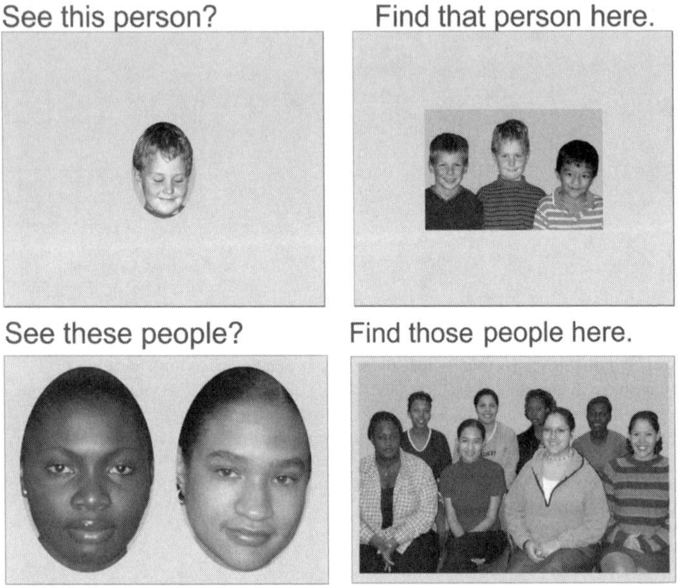
See this person?
Find that person here.
See these people?
Find those people here.

FIGURE 3.11 Illustration of a visual processing (*Gv*) subtest that requires visual memory (KABC-II Face Recognition).
Note. From *Kaufman Assessment Battery for Children, Second Edition (KABC-II)*, by A. S. Kaufman and N. L. Kaufman, 2004, Circle Pines, MN: American Guidance Service.

Quantitative Thinking (*Gq*)

Gq is a person's "ability to use quantitative information and manipulate numeric symbols" (Flanagan et al., 2007, p. 282). It is math, an aspect of academic achievement. CHC theory lists it as a broad ability, but it's school achievement, not IQ.

Reading and Writing (*Grw*)

Grw is a person's "acquired store of knowledge that includes basic reading, reading fluency, and writing skills required for the comprehension of written language and the expression of thought via writing" (Flanagan et al., 2007, p. 283). Again, it's school achievement, not IQ.

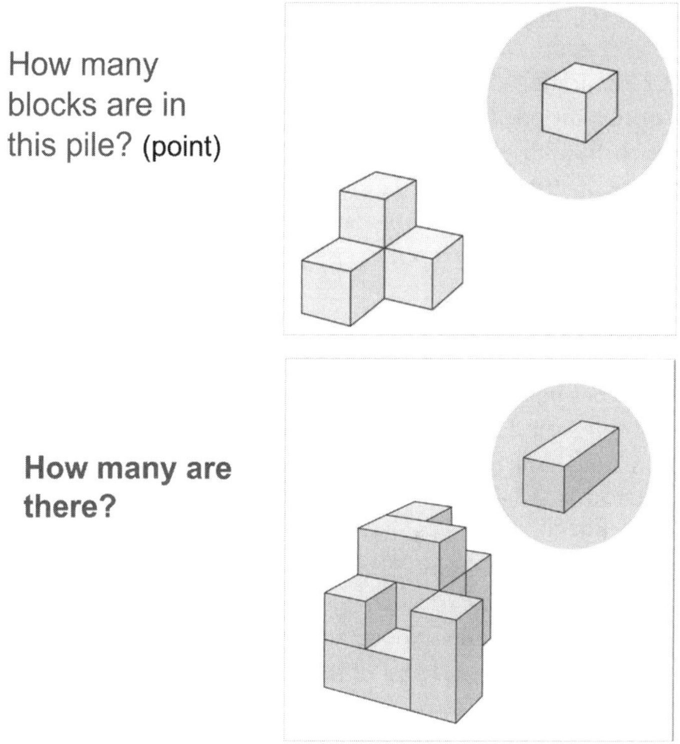
How many blocks are in this pile? (point)
How many are there?

FIGURE 3.12 Illustration of a visual processing (*Gv*) subtest that requires visual-spatial reasoning (KABC-II Block Counting).
Note. Number of blocks: 4 (1st item) and 8 (2nd item). *Kaufman Assessment Battery for Children, Second Edition (KABC-II)*, by A. S. Kaufman and N. L. Kaufman, 2004, Circle Pines, MN: American Guidance Service.

Decision Speed/Reaction Time (*Gt*)

Gt is a person's quickness in reacting and making decisions, reflecting the immediacy of responding to a stimulus (measured in seconds or fractions of seconds), whereas *Gs* reflects rapid responding at intervals of 2 or 3 minutes (Flanagan et al., 2007). "None of the major IQ tests measure *Gt*, although Speed of Information Processing on the DAS and DAS-II—with several sets of very brief scanning tasks rather than one long one—may come closer to *Gt* than do other *Gs* tasks" (J. O. Willis, personal communication, November 2, 2008). Research measures of *Gt* are often included in the kind of reaction time experiments that stretch back to Galton's early sensory-motor tests. These tasks are usually used in investigations of Spearman's *g* theory of intelligence; surprisingly, these tasks correlate substantially with *g* when they involve both decision speed and reaction time (Jensen, 1998).

Long-Term Retrieval (*Glr*)

Glr is a person's ability to store information (either newly learned or acquired in the past) and efficiently retrieve the information from long-term memory. "*Gc, Gq,* and *Grw* represent *what* is stored in long-term memory, whereas *Glr* is the *efficiency* with which this information is initially stored in and later retrieved from long-term memory" (Flanagan et al., 2007, p. 289). *Gsm* measures immediate recall after a few seconds, while *Glr* begins "within a few minutes or hours of performing a task" (Flanagan et al., 2007, p. 289). Several of the *Glr* narrow abilities, such as naming facility, are associated with divergent-production from Guilford's theory, but creativity is virtually buried in the depths of CHC theory in contrast to the featured role it played in Guilford's conception of intelligence. In modern IQ tests, most notably the WJ III and KABC-II, *Glr* is measured primarily by paired-associate learning tasks, as in the KABC-II Rebus subtest (which was illustrated in Figure 3.5 with items from the similar KAIT Rebus Learning subtest). These learning tasks require the person to learn and retain the new information during a "teaching-and-learning" session that lasts for about 10 to 12 minutes. *Glr* over a longer time frame is also measured by delayed-recall tasks. After administering a few more subtests to the person, the examiners give a pop quiz, without warning, to see how much the person remembers. On the KABC-II, the interval is about 30 minutes; on the WJ III, the delayed versions of the learning tasks are given anywhere from 30 minutes to 8 days later.

Speaking of the WJ III, I have to admit that our KABC-II learning subtests are modeled after ingenious tests developed by Woodcock for the original WJ (Visual-Auditory Learning, which inspired Rebus) and for the WJ-R (Memory for Names, which led to Atlantis). Years ago, I asked Dr. Wechsler why he took subtests—sometimes exact test items—directly from the Binet or from the nonverbal tests developed during World War I. He smiled, and said, "There are only 9 commandments for test developers, not 10. The one that is missing is 'Thou shalt not steal.'" He was right. Woodcock's ideas were too good to ignore, because tests of learning ability translate directly to the classroom. Understanding how well children learn is usually the reason we test children in the first place. So we paid Dr. Woodcock the highest form of flattery—imitation! (And other test developers have returned the compliment to us by "borrowing" our novel ideas for tests like Riddles and Spatial Memory.) Imitation also has its benefits: Inclusion of well-researched item types allows examiners to draw on that research history when interpreting new tests.

Tests Built from *Gf-Gc* or CHC Theory

Ultimately, both the Cattell-Horn and Carroll models started from the same point—Spearman's (1904) *g*-factor theory—and ended up with remarkably consistent conclusions about the spectrum of human abilities. That consistency has formed the foundation for most contemporary IQ tests, and for the most prominent, research-based approach to the interpretation of all IQ tests from the CHC model: the cross-battery approach, developed by Dawn Flanagan and her colleagues (e.g., Flanagan & McGrew, 1997; Flanagan et al., 2007), which is rooted in Woodcock's (1990) seminal work. The cross-battery approach urges the selection of tasks from virtually all IQ tests, rather than relying on a single instrument, in order to assess a more complete array of broad and narrow abilities.

The first individually administered comprehensive tests of intelligence to be loosely grounded in *Gf-Gc* theory were the K-ABC (Kaufman & Kaufman, 1983) and the fourth edition of the Stanford-Binet (Binet-IV; Thorndike et al., 1986). As we stated way back when (Kaufman & Kaufman, 1983), "The Achievement Scale resembles closely the crystallized abilities, and the two Mental Processing scales together resemble the fluid abilities that characterize the Cattell-Horn theory of intelligence (Cattell, 1971; Horn, 1968; Horn & Cattell, 1966)" (p. 2). However, as already discussed, the K-ABC was rooted in neuropsychological theory and was only incidentally tied to *Gf-Gc* theory.

The Binet-IV offered a hierarchical model of intelligence (Thorndike et al., 1986): "This model had a general reasoning factor, *g*, at the top level. The second level consisted of three broad factors—crystallized abilities, fluid-analytic abilities, and short-term memory. The third level consisted of three more specific factors—verbal reasoning, quantitative reasoning, and abstract/visual reasoning" (p. 9).

The K-ABC did not do a very good job of translating *Gf-Gc* theory into practice. The K-ABC's separation of intelligence from achievement, which was done primarily for *practical* reasons concerning fairness to children from different ethnic groups, violated the basic premise that *Gf* and *Gc* were two types of intelligence. Furthermore, the K-ABC's measure of intelligence, said to measure *Gf*, really had only a few subtests that measured abstract reasoning ability.

And the Binet-IV did not fare any better. Thorndike and colleagues (1986) based the test on a blend of *g* theory and theories of multiple cognitive abilities, but they failed to disclose exactly which theories were most influential. They used Cattell-Horn terminology for two of their second-level abilities, and one can infer from their historical introduction to the manual that they were also influenced by Thurstone (1938); Guilford (1967); and Hunter, Schmidt, and Jackson (1982). From a *Gf-Gc* perspective, they missed the mark. They subdivided crystallized abilities into two scales: Verbal Reasoning and Quantitative Reasoning, even though the latter scale is known to be more closely aligned to *Gf* than *Gc*. Not surprisingly, the statistical method that identifies the abilities or constructs that underlie a battery of tests—factor analysis—did *not* support the meaningfulness of the Binet-IV scales (Reynolds, Kamphaus, & Rosenthal, 1988). As I wrote about the Binet-IV a few years after it was published (Kaufman, 1990, p. 608), "Had it not been for its venerated name, the new battery probably would have died a quick death, following at least one reviewer's proposal to heed a eulogy proposed previously for the old Binet: 'To the S-B IV, *requiescat in pace*: and so it should have stayed' (Reynolds, 1987, p. 141)."

The real hero in developing a *Gf-Gc*-based test of cognitive abilities was Dick Woodcock. His first comprehensive test battery, the WJ (Woodcock & Johnson, 1977), was deliberately nontheoretical; it was built to address the practical psychoeducational concerns of psychologists, special educators, and teachers, and it included an array of novel measures of intelligence. In a review I wrote of the test, I concluded that the WJ "is a mixture of extremes, possessing some outstanding qualities, yet hampered by glaring liabilities. . . . The [WJ] represents a monumental and creative effort by its authors" (Kaufman, 1985, p. 1762). One of its "glaring liabilities" was the total absence of a theoretical model, a liability that Woodcock walked the extra mile to address. He spent several years at the University of Southern California in order to study directly with John Horn and be mentored by the great man in the nuances of *Gf-Gc* theory. Horn excelled as a mentor (something I learned firsthand when my son James studied with him as an undergraduate at USC). And Dr. Woodcock excelled as Horn's student (so did James).

Woodcock revised his original test so thoroughly that the WJ was barely recognizable in its rebirth as the WJ-R. Woodcock retained, or modified, the original WJ tasks so long as they fitted nicely into *Gf-Gc* theory. The 1986 meeting I mentioned earlier that included Horn, Carroll, and Woodcock, the one that paved the way for future developments in *Gf-Gc* and CHC theory (McGrew, 2005), was part of the elaborate test-development process for the WJ-R. Overall, the revised, theory-based edition of the WJ measured seven of the broad abilities posited by Horn (1989) in his expansion and refinement of the original two-ability Cattell-Horn model. From personal conversations I had with Dr. Horn in the early 1990s, I found that he was clearly impressed with Woodcock's adept translation of theory to practice. Horn would surely have agreed with Esters, Ittenbach, and Han's (1997) review of the WJ-R, stating that "Quite possibly the best and purest example of *Gf-Gc* theory as operationally defined by an IQ test is the [WJ-R]" (p. 212). I marveled: "In particular, it includes fairly pure measures of *Gf* as well as true learning tasks (such as the *Glr* paired-associate subtests) that are basically excluded from Wechsler's system" (Kaufman, 2000b, p. 464). And I also relished Dick Woodcock's comment to me some years ago that my 1985 review of the WJ was a wake-up call that impelled him to action to seek out the best possible theory on which to build the WJ revision.

The WJ-R measured seven of Horn's broad abilities. In addition to *Gf,* referred to by Woodcock as fluid reasoning, and *Gc,* labeled comprehension-knowledge, the WJ-R provided reliable and valid measurement of long-term retrieval (*Glr*), short-term memory (*Gsm*), processing speed (*Gs*), auditory processing (*Ga*), and visual processing (*Gv*). Examiners who administered the complete WJ-R, including the tests of achievement, could also assess an eighth broad ability from Horn's model, quantitative thinking (*Gq*).

This same theoretical structure formed the foundation of the WJ III (Woodcock et al., 2001), but by the time this theory-based test was published, the Cattell-Horn and Carroll systems had been merged and CHC theory provided the theoretical underpinnings of the WJ III. The seven primary broad CHC factors, as they are called on the WJ III, are essentially the same as the WJ-R scales. In addition, administration of the WJ III achievement tests provides measurement of *Gq* and *Grw* (reading and writing). Therefore, the WJ III, in its entirety, measures 9 of the 10 primary broad factors that comprise Stratum II of the CHC model.

Extent of the Influence of CHC Theory on IQ Tests

What started more than a generation ago as an easy analogy with which to interpret Wechsler's Verbal and Performance IQ scales (Matarazzo, 1972) has grown to mammoth proportions in terms of its impact on contemporary IQ tests. As Horn expanded the *Gf-Gc* dichotomy to encompass many broad abilities, it became increasingly clear that Wechsler's Verbal IQ measured not only *Gc* but also *Gsm* and *Gq,* and that his Performance IQ measured more than *Gf,* providing measurement of *Gv* and *Gs;* indeed, Woodcock (1990) argued that older versions of Wechsler's scales measured *Gv* and not *Gf* at all.

That has all changed. New versions of the Wechsler scales include Matrix Reasoning and other subtests measuring *Gf* as well. The WAIS-IV includes three new subtests, as illustrated in Figure 3.13—Figure Weights (*Gf*), Visual Puzzles (*Gv*), and Cancellation (*Gs*). Like the KABC-II's Block Counting, Visual Puzzles is a good example of spatial reasoning. This new WAIS-IV subtest is similar to the Woodcock-Johnson's Spatial Relations subtest, and both, undoubtedly, were inspired by age-old paper formboard tasks that date back to the late 1920s (Roszkowski, 2001).

But even if some new Wechsler subtests have old roots, the look of the latest versions of Wechsler's scales is decidedly new. The two IQ scales (Verbal and Performance) have been replaced by four separate scales, each interpretable according to CHC theory (Flanagan & Kaufman, 2004, 2009). And many current IQ tests are built from CHC theory, including these:

- WJ III (Woodcock et al., 2001; see Table 3.2) for ages 2 to 95+ years
- Stanford-Binet-5 for ages 2 to 85+ years (Binet-5; Roid, 2003; see Table 3.3)
- DAS-II for ages 2½ to 17 years (Elliott, 2007; see Table 3.4)

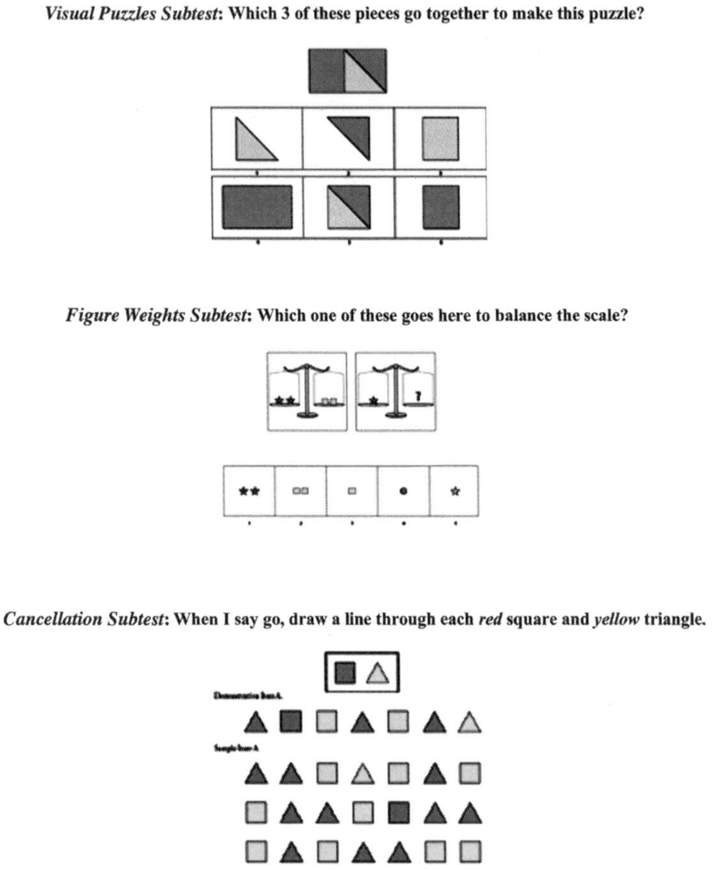
Visual Puzzles Subtest: Which 3 of these pieces go together to make this puzzle?
Figure Weights Subtest: Which one of these goes here to balance the scale?
Cancellation Subtest: When I say go, draw a line through each *red* square and *yellow* triangle.

FIGURE 3.13 Three new WAIS-IV subtests.
Note. Sample items similar to items in the *Wechsler Adult Intelligence Scale—Fourth Edition (WAIS-IV)*, by D. Wechsler, 2008, San Antonio, TX: The Psychological Corporation. Copyright © 2008 by NCS Pearson, Inc. Reproduced with permission. All rights reserved. "Wechsler Adult Intelligence Scale" and "WAIS" are trademarks, in the United States and/or other countries, of Pearson Education, Inc., or its affiliate(s).

- Reynolds Intellectual Assessment Scales (RIAS; Reynolds & Kamphaus, 2003), which were developed to measure *Gf* and *Gc* efficiently and to provide a separate scale that assesses *Gsm*
- KABC-II for ages 3 to 18 years (Kaufman & Kaufman, 2004a; see Table 3.5, which shows its dual theoretical foundation)

TABLE 3.2 WOODCOCK-JOHNSON III (WJ III) FOR AGES 2–95+ YEARS

- Global Ability: General Intellectual Ability
- CHC Ability Factors:
  - Fluid reasoning (*Gf*)
  - Comprehension-knowledge (*Gc*)
  - Long-term retrieval (*Glr*)
  - Visual-spatial thinking (*Gv*)
  - Short-term memory (*Gsm*)
  - Auditory processing (*Ga*)
  - Processing speed (*Gs*)

TABLE 3.3 STANFORD-BINET-5 FOR AGES 2–85+ YEARS

- Global Ability: Full Scale IQ
- Factor Indexes:
  - Fluid reasoning (*Gf*)
  - Knowledge (*Gc*)
  - Quantitative reasoning (*Gq*)
  - Visual-spatial processing (*Gv*)
  - Working memory (*Gsm*)

TABLE 3.4 DIFFERENTIAL ABILITY SCALES—2ND ED. (DAS-II) FOR AGES 2½–17 YEARS

- Global Ability: General Conceptual Ability (GCA)
- Cluster Scores:
  - Verbal ability (*Gc*)
  - Nonverbal reasoning ability (*Gf*)
  - Spatial ability (*Gv*)
  - Processing speed (*Gs*)—*diagnostic*
  - Working memory (*Gsm*)—*diagnostic*

TABLE 3.5 KAUFMAN ASSESSMENT BATTERY FOR CHILDREN–2ND ED. (KABC-II) FOR AGES 3–18 YEARS

Luria Term	CHC Term	Name of KABC-II Scale
Learning ability	Long-term storage and retrieval (*Glr*)	Learning/*Glr*
Sequential processing	Short-term memory (*Gsm*)	Sequential/*Gsm*
Simultaneous processing	Visual processing (*Gv*)	Simultaneous/*Gv*
Planning ability	Fluid reasoning (*Gf*)	Planning/*Gf*
	Crystallized ability (*Gc*)	Knowledge/*Gc*
Mental Processing Index (MPI)	**Fluid-Crystallized Index (FCI)**	

Just as the WJ III Cognitive and Achievement tests were conormed, so too were the KABC-II and the Kaufman Test of Educational Achievement—Second Edition (KTEA-II; Kaufman & Kaufman, 2004c, 2005). The combination of Kaufman tests provides examiners with eight broad abilities. The KABC-II measures five (*Gf, Gc, Gv, Glr, Gsm*) and the KTEA-II measures quantitative thinking (*Gq*), reading and writing (*Grw*), and auditory processing (*Ga*), as well as additional *Glr* narrow abilities.

Indeed, most cognitive tasks can be viewed in different ways and are equally valid from one theoretical perspective as from another. That is one reason why we chose to base the KABC-II on the dual theoretical models of Luria and CHC. Another reason for the dual model is that Nadeen, an astute clinician, is immersed in the clinical nature of Luria's neuropsychological model, a theory that evolved from Luria's clinical work with neurological patients; in contrast, my psychometric, research-based, and statistical orientation is more in tune with the data-driven CHC theory.

For a thorough history of CHC theory, with an emphasis on the WJ-R and WJ III, see McGrew (2005). Also see Flanagan et al.

(2007) for a comprehensive application of CHC theory to the interpretation of all current IQ tests.

Extent of the Influence of IQ Tests on CHC Theory

I've already mentioned the 1986 meeting in Dallas attended by theorists, test authors, and the WJ-R test publisher. Now consider the meeting that took place in 1999 in Chapel Hill, North Carolina, organized by Riverside, the publisher of both the WJ III and the Binet-5. That meeting was attended by authors of the WJ III (Dick Woodcock, Kevin McGrew) and Binet-5 (Gale Roid), two theorists (John Horn and John Carroll), and staff members from Riverside. The goal was "to seek a common, more meaningful umbrella term that would recognize the strong structural similarities of their respective theoretical models, yet also recognize their differences" (McGrew, 2005, p. 149). The net result of that meeting was the merger of the Cattell-Horn and Carroll systems into CHC theory. Talk about the tail wagging the dog! What had begun back in the late 1970s and early 1980s as a search for the best theories on which to build an IQ test had come full circle: Two decades later, the needs of test publishers and test authors forged the theory that underlies almost all current-day IQ tests.

SO WHAT IS THE RIGHT NUMBER OF ABILITIES?

Theory has ultimately merged thoroughly with practice. It has infiltrated all IQ tests and dominated most. What is the "right" number of abilities for an IQ test to measure? Surely not the 1 posited by Spearman or the 120 or more that came with Guilford's territory. And not the 2 that were popular for so long when Wechsler's Verbal and Performance IQs pervaded schools, clinics, and the psychology literature—or the 2 of *g* that characterized the original Cattell-Horn dichotomy, or the 2 mental processes on which the K-ABC was built. Two abilities were not enough.

Wechsler's scales now feature four indexes (see Table 3.6), the same number as the PASS processes in the Luria-based CAS. Glancing over Tables 3.2 to 3.4, we see that the tests built from CHC theory measure five to seven abilities. The KABC-II (Table 3.5), founded on two theoretical models, measures either four or five depending on whether the CHC or Luria model is selected. The CHC model of the KABC-II yields scores on five abilities, whereas the Luria model measures four processes. The difference? We included the Knowledge/*Gc* scale in the CHC model, because *Gc* is such a key ingredient of *Gf-Gc* theory. But tests of factual knowledge and language ability are deliberately excluded from the Luria model, which emphasizes mental processing rather than acquired knowledge and is especially useful for the ethnically fair assessment of children from bilingual and bicultural backgrounds.

So, a contemporary answer to "What is the right number of abilities to measure?" is somewhere between four and seven. These numbers allow examiners to identify important areas of strength and weakness for each person tested. The four abilities measured by Wechsler's scales (Table 3.6)—verbal comprehension, perceptual reasoning, working memory, and processing speed—display distinctly different growth curves as adults travel the rocky road from young adulthood to old age (a hot topic

TABLE 3.6 WISC-IV FOR AGES 6–16 YEARS AND WAIS-IV FOR AGES 16–90 YEARS

- Global Ability: Full Scale IQ (FS-IQ)
- Factor Indexes:
  - Verbal Comprehension Index (VCI) (*Gc*)
  - Perceptual Reasoning Index (PRI) (*Gv-Gf*)
  - Working Memory Index (WMI) (*Gsm*)
  - Processing Speed Index (PSI) (*Gs*)

discussed in chapter 8). Also, the four to seven abilities and processes measured by current IQ tests are in lockstep with the federal definition of specific learning disabilities, which stipulates a disorder in a basic psychological process. But whether or not that disorder really needs to be measured is another story—a hot topic discussed in chapter 9.

DAVID WECHSLER'S LEGACY

As I've discussed at length in this chapter, theory-based tests began to appear throughout the decade of the 1980s, notably the K-ABC, Binet-IV, and WJ-R. All of these theory-based tests have been successful, as have the latest editions of each test, published in the early 2000s. They have met with worldwide success in some instances (e.g., Kaufman & Kaufman, 1993; Melchers & Preuß, 1991).

Nonetheless, Wechsler's scales for children, adolescents, and adults have withstood challenges by the theory-based tests. Though not specifically developed from CHC theory, Wechsler's modern-day tests were specifically revised in the 1990s and 2000s to incorporate CHC theory and state-of-the-art research on working memory and other executive functions. And the most popular interpretations of profiles yielded by Wechsler's children's and adult scales are decidedly CHC in origin (Flanagan & Kaufman, 2004, 2009; Kaufman & Lichtenberger, 2006; Keith et al., 2006). Theory-based tests such as the WJ III, KABC-II, RIAS, CAS, Binet-5, and DAS-II are of high quality and are frequently used, but they mainly serve as members of Wechsler's royal court. Make no mistake about it: More than seventy years after he published his first IQ test and nearly a century since several of his performance tasks were developed by World War I psychologists, the Wechsler scales are the most popular tests in the United States (Prifitera, Saklofske, Weiss, Rolfhus, & Holdnack, 2005) and throughout the world (Georgas, Weiss, van de Vijver, & Saklofske, 2003). David Wechsler is still the king.

4

The IQ Construct, Part 1: We All Know What IQs Are—Don't We?

Marilyn vos Savant, an entertaining columnist for *Parade* in Sunday newspapers everywhere, is billed as the smartest person in the world. She was listed in each annual edition of the *Guinness Book of World Records* (McFarlan, 1989) between 1986 and 1989 as the all-time IQ champion, in a section called "Highest IQ." The IQ blurb was found easily, nestled between "Smallest Brains" and "Largest Chest Measurements." The *Guinness Book* told its readers authoritatively that Intelligence Quotients or IQs equal the person's Mental Age (MA) divided by Chronological Age (CA) multiplied by 100, and that the highest childhood IQ was earned by Marilyn vos Savant, who at age 10 achieved an MA of 22 years 10 months, giving her an IQ of 228.

Little Miss Savant was given an old version of the Stanford-Binet (Terman & Merrill, 1937), which did, indeed, use the antiquated formula of MA/CA × 100. But in the test manual's norms, the Binet does not permit IQs to rise above 170 at any age, child or adult. And the authors of the old Binet stated: "Beyond fifteen the mental ages are entirely artificial and are to be thought of as simply numerical scores" (Terman & Merrill, 1937, p. 31). In short, Marilyn vos Savant has always been unusually bright, amazingly gifted, and an extremely funny and entertaining columnist and author. Her "Ask Marilyn" column is often witty and brilliant. However, the psychologist who came up with an IQ of 228 committed an extrapolation of a misconception, thereby violating most every rule imaginable concerning the meaning of IQs. Does an IQ of 228 make any sense? For an expert opinion, "Don't Ask Marilyn."

I have gone into depth in the previous chapters on the history of IQ testing and the neuropsychological and cognitive theories that underlie contemporary tests. But I have not yet discussed the psychometrics of IQ tests, namely their statistical aspects. That is the goal of this chapter and also chapter 5.

THE IQ IS NOT A QUOTIENT

IQs stand for Intelligence Quotients, but they haven't been quotients for two generations. They began as quotients in Terman's (1916) original Stanford-Binet, and the idea made a good bit of sense at the time. Terman's grouping of tasks by age level made it easy for people to grasp the concept of mental age—for example, consider a female who passed all tasks for Ages 2 through 8, passed half the tasks at Age 9, and then failed all tasks at Age 10. She performed midway between the average 8-year-old and the average 9-year-old, thereby achieving an MA of 8½. Whether she was 3, 6, 9, or 20 years of age, she performed as well as the average child of 8½ years. Terman needed to find a way to distinguish between people who all earned identical MAs but differed in their actual or chronological age. His solution was the clever formula shown above: Divide MA by CA, and then multiply the quotient by 100. Actually, the German psychologist William Stern (1914) was the creative force who invented the MA/CA quotient. But Terman didn't like decimals so he multiplied Stern's Mental Quotient by 100 and spawned the infamous formula for computing IQ.

IQ = MA/CA × 100 is a simple formula and the computations of IQ are even simpler. Consider three different people who earned the same MA of 7.

Mental Age (MA)	Chronological Age (CA)	MA ÷ CA	The Quotient	× 100 = IQ
7	5	7 ÷ 5	1.40	140
7	7	7 ÷ 7	1.00	100
7	11	7 ÷ 11	0.64	64

The same MA yields very superior, average, or low-functioning intelligence, depending on the age of the child, making the IQ a yardstick for comparing people's intelligence across the age range.

The IQ concept was valuable, even sophisticated—for 1916. But it proved to be a rubber yardstick. As mentioned in chapter 1, a year's growth doesn't have a constant meaning from year to year for mental ability or for height. Enormous mental growth occurs at the preschool ages, but that accelerated growth slows down to a crawl by the teenage years. And how do you deal with adults? Terman (1916) used a CA of 16 as the denominator for adults in the original Stanford-Binet but dropped it to 15 for the next revision of the test (Terman & Merrill, 1937) because he found that the average score stopped increasing in the middle teen years. His best guess (and it was just a guess, because he tested no one older than 18 when he revised the Binet) was that "A mental age of fifteen years represents the norm for all subjects who are sixteen years of age or older" (Terman & Merrill, 1937, p. 31). He was wrong about that (see chapter 8 on aging and IQ), but he was right to sense that the MA/CA formula wouldn't work for adults, that both the MA and the CA had built-in flaws, and, no question, that the formula was too simplistic for a complex concept like human intelligence.

The result of the elastic Intelligence Quotient formula was a weird set of IQs, a set that might change wildly for a person tested several times in the course of a few years—even if that person's intelligence remained fairly static. Lewis Terman recognized the problem and was aware that the *variability* of IQs at each age level (measured by a statistic called the *standard deviation* or *sigma*) differed from age to age. The standard deviation, or *SD,* ranged from about 12 to 20 across the different age groups between 2 and 18 years, with an average of 16. Mostly, Terman attributed the differences in variability from age group to age group to chance fluctuations, though the huge *SD* = 20 at age 12 caused him to reflect that "the high variability at age 12 might conceivably be ascribed to the differential age of the onset of pubescence, although it has yet to be demonstrated that pubescence is significantly related to the rate of mental growth" (Terman & Merrill, 1937, p. 41).

Regardless of why the variability in IQ differed markedly from age to age, the simple answer, even in 1937, should have been to eliminate the MA/CA formula for computing Stanford-Binet IQs. A more sophisticated statistic, the *standard score,* immediately solved the problem of age-by-age fluctuations. Terman and Merrill (1937) wrote about standard scores in the Binet test manual, provided a table with which to convert formula-based IQs to standard-score IQs, and recognized that, "from the statistical point of view, every advantage is in favor of the standard score" (p. 27). But they perpetuated the outdated formula primarily because "the majority of teachers, school administrators, social workers, physicians, and others who utilize test results have not learned to think in statistical terms. To such a person a rating expressed as '+2 sigma' is just so much Greek" (pp. 27–28).

Fortunately, just a couple of years later, David Wechsler (1939) was not so condescending to test users and replaced the MA/CA formula with standard scores when he published his landmark Wechsler-Bellevue Intelligence Scale. The Stanford-Binet would wait two more decades before swapping the formula-based IQ for standard scores (Terman & Merrill, 1960), ending the formula-based IQ's use about midway through the last century. It is time to let the formula stay in the past. Marilyn vos Savant is smart. Perhaps she deserves to be in the Guinness Hall of Fame, as her columns sometimes claim. More likely, the psychologist who evaluated her should be in the Guinness Hall of Shame for blatant test abuse. An IQ of 228 is an imaginary number, and it violates the rules in the test manual. It made no sense when she was tested as a child in 1956, on a test that was almost two decades old at the time, and it makes even less sense now.

STANDARD SCORES

Standard scores depend on the normal curve, and they yield IQs that have a clearly defined meaning from age to age. David Wechsler called these scores *deviation IQs* (because they were based on the concept of the standard deviation) to distinguish them from the Stanford-Binet's *ratio IQs* (i.e., MA/CA). But the label was short-lived and Wechsler's scores were simply referred to as IQs. Wechsler chose 100 as the mean or average because that notion had become well accepted thanks to the MA/CA formula. The choice was arbitrary. Wechsler set the value of the *SD* at 15 for IQs, but again the choice was arbitrary. He chose 15 because it was a nice, easily divisible number that was quite close to the value of 16 that Terman and Merrill (1937) had identified as the average *SD* using the IQ formula. Wechsler could have chosen a mean of 500 (with *SD* = 100), the values originally used by the College Entrance Examination Board (CEEB) for the Scholastic Aptitude Tests (SATs) and by the Educational Testing Service (ETS) for the Graduate Record Exam (GRE) and other professional school admission testing programs. Or Wechsler could have chosen a mean of 50 and an *SD* of 10, the parameters of the *T* scores that are used by popular personality tests such as the MMPI-2. Or he could have chosen any set of values he wished. His choices of 100 and 15, however, were sensible because they yielded a range of numbers that the public had internalized ever since Terman published the Stanford-Binet in 1916.

I won't try to explain the mathematical meaning of *SD* or go into its formula, because I'd like you to continue reading this book (I've always had a hard time conveying the mathematics of *SD*s to my doctoral students). It is the properties of the *SD* that are important. If you subtract one *SD* from the mean (100 – 15 = 85) and add one *SD* to the mean (100 + 15 = 115), then you have identified the middle 2/3 of human intelligence. That is to say, about 2/3 of all people (actually 68.26%) earn Wechsler IQs between 85 and 115. And about 95% score within 2 *SD*s of the mean (between 70 and 130). That's where we get the common cut-offs for identifying individuals with possible intellectual disability (<70) or giftedness (>130). The cut-off points are not based on some type of absolute level of deficiency or brilliance; they're based strictly on the number of people in any population who score very low or very high. Just over 95% of people earn IQs between 70 and 130, which leaves a bit less than 5% for the extremes—about 2¼% in the lower tail of the normal curve who score below 70 and the same percentage above 130. If someone ever invented a pill that raised *everyone's* IQ by about 30 points, the lowest 2¼% would *still* be considered intellectually disabled. And the bar for qualifying as gifted would be raised considerably but that elite group would still constitute 2¼% of the population. It's simply built into the IQ-as-standard-score concept, and we can't escape it.

But the normal curve has some advantages that make standard scores neat statistics; for example, they possess the special feature of forming an *interval* scale. Ten points, for example, denotes the exact same interval regardless of where on the normal curve the IQs reside and regardless of the examinee's age. The distance from an IQ of 53 to an IQ of 63 equals the exact distance between IQs of 95 and 105 or IQs of 126 and 136. That is not a feature enjoyed by the formula-driven ratio IQ.

Converting Standard Score IQs to Percentile Ranks and Verbal Labels

The use of standard scores for IQs has a lot of benefits, not the least of which is giving IQs a common meaning regardless of how old you are when you are evaluated. Your IQ corresponds to a percentile rank, which tells the percentage of people your own age who earned lower IQs than yours. A Wechsler IQ of 120, for example, corresponds to the 91st percentile, and it doesn't matter whether it was obtained by a boy of 4 on Wechsler's preschool battery (the WPPSI-III) or a woman of 79 on his adult battery (the WAIS-IV). Or it could be obtained on other IQ tests such as the KABC-II, Binet-5, RIAS, or DAS-II. Or it could be obtained on a scale such as the WISC-IV Verbal Comprehension Index (VCI) or the KABC-II Planning/*Gf* scale. So long as the mean is 100 and the *SD* is 15, score 120 and you have done better than 91% of the people your age—people who were given the same questions and problems that you were given, with the psychologist using the same *standardized* procedures each time.

Table 4.1 shows the percentile ranks that correspond to selected IQs. As shown, an IQ of 130 ranks you ahead of 98% of the people your age. Get a 65, and you are ahead of a mere 1%. Extremely high or low IQs (in the distant tails of the normal curve) are quite rare. An IQ of 155, for example, is a 1 in 10,000 occurrence, as is its polar opposite, an IQ of 45. Percentile ranks (usually just called percentiles) are pretty easy to understand, but some people prefer a blend of numbers and words. So IQs are converted to verbal labels to facilitate the psychologist's communication of test results to parents, teachers, and the children and adults who are evaluated.

TABLE 4.1 PERCENTILE RANKS CORRESPONDING TO SELECTED IQs (STANDARD SCORES)

IQ	Percentile Rank	IQ	Percentile Rank
160	99.997	95	37
155	99.99	90	25
150	99.91	85	16
145	99.87	80	9
140	99.62	75	5
135	99	70	2
130	98	65	1
125	95	60	0.38
120	91	55	0.13
115	84	50	0.04
110	75	45	0.01
105	63	40	0.003
100	50		

Terman (1916, p. 79) gave us the first classification system when he published the original Stanford-Binet:

IQ	Classification
Above 140	Near genius or genius
120–140	Very superior intelligence
110–120	Superior intelligence
90–110	Normal, or average, intelligence
80–90	Dullness, rarely classifiable as feeble-mindedness
70–80	Border-line deficiency, sometimes classifiable as dullness, often as feeble-mindedness
Below 70	Definite feeble-mindedness

Following Esquirol (1828, 1838), Terman (1916) further subdivided low-functioning individuals: "Of the feeble-minded, those between 50 and 70 IQ include most of the morons (high, middle, low), those between 20 or 25 and 50 are ordinarily to be classified as imbeciles, and those below 20 or 25 as idiots" (p. 79). He also philosophized about the people who flunked his test: "The fact is, the more one sees of feeble-minded children, the less reliance one comes to place upon facial expression as a sign of intelligence. Some children who are only slightly backward have the general appearance of low-grade imbeciles" (Terman, 1916, p. 30). And he had a decidedly dim view of *anyone* who scored below the mean on his IQ test: "In the literal sense every individual below the average is more or less mentally weak or feeble" (Terman, 1916, p. 80).

Terman's classification system provided the rudiments of future systems, but subsequent approaches were modified (e.g., an IQ of 120 was required to be called *superior,* not 110) and the category systems were refined. Table 4.2 presents common labels for various IQ ranges, labels that probably have caused far more trouble than they're worth. This table shows the labels that have been used to classify IQs since the middle of the 20th century, for both the Stanford-Binet and Wechsler scales. The labels and the IQ ranges tend to be similar for the Binet and the Wechsler, and little has changed between the middle of the last century and the first decade of this century. *Average* usually corresponds to IQs of 90 to 109, the middle 50% of humanity on the Wechsler scales (and a bit less than 50% on the Binet for reasons I'll explain later). The main difference between the 1950s and now is the political correctness of the labels nowadays, especially for low-functioning individuals.

Borderline and Dull Normal

The traditional name for IQs in the 70–79 range (*borderline*) is my favorite troublemaker. Terman (1916) coined the term *Borderline Deficiency*: "The border-line cases are those which fall near

TABLE 4.2 TRADITIONAL VERBAL LABELS FOR RANGES OF IQ

Stanford-Binet, Form L-M, 1960		Stanford-Binet–Fifth Edition, 2003	
Label	*IQ Range*	*Label*	*IQ Range*
Very superior	140–169	Very gifted or highly advanced	145–160
Superior	120–139	Gifted or very advanced	130–144
		Superior	120–129
High average	110–119	High average	110–119
Normal or average	*90–109*	*Average*	*90–109*
Low average	80–89	Low average	80–89
Borderline defective	70–79	Borderline impaired or delayed	70–79
Mentally defective	30–69	Mildly impaired or delayed	55–69
		Moderately impaired or delayed	40–54

Wechsler Intelligence Scale for Children				
WISC 1949 Label	*WISC-R 1974 Label*	*WISC-IV 2003 Label*	*IQ Range*	*Percent*
Very superior	Very superior	Very superior	130 and above	2.2
Superior	Superior	Superior	120–129	6.7
Bright normal	High average (bright)	High average	110–119	16.1
Average	*Average*	*Average*	*90–109*	*50.0*
Dull normal	Low average (dull)	Low average	80–89	16.1
Borderline	Borderline	Borderline	70–79	6.7
Mental defective	Mentally deficient	Extremely low	69 and below	2.2

Note. Classifications are from Terman and Merrill (1960, Table 1); Roid (2003, Figure 5.2); Wechsler (1949, Table IX; 1974, Table 8); and The Psychological Corporation (2003, Table 6.3).

the boundary between that grade of mental deficiency which will be generally recognizable as such and the higher group usually classified as normal but dull. They are the doubtful cases, the ones we are usually trying (rarely with success) to restore to normality" (p. 87). In other words, borderline means that the psychologist isn't sure. I always imagine parents bringing their child to a private clinic for an evaluation, only to be told that their child is borderline. I picture the parents displaying justifiable anger, saying, "You are charging me $1,000 and you aren't sure?!?" The use of borderline for IQs in the 70s is also confusing to parents and professionals alike, because a borderline personality disorder is a common and well-known psychiatric diagnosis for individuals whose personality structure is on the boundary of psychosis and what used to be known as neurosis (*neurotic* has been replaced in the classification system by Axis II *personality disorders*—even though we all know people who are so clearly neurotic).

Whenever psychologists perform the slow computations necessary to generate a person's profile of scores on an IQ test (or, more likely, use a computerized scoring program), there is always a bit of anxiety after the testing is completed and before the psychologist sees the test results. Even examiners who are not especially religious become pious during this interval, praying, "Please, let the IQ be in the 60s or the 80s, but don't make me explain an IQ of 75."

Happily, the term *dull* has dropped out of the vernacular of the classification systems. Terman (1916) used this label. Wechsler used the term a lot when speaking about low-functioning children and adults, and his category systems (during his lifetime) classified IQs of 80 to 89 as *low average* (dull) or *dull normal.* Dull is just a downright offensive term. I think about the child who might have earned an IQ of 88, say, a girl born into poverty with a home environment that was less than enriching. She took an IQ test and zoomed past the "Less than 70" category, and all the offensive subdivisions of that category foisted on the world by Esquirol and Terman (morons, imbeciles, and idiots); she even avoided the ambiguity of borderline ability and landed feet-first in the dull normal category. "How'd my daughter do on the IQ test?" her mother might have asked. "Fine, just fine, no problem. She's in the normal category. Just a little dull, that's all." It could have been worse. Wechsler might have decided that the real opposite of high average (bright) was low average (dim).

IQs Below 70

The problem with the labels for individuals who score below 70 on an IQ test is no joke, however. Even Terman abandoned the term *feebleminded* when he published his revised Binet in 1937. He virtually avoided calling low-functioning individuals *anything* in the test manual for Forms L and M; the closest he came was to talk about "the mentally less advanced" (Terman & Merrill, 1937, p. 39). In the 1950s and 1960s, as shown in Table 4.2, people who scored below 70 were called *mentally defective,* not a huge leap from Terman's feebleminded or Esquirol's imbeciles and idiots. In the fourth edition of the Binet, this term evolved into *mentally retarded* (Thorndike et al., 1986) and in the fifth edition in 2003 into the benign *mildly impaired or delayed*. In Wechsler's scales, the label was transformed into *mentally deficient* in 1974 (WISC-R), *mentally retarded* in 1981 (WAIS-R), *intellectually deficient* in 1991 (WISC-III), and *extremely low* in 1997 (WAIS-III). Extremely low, a variant of the term *lower extreme* that we introduced in 1983 for the K-ABC (Kaufman & Kaufman, 1983), is just a mere statement of fact, designed to offend no one.

But the labels such as mentally retarded or mentally deficient that were popular into the early 1980s, printed right in the test manuals, were more than just politically incorrect; they were encouraging blatant test abuse. The guidelines for diagnosing intellectual disabilities, mental retardation, mental deficiency—by any name—have stipulated for decades that such a diagnosis cannot be made based solely on the results of an IQ test. That diagnosis requires poor functioning on both an IQ test and a measure of *adaptive behavior* (i.e., the ability to perform age-appropriate social tasks and daily activities). The sociologist Jane Mercer (1973) popularized the measurement of adaptive behavior in the 1970s, even though her own test of adaptive behavior, the SOMPA (Mercer & Lewis, 1978), was not very user friendly and never became very popular. But as a speaker and writer, Mercer (1973, 1977) was dynamic. She wrote about "the struggle for children's rights" and the unfairness of IQ tests for children from ethnic minorities. She spoke about the "six-hour retardate," a phrase that was meant to be deliberately provocative. It referred to the teenage boy or girl, typically from an African American or Hispanic family, who scored 65 or so on an IQ test and was forced to attend a special class for mentally retarded students from 9 A.M. to 3 P.M.—but after school, he or she went to the market to purchase food for dinner, went home to prepare the family's meal, and supervised and disciplined his or her younger brothers and sisters until their parents came home from work. In short, a child or adolescent who was considered retarded in school but whose adaptive behavior was normal, even exemplary, for his or her age.

Why were so many children and adolescents misclassified as intellectually disabled (by whatever name) in the past? Because reliable, valid, well-normed, user-friendly tests of adaptive behavior didn't really exist until the early 1980s, when Sara Sparrow and her colleagues revised Edgar Doll's (1965) Vineland Social Maturity Scale and published the Vineland Adaptive Behavior Scales (Sparrow, Balla, & Cicchetti, 1984). Before that, psychologists focused almost totally on IQ for deciding if someone was mentally retarded. Doll's Vineland, first developed in the mid-1930s, operationalized the concept of social competence, or adaptive behavior, but his test fell far short of the psychometric excellence of IQ tests like Terman's or Wechsler's and was not often administered by psychologists. The most popular measure of adaptive behavior through the 1970s was facetiously known as the EBTAB—the "Eyeball Test of Adaptive Behavior." The test went something like this: If a child or adult scored below 70 on an IQ test, you "eyeballed" him or her and concluded, "Yep, sure looks retarded to me!" An alternate form of the EBTAB is what my colleague John Willis (personal communication, October 9, 2008) refers to as the SWAG—"Scientific Wild Ass Guess").

In the late 1970s, when Mercer's voice was heard everywhere, I learned firsthand that people with IQs below 70 are not always intellectually disabled. A case in point is a man I met back in 1979 when I was associate director of a psychology clinic for the developmentally disabled. Dennis, then 32 years old, had been in various sheltered workshops for the mentally retarded since 1965. It seems that no matter how many times he was given Wechsler's or Binet's IQ tests, he earned IQs somewhere in the 50s or 60s. Based on the EBTAB, Dennis was labeled mentally retarded. He was sent to the clinic for yet another evaluation and kept alive his streak of never once approaching the 70 barrier. The trouble was that Dennis was no more intellectually disabled than the psychologists who kept testing him, a fact that I discovered when he silently handed me the poignant letter reprinted in Figure 4.1. A subsequent clinical neuropsychological evaluation revealed that Dennis had a language disorder that impacted his ability to communicate orally and affected his ability to comprehend the examiner's directions on visual-motor problem-solving tasks. Masked by his profile of scores on the IQ tests were his good thinking ability and social-adaptive skills in communication (written, not oral), self-help, gross and fine motor coordination, and interpersonal skills; indeed, his social awareness is evident in his comments about being uncomfortable with young staff members and embarrassed being with the "retarted." He was immediately taken out of the sheltered workshop and through intensive occupational therapy was trained for a semiskilled job in a sewing machine factory that people with IQs of 50 or 60 are not supposed to be able to do.

Mercer's (1973, 1977) preaching about the importance of adaptive behavior, coupled with the development of excellent measures of adaptive behavior—most notably the Vineland (Sparrow et al., 1984, 2005)—changed the way psychologists diagnosed intellectual disability to include measures of *both* IQ *and* adaptive behavior. Tests like the Vineland Adaptive Behavior

Scales—which measure social-role functioning in areas such as communicating with language, practicing daily living skills (eating, dressing, handling money), getting along with others, and motor coordination—have been routinely administered in psychological evaluations for a generation. And the category systems in test manuals finally stopped using diagnostic labels such as mentally retarded and replaced them with terms like extremely low to avoid the implication that a low IQ, by itself, means an intellectual disability.

IQs Above 130

At the opposite end of the continuum, innocuous terms have typically been used to denote IQs of 130 or 140 and higher, rather than more diagnostic labels like *gifted.* Terman (1916), as I indicated, used *near genius or genius* for IQs above 140, but mostly *very superior* has been the label of choice (and thank goodness no one has used *very inferior* to denote its opposite—except for the U.S. Army during World War I to identify the soldiers who performed poorly on the verbal Army Alpha or the nonverbal Army Beta tests; Yoakum & Yerkes, 1920, p. 17). The 2003 edition of the Binet surprisingly used the terms very gifted and gifted for high IQs (see Table 4.2), even though giftedness, like intellectual disabilities, should be identified using multiple criteria, such as intelligence and creativity (J. C. Kaufman, 2009). However, at the upper tail of the normal curve, no one gets too upset if the label for high IQs overlaps a bit with the diagnosis of intellectual giftedness.

Nonetheless, with the K-ABC, and again with the KABC-II, we got rid of all evaluative terms (like superior), ambiguous terms (like borderline), and offensive terms (like dull) and replaced them with neutral, descriptive terms (Kaufman & Kaufman, 1983, 2004a). Instead of very superior or gifted, we used upper extreme for IQs above 130, and we used the boring and benign term well below average instead of borderline. In fact, all of our labels were deliberately boring (e.g., well above average, below average) in the belief that descriptive labels rather than

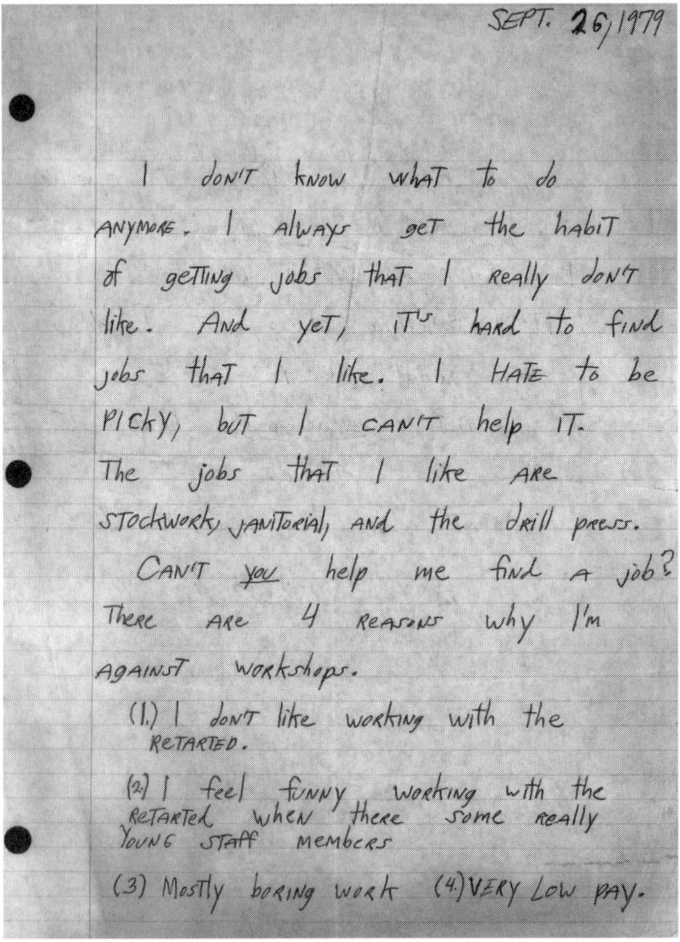

SEPT. 26, 1979

I don't know what to do anymore. I always get the habit of getting jobs that I really don't like. And yet, it's hard to find jobs that I like. I hate to be picky, but I can't help it. The jobs that I like are stockwork, janitorial, and the drill press.

Can't <u>you</u> help me find a job? There are 4 reasons why I'm against workshops.

(1.) I don't like working with the retarted.

(2.) I feel funny working with the retarted when there some really young staff members

(3) Mostly boring work (4.) Very low pay.

FIGURE 4.1 Letter originally handwritten by Dennis, aged 32, who earned IQs in the 50s and 60s.

jargon would communicate more directly with parents, students, and school staff. We developed the most boring labeling system in the history of assessment, one that might make Esquirol squirm in his grave as his soul reflects on his legacy of imbeciles and low-grade morons.

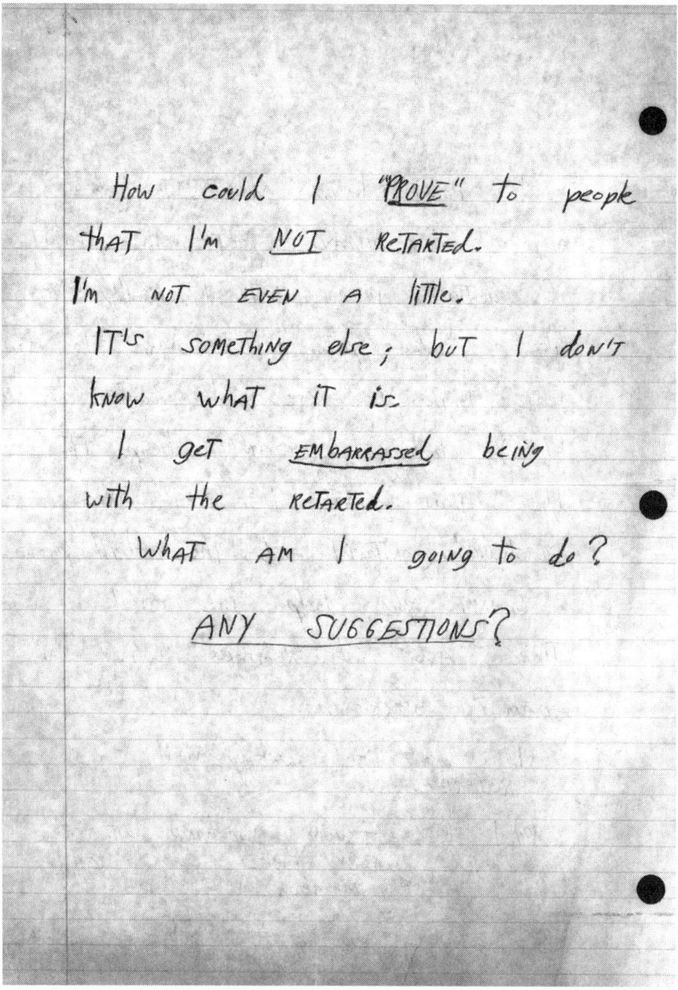

How could I "PROVE" to people
that I'm NOT retarted.
I'm not even a little.
IT's something else; but I don't
know what it is.
I get embarrassed being
with the retarted.
What am I going to do?
ANY SUGGESTIONS?

FIGURE 4.1 Letter originally handwritten by Dennis, aged 32, who earned IQs in the 50s and 60s. (*Continued*)

Direct Communication

Alas, communication has not always been foremost in the minds of test developers, a problem that stems from an early feud of sorts between the developers of the Stanford-Binet and Wechsler scales.

Table 4.1 presents percentile ranks for selected IQs, but these percentile ranks apply only to IQs with mean = 100 and *SD* = 15, the parameters inaugurated by Wechsler (1939) when he published his first test, the Wechsler-Bellevue. The percentiles in Table 4.1 do not apply to IQ tests that use *SD* = 16, the value that Terman and Merrill (1960) selected when they finally agreed to use standard scores instead of the MA/CA formula to derive IQs. When the *SD* is set at 16, the percentiles shown in Table 4.1 are just a little off. An IQ of 115, for example, corresponds to the 83rd percentile, not the 84th, which it corresponds to when the *SD* is 16 instead of 15; 70 corresponds to the 3rd percentile, not the 2nd; and so forth. Not a big deal? Actually it is when IQs are used (rightly or wrongly) for classification purposes. IQs that are more than two *SD*s below the mean have traditionally been used to identify whether children's IQs are low enough for them to qualify as mentally retarded, mentally deficient, intellectually disabled, or whatever term was current (assuming that their adaptive behavior was likewise low). On Wechsler's scales, that value has always corresponded to an IQ of 70, a nice round number; but on the Stanford-Binet, with *SD* = 16, the equivalent value for 2 *SD*s below the mean is 68. Similarly, at the upper end, 130 on Wechsler's scales (2 *SD*s above the mean) is equivalent to an IQ of 132 on the Binet.

Even in the middle of the IQ range there has been ambiguity. With an average range set at 90 to 109, an *SD* of 15 neatly fits the normal curve such that exactly 50% of the children and adults at all ages will be considered average. Change it to *SD* = 16, and the average group of children includes only about 45%. The net result: confusion for the professional groups who have had to develop guidelines and the practitioners who have had to adhere to the guidelines. The American Association on Mental Deficiency (now renamed politically correctly as the American Association on Intellectual and Developmental Disabilities) has had to provide two sets of criteria to determine whether a person's IQ was sufficiently low—"Less than 70" on the Wechsler Scales and "Less than 68" on the Stanford-Binet. Ridiculous!

The *SD* of 16 lasted in the Stanford-Binet into the first decade of the 2000s, until Gale Roid (2003) finally decided to change the value to 15 for the fifth edition; Thorndike et al. (1986) stubbornly held onto its traditional value of 16 for the fourth edition. Some other tests also held onto the *SD* of 16 for way too long, especially tests developed by Terman's doctoral students Arthur Otis and Nancy Bayley. Otis (1919) developed a group-administered version of the Stanford-Binet, and Bayley (1933, 1969) extended the measurement of mental development down into infancy. The Bayley Scales of Infant Development used *SD* = 16 until the 1990s, when the second edition switched to the more user-friendly *SD* of 15 (Bayley, 1993). The current version of Otis's group test, the eighth edition of the Otis-Lennon School Ability Test (OLSAT 8; Otis & Lennon, 2006), still uses *SD* = 16, but that is the exception to the rule. And because the OLSAT is a group-administered test, as opposed to an individual test administered by a psychologist for clinical purposes (the focus of *IQ Testing 101*), it doesn't muddy the water too much. Yet OLSAT 8, by retaining *SD* = 16, still has the potential to cause confusion. For example, as of 2007, the New York City Department of Education began to use the OLSAT 8, along with a readiness test, for admission to gifted and talented programs in prekindergarten through second grade. Nonetheless, almost complete harmony has been achieved in the field of clinical assessment of IQ, as all major clinical tests of children's and adults' intelligence use the identical metrics of mean = 100 and *SD* = 15.

Why did the Stanford-Binet and Wechsler scales have slightly different *SD*s for more than 60 years? For the same reason that the Capulets and Montagues would never have agreed on a restaurant for Romeo and Juliet's rehearsal dinner. As I've mentioned, the actual index of variability (i.e., *SD)* averaged 16, when using the old MA/CA formula. Terman and Merrill (1937) provided a table of standard scores "for purposes of research" (p. 42) and indicated that the appropriate *SD* for standard scores should be 16; they used mean = 100 and *SD* = 16 in the conversion table they provided for researchers.

But when Wechsler (1939) published the Wechsler-Bellevue a couple of years later, eliminating the "quotient" from "IQ," he figured that 16 was a silly number to pick as the *SD* when 15 is so close to the "real" value and yet has the advantage of being divisible by 5. That advantage translated to simplicity for examiners because it produced "round" benchmark numbers like 85 (1 *SD* below the mean) and 130 (2 *SD*s above the mean). Still, he might have done psychologists and teachers a favor by sticking to Terman's 16, because the Binet people were not going to capitulate to the upstart Wechsler. When they finally decided to switch to Wechsler's notion of standard scores for the 1960 edition of the Stanford-Binet, they chose 16 as the *SD*; after all, Binet developed the IQ test and Terman (from Stanford University) popularized the IQ formula. Why should they flinch?

Both test developers stubbornly refused to yield to the other: In 1986, the fourth edition of the Stanford-Binet departed from its ancestors in every way imaginable—the developers used Wechsler-like subtests for all age groups instead of using their traditional "age level" approach, they abandoned the term IQ, and they even eliminated Terman and Merrill as authors—but they insisted on keeping the *SD* at 16 (Thorndike et al., 1986). Yet, in fairness, other test developers from years past have made life more difficult for psychologists and educators than has the petty rift over 15 versus 16. Although everyone is used to dealing with a mean of 100 (IQ) or 500 (SATs) or even 50 (*T* scores on personality tests), round numbers all, Sam Kirk gave us a mean of 36 on the Illinois Test of Psycholinguistic Abilities (ITPA; Kirk, McCarthy, & Kirk, 1968). Kirk was a pioneer who coined the term *learning disabilities* in 1963, but the test he developed to help diagnose dyslexia and related disorders, the ITPA, made many psychologists and special educators feel like *they* had a learning disability in math. Kirk used *SD* = 6 to accompany the mean of 36. That meant that so-called very superior or gifted performance (more than 2 *SD*s above the mean) corresponded to a standard score greater than 48 and the opposite pole corresponded to a standard score below 24. The numbers meant nothing, intuitively, to anyone. No one I knew who used this test (which happened to include some novel and interesting tasks) could easily remember just which scores were very good or poor. Indeed, most professionals didn't have a clue how to relate children's standard scores on the ITPA to their IQs on the Wechsler or Binet.

Even Richard Woodcock, a great test developer and innovator with a keen mathematical mind, used metrics that boggled the minds of professionals when he first published the Woodcock-Johnson in the late 1970s (Woodcock & Johnson, 1977). The scores were derived from a sophisticated procedure called Rasch latent-trait scaling and were known as W-Ability scores (now simply referred to as *W* scores). The mean W-Ability score was set at 500, but that mean corresponded to the average performance of a 10-year-old. Whether you were testing a 3-year-old, a 15-year-old, or a 60-year-old, a score of 500 equaled the mean performance of children at the beginning of fifth grade (I swear I am not making that up!). When professionals had difficulty understanding the W-Ability scores and the other novel scores (such as the relative proficiency index, or RPI), Woodcock published tables of standard scores by age level and grade level (mean = 100, *SD* = 15) to facilitate understanding of the unusual scores. The WJ-R (Woodcock & Johnson, 1989) and WJ III (Woodcock et al., 2001) continued to feature the W-Ability scores and the other esoteric scores, but tables of standard scores were always provided as well to ease the translation to IQs earned on other tests. When McGrew, Woodcock, and Ford (2006) listed the seven types of scores yielded by the WJ III, it is clear that the *W* score is still the favorite. It is discussed first and standard scores are discussed last (and briefly), but "The standard score is the score most commonly reported in clinical practice" (p. 579).

Scaled Scores

There is one other type of standard score that is popularly used for IQ tests that I haven't discussed yet but need to touch on briefly—the *scaled score,* or subtest score, that a person earns on each separate subtest making up a comprehensive IQ test. Wechsler (1939) introduced these standard scores when he first published the Wechsler-Bellevue, assigning them a mean of 10 and *SD* of 3. Scaled scores typically range from 1 to 19, and these scores are now universal, applying to subtests on most major IQ tests such as the KABC-II and Binet-5. Wechsler chose 10 and 3 (instead of 100 and 15) for the subtests to prevent people from coming up with a "Vocabulary IQ" or a "Block Design IQ." He wanted people to focus on the global IQs (Verbal, Performance, and Full Scale), not on each separate task, but he also wanted to provide scores that were simple. By making the average score 10, and limiting the range of scores to ± 3 *SD*s from the mean, he accomplished just that. Psychologists and educators have internalized the concept of scaled scores on separate subtests, and they do not confuse them with IQs. Importantly, a scaled score of 6 or 9 or 14 on Wechsler's scales has the same meaning regardless of whether the subtest measures verbal ability, visual-spatial ability, working memory, or processing speed, and regardless of the age of the child or adult. And because other IQ tests have adopted Wechsler's scaled scores for their tests, these scores have the same meaning from test battery to test battery. For example, a scaled score of 13 equals the 84th percentile (1 *SD* above the mean) and a score of 4 equals the 2nd percentile (2 *SD*s below the mean) regardless of age or subtest.

HOW DO YOU IDENTIFY AVERAGE INTELLIGENCE?

Setting the mean for IQs at 100 and the *SD* at 15 is the easy part. So is setting the mean and *SD* for subtest scaled scores at 10 and 3, respectively. Those are arbitrary decisions that can be made in an armchair. But how do you figure out just what is average, or superior, or extremely low performance? How do you determine what level of success is needed to be at a 130 IQ level, or what degree of failure translates to IQs in the 50s or 60s? And just what do we mean by average intelligence? I'm not talking about what range of IQs is considered average. That range has traditionally been 90–109, following the Terman-Wechsler tradition. Or sometimes it is defined as ± 1 *SD* from the mean (i.e., 85–115), which considers the middle two thirds of people to represent average or normal intelligence, instead of the middle 50%. My colleagues and I have recently begun to consider average to be within 1 *SD* of the mean, because the "number of *SD*s from the mean" has become an increasingly popular way of communicating test results (Flanagan & Kaufman, 2004, 2009; Kaufman & Kaufman, 2004a). But I am not concerned with *what* IQs are considered average; I want to explain *how* average levels of performance are determined.

As I said before, IQ is a relative concept, not an absolute one. Before any IQs can be assigned, we must find out how well large groups of people perform on the questions and novel problems included in the IQ test. These groups are called *standardization* samples or *norms* groups. But they can't be made up of just any people. If you want to know your 9-year-old daughter's IQ, you must compare the number of questions she answered correctly to the number gotten right by other 9-year-olds. But not just any 9-year-olds. If all the children in the age 9 norms group had parents with MD and PhD degrees, she would be unfairly penalized. The norms would be too "steep" because the reference group would have set the bar for "average performance" too high; as we will see in Table 4.3, adults with MDs and PhDs average about 125 on IQ tests, and their children also score well above average on tests like the WISC-IV, KABC-II, and Stanford-Binet-5. However, if all the 9-year-olds in the sample were the children of parents who dropped out of elementary school (whose average IQ is in the low 80s), then the norms would be biased in the opposite direction—too easy or "soft." To avoid built-in bias, the sample must be representative of children aged 9 living in the United States. For teens and adults, the age ranges are broader (for example, 16–17, 20–24, or 35–44), but the principle is the same: To determine IQ,

TABLE 4.3 AVERAGE ADULT IQs ASSOCIATED WITH REAL-LIFE ACCOMPLISHMENTS

Average IQ	Real-Life Accomplishment
125	MDs or PhDs
115	College graduates
105–110	1 to 3 years of college
100–105	Clerical and sales workers
100	High school graduates Skilled workers (e.g., electricians, cabinetmakers)
95	1 to 3 years of high school (completed 9–11 years of school)
90–95	Semi-skilled workers (e.g., truck drivers, factory workers)
90	Elementary school graduates (completed eighth grade)
80–85	Elementary school dropouts (completed 0–7 years of school)
75	Have 50/50 chance of reaching high school Adults can keep small store
60	Adults can harvest vegetables, repair furniture
50	Adults can do domestic work, simple carpentry
40	Adults can mow lawns, do simple laundry

Note. This table is based on data and information from Kaufman and Lichtenberger (2006, Figure 1.1 and chapter 4). The IQs are predominantly Full Scale IQs obtained on Wechsler's adult scales (the Wechsler-Bellevue, WAIS, WAIS-R, and WAIS-III). Lower IQs also are based on early versions of the Stanford-Binet.

a person's test performance must be compared to the test performance of *representative* groups of children, adolescents, or adults of approximately the same age as the person tested.

The method is simple, at least conceptually. In practice, it's time consuming and expensive. First, you must study the U.S. Census data on key variables like gender, ethnicity, socioeconomic status (SES), geographic region, and community size to determine the proportions that characterize the United States. Then you must select the standardization sample for your IQ test to match the census proportions. For example, the distribution of children ages 3–18 years living in the four geographic regions of the United States is as follows, according to the March 2001 *Current Population Survey*: 19.2% in the Northeast, 22.1% in the North Central region, 34.7% in the South, and 24.1% in the West (Kaufman & Kaufman, 2004a, Table 7.5). To be representative, an IQ test's standardization sample for children and adolescents needs to match the regional percents of the United States as a whole.

SES is usually defined as educational attainment (years of schooling) or occupational category for adult samples; for children's samples, it is typically defined as parents' education or occupation. From the 2001 U.S. Census, for example, 34.3% of African American children and adolescents had parents who attended college for 1–3 years and 12.8 percent had parents who graduated from college (Kaufman & Kaufman, 2004a, Table 7.6). When testing children for a standardization sample, you need to match those percentages as closely as possible—and do the same for all ethnic groups, SES categories, geographic regions, and so forth—to ensure that your normative group is unbiased and representative of the United States.

The average scores earned by truly representative samples at each age reflect average performance (IQ = 100 or scaled score = 10). On Wechsler's children's and adult scales, for example, children are asked questions about general facts on the Information subtest (e.g., What is steam made of? What is the capital of France? Who wrote *Tom Sawyer*?), and they are asked to solve nonverbal reasoning problems (Matrix Reasoning subtest). Figure 4.2 illustrates an easy Matrix Reasoning item and Figure 4.3 provides a difficult item, one that resembles the kind of fluid reasoning that is needed to solve the harder Matrix Reasoning items (also see Figure 3.6 for an example of a medium-difficulty matrices item).

The WISC-IV includes 33 Information items and 35 Matrix Reasoning items. How many of the 33 Information items must

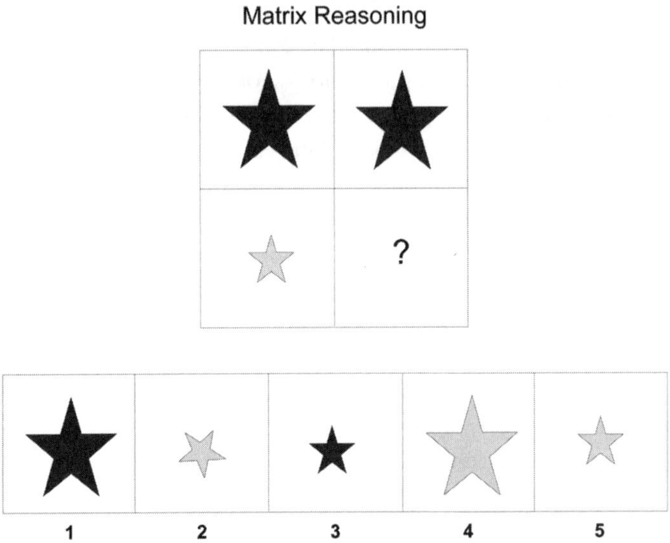

FIGURE 4.2 Example of Wechsler's Matrix Reasoning subtest.
Simulated items similar to those in the *Wechsler Intelligence Scales for Adults and Children*, San Antonio, TX. Copyright © 2005 by Harcourt Assessment, Inc. Reproduced with permission.

be answered correctly to be considered average? superior? extremely low? What about the number of nonverbal reasoning problems? Will solving 25 of the 35 correctly yield a high score? There is no way to answer these questions without first obtaining a representative standardization sample and determining how many items were solved correctly by the average child or adolescent at each age in the sample. Looking at the norms for the WISC-IV (Wechsler, 2003, Table A.1), we learn that the average 7½-year-old answered 12 of the 33 Information items correctly and solved 13 to 14 of the 35 Matrix Reasoning items. For age 10½, those average values are 17 and 20–21, respectively, and at age 15½, the averages are 22 to 23 Information items and 25 to 26 Matrix Reasoning items.

Now we know what average performance means on those two subtests. Remember that 10 is the average scaled score on

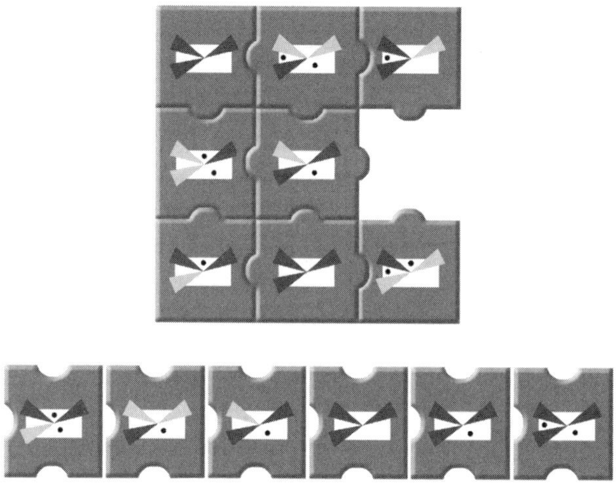

FIGURE 4.3 Example of a hard *Gf* matrices item (similar to items on the KBIT-2 Matrices test).

Note. The correct response is fourth from the left. The key is to focus on (a) the number of dark gray triangles in each design (either 1, 2, or 3, going both across and down) and (b) the number of dots in the design (either 0, 1, or 2, going both across and down). The missing puzzle piece must have 3 dark gray triangles and 0 black dots to "fit" the overall pattern in the 3 × 3 matrix. From *Kaufman Brief Intelligence Test—Second Edition (KBIT–2)*, by A. S. Kaufman and N. L. Kaufman, 2004, Circle Pines, MN: American Guidance Service.

each subtest at each age. To earn a score of 10 on Information, you must get 12 items right if you are 7½ years old, 17 if you are 10½, and 22 or 23 if you are 15½. If you are a child of 7 or 8 and you answer 20 Information items correctly, you are surely substantially above average and your score will be higher than 10. If you solve only 5 Matrix Reasoning items correctly, you will be below average and your score will be in single digits. How much above or below? That is again determined by the variability in test scores for individuals of about your age. It involves the *SD* or variability on each subtest at each age as well as the normal curve to determine exactly how high or low the scaled score is. Score higher than 98% of your age-mates on Information or Matrix Reasoning, or any other subtest, and your scaled score will be 16. Score higher than only 9%, and your scaled score will be 6.

How do you get to your WISC-IV Full Scale IQ? You put all 10 of the core WISC-IV subtests together and again compare a person's performance to his or her age-mates' performance on the test as a whole. Based on the *SD* and the normal curve, IQs will be assigned to each level of performance. If you are 12 years old and you performed better than 25% of other 12-year-olds on the WISC-IV, your Full Scale IQ will be 90; if you are 60 and you performed better than 75% of other adults about age 60, your WAIS-IV Full Scale IQ will be 110 (see Table 4.1). And so forth for IQs yielded by the KABC-II or the WJ III or the DAS-II or the Stanford-Binet-5.

There is no particular criterion to reach. The set of general information questions on Wechsler's Information subtest does not include key facts to master. "Good" for children or adults is defined by the performance of others the same age. If you get more questions right or solve more problems than most people your own age, then your IQ will be above 100. If you perform below the norm for your age-mates, then your IQ will be below 100, maybe well below. When you take an IQ test you may feel that you did great on one subtest and terribly on another. But you can never be sure until your right and wrong answers are tallied and your scores are put to the supreme test: How did you stack up in each area when compared to the representative sample of Americans about your age that were given the IQ test when it was standardized?

If you left the norms group panting in the dust and aced all the parts of the test with flying colors—for example, if you earned an IQ of 145, only 2 light years behind Marilyn vos Savant but better than about 999 of 1,000 people in the human species (Table 4.1)—then dreams of dean's lists, doctorates, and prestige may legitimately permeate your fantasies. But if you just couldn't hack it, and you scored somewhere in the mid- or high

80s (dull normal before political correctness became the vogue), then maybe those dreams had better shift to a factory assembly line or to a career in politics.

And don't think for a second that you can determine your IQ on a Web site that promises you that it can pinpoint your own intelligence. The people who develop these Web sites don't use theory to develop their tests. They don't spend the considerable amount of money it takes to refine each and every item and to standardize the IQ tests to provide a large, representative reference group on which to base a person's IQ. When it comes to quick-and-dirty IQ tests on the Internet, or from books that advertise "Know Your IQ"—forget about it!

And just because a test is published, don't assume that its norms are representative of the United States. Sometimes test publishers take short cuts, as my colleague Ron Dumont (personal communication, October 9, 2008) reminded me. He pointed out that the original norms for the Halstead-Reitan, a popular test used by neuropsychologists, were based on a tiny and inadequate sample of 21 men and 8 women. Ten of the subjects were servicemen who were available to be tested because of "minor" psychiatric problems; another was awaiting sentencing for a capital crime; four were awaiting lobotomies; and yet another person was tested twice (bringing the grand total to 30) because he was still in the hospital, so he decided to take the test again (Boll, 1981). Not exactly a "normal" sample! And Ron also joked about the normative sample for the published Boston Naming Test, also a neuropsychological test: "At age 18, the norming sample was a grand total of one. . . . his name was Norm, so they let him in."

A REAL-LIFE PERSPECTIVE ON IQs—WHO SCORES WHAT?

Table 4.3 (p. 126) puts IQs into a little more perspective by showing the IQs that correspond to a variety of education levels and jobs, ranging from the IQ needed to mow lawns and do simple laundry to the average IQ of physicians and university professors. This table shows the approximate average IQ earned by people with different educational and occupational backgrounds, and it also indicates the type of work that adults with IQs between 40 and 75 are capable of doing. Not only do adults in high status occupations earn higher IQs than adults in low status occupations, but so do their children (see Table 4.4). Adults in prestigious occupations often earn more money and are better educated than adults in less prestigious occupations, and they tend to provide a more stimulating environment for their children. Logic tells us that adults in professional jobs and their children ought

TABLE 4.4 AVERAGE WAIS-R FULL SCALE IQs EARNED BY ADULTS (AGES 20–54) IN VARIOUS OCCUPATIONAL GROUPS AND AVERAGE WISC-R IQs EARNED BY CHILDREN (AGES 6–16) WHOSE PARENTS ARE IN THE SAME OCCUPATIONAL GROUPS

	Average Full Scale IQ of:	
Occupational Group	*Adults in These Occupations*	*Children Whose Parents Are in These Occupations*
Professional and technical	112	108
Managers and administrators	104	103
Clerical workers; sales workers; skilled workers, craftsmen, and foremen	101	100
Semi-skilled workers (operatives, service workers, including private household; farmers and farm managers)	92	96
Unskilled workers	87	87

Note. WAIS-R data are from Reynolds, Chastain, Kaufman, and McLean (1987); WISC-R data are from Kaufman and Doppelt (1976).

to be more intelligent than unskilled laborers and their family members. It makes no difference what the cause and effect are. Maybe smart people set and reach higher goals; maybe the intelligence emerges as the fruits of the work it takes to achieve those goals; maybe a little bit of both. No matter. The Wechsler IQs of adult professionals are 25 points higher than the IQs of unskilled workers. Children of professionals outstrip children of unskilled laborers by 21 points.

But don't take the numbers in Tables 4.3 or 4.4 too literally or think of them too rigidly. I just want to use the tables to install a few commonsense guideposts to make the IQ number system a bit more meaningful. Average IQs don't speak for everyone within a given occupational group or with the same level of education. People vary; there is a good deal of variability around every mean or median score. Adults with bachelor's degrees earn an average IQ of 115, which is 20 points higher than the average IQ of adults who dropped out of high school (9–11 years of schooling). Yet, not all of the adults with bachelor's degrees scored 115. In fact, in one study, their IQs spanned the wide range from 87 to 148 (Reynolds, Chastain, Kaufman, & McLean, 1987). The range for adults with 1 to 3 years of high school was 59 to 146. Quite a few high school dropouts shine brighter than college grads when sent into battle with an IQ test. So do some semiskilled workers (IQ range of 56–135) when they are compared to professionals (81 to 148). In fact, high IQs are found at all levels of education and within every occupational category (Kaufman & Lichtenberger, 2006). The biggest difference invariably occurs at the low end of the IQ continuum. While it is fairly common to find high school dropouts and semiskilled workers with IQs below 80, only an occasional college graduate or professional scores below 90.

The ability for IQs to distinguish among groups of people who should logically differ from each other (such as professionals vs. unskilled workers or college graduates vs. high school dropouts) provides evidence that the IQ is a *valid* construct. Even more compelling is the fact that these IQ differences between groups emerge for nonverbal as well as verbal tasks (Manly, Heaton, & Taylor, 2000; Reynolds et al., 1987)—that is to say, for measures of fluid reasoning (*Gf*), which are not taught in school, as well as for tests of crystallized knowledge (*Gc*). In fact, *Gf* shows about the same differences among adults categorized by years of schooling as do both *Gc* and traditional measures of academic skills like reading, math, and writing (Kaufman, Kaufman, Liu, & Johnson, in press).

Like adults, children and adolescents from different socioeconomic backgrounds differ in the predicted direction on both verbal and nonverbal scales. Weiss et al. (2006) presented interesting data on the WISC-IV Spanish (Wechsler, 2005), an adaptation of the WISC-IV for use with Spanish-speaking children in the United States and Puerto Rico. These researchers grouped Spanish-speaking children living in the United States into five categories based on (a) their opportunities for acculturation (the percentage of the children's education in U.S. schools) and (b) SES (parent education). The children differed just as much on the WISC-IV Perceptual Reasoning Index (PRI), a nonverbal measure of *Gf* and visual processing (*Gv*), as they did on the Verbal Comprehension Index (VCI), a measure of *Gc*, as shown here (Level V is the highest level of acculturation and SES, and Level I is the lowest):

Category	**Perceptual Reasoning Index (PRI)**	**Verbal Comprehension Index (VCI)**
V	105	103
IV	102	98
III	97	96
II	90	91
I	82	85

So what can we conclude? IQs are no longer quotients, but they are valid standard scores that discriminate among groups of children and adults who would be expected to score either high or low on an intelligence test. But are they error free? Are they determined to some extent by genetics? Are they malleable, based on the impact of environment? Do they increase or decrease as we get older? These topics are covered in the next four chapters.

5

The IQ Construct, Part 2: How Accurate Are IQ Tests?

Francis Galton, following a pure scientist's credo, denied that it was necessary to accept measurement error when measuring intelligence. Alfred Binet knew better. If you try to measure someone's intelligence, you can't do it with pinpoint accuracy. It's not the same as measuring someone's height with a ruler or weight with a scale. There's no common yardstick, no universal set of questions that makes up "intelligence." Get 20 experts in psychology together, and you'll get almost as many divergent views of what intelligence is. Get them to agree that CHC theory is the best way to define intelligence, and that still doesn't solve the problem of how to measure it. If you decide that knowing the meaning of many words is a sign of *Gc*, then how do you test it? Have people name pictures of objects? Tell them a word and have them define it? Both are acceptable IQ tasks, but some people who can name pictures of esoteric objects like *hygrometer* and *calyx* just can't put their ideas into words to describe the meaning of *infidelity* or *petulance.*

Or suppose that everyone agrees that defining words is a good way to test *Gc.* Which words do you choose? Are some more important than others? Are you more intelligent if you are able to define adverbs and adjectives rather than just nouns and verbs? Abstract concepts versus concrete objects? Practical considerations mean that only a few words (maybe 25 or 35) can be included in the vocabulary test (you can't lock a person in a room for 48 hours and test him or her until one of you passes out). Thus, the person's success or failure on the specific words is only an estimate of how many words the person knows.

ERRORS OF MEASUREMENT

Sources of error abound when measuring any skill. Sticking with vocabulary as a measure of *Gc* as an illustration, people are likely to get more words right if they are calm, rested, and attentive than if they are tense, tired, and tuned out. Sometimes they will have just learned a specific word or two from a recent conversation, TV show, or school lesson. If you had tested them the previous week, they wouldn't have heard of the words; test them next week, and they might display the T-O-T or tip-of-tongue phenomenon ("It's on the tip of my tongue, but I can't remember it"). An examinee might narrow down possible responses to two choices (I know a stalagmite is either on the roof or on the floor of a cave) and have a 50/50 chance of guessing right on any given day.

Or the same answer might be scored differently by two different examiners, because no scoring guide, no matter how thorough, can anticipate all possible definitions that people give when asked, "What do we mean by *obnoxious*?" On Wechsler's scales, the scoring guide gives samples of 2-point, 1-point (partially correct), and 0-point responses. So why do so many people seem to give precisely "1½-point answers"? Examiners also differ in the kinds of answers they choose to follow up with neutral questions ("Tell me more about it"). Examiners are told to query verbal responses that are ambiguous or incomplete, and the scoring guide illustrates the kinds of answers that must be questioned. But it's often mud-clear whether a given answer should be queried, and examiners differ in their testing styles. Some will question nearly everything, including burps and grunts ("Gotta give the kid every chance to get an A-1 IQ"), while others need to be placed in a hammer-lock before probing an answer ("Don't wanna shatter the kid's confidence by saying 'Tell me more, tell me more, tell me more!'").

The net result of the human and emotional side of IQ testing is error. It's built into IQ tests, all IQ tests, from the beginning. You try to minimize it as much as possible, but with complex tasks you just can't get it to go away. It afflicts all mental tasks, verbal or nonverbal, problem solving or rote memory, convergent or creative. The scoring problems associated with subjective tests like vocabulary tests shouldn't affect objectively scored nonverbal tasks, should they? Copying an abstract design using red-and-white cubes or putting together a picture puzzle is either right or wrong—right? Not quite. Wechsler's tests give bonus points on some tasks for people who solve items very quickly; so do other tests like the KABC-II. Copy one design with blocks in 10 seconds or less, and earn a score of 7; get the same design right, but take more than 20 seconds, and you wimp out with 4 points. But psychologists can't always be sure when a person is done. Some tell the examiner, some don't. Some look up, others continue to stare at the blocks they put together while they're thinking about tonight's date or tomorrow's lunch. When do you turn off the stopwatch? What do you do if you turn off the stopwatch, and then the person starts rearranging the blocks once more? IQ testing just isn't a precise science. And some of the best clinicians in the world are lousy clerks. They might succeed in giving an IQ test to a psychotic child or adult branded "untestable!" by previous examiners, and then make an error in adding up a column of numbers, or enter the wrong table to compute the IQs, or score some items wrong.

In one study, psychology graduate students were asked to score a written record of a client's responses to all items on Wechsler's adult test, and then compute the IQs (Ryan, Prifitera, & Powers, 1983). If scored correctly, the client would have earned a Full Scale IQ of 110. These psychology students came up with IQs ranging from 108 to 117. The sad truth is that the carelessness doesn't seem to disappear with practice. Bad clerks abound even after earning PhDs and having years of experience. In that same study, a group of experienced psychologists produced a set of IQs for the client that ranged from 107 to 115. And numerous other studies have found the same thing. Fifteen graduate students averaged 7.8 errors per WISC-III protocol in one study (Alfonso, Johnson, Patinella, & Rader, 1998); seven master's level psychologists made clerical errors on 42% of the WISC-III protocols they scored in another study (Klassen & Kishor, 1996); and the list goes on.

Robert Gregory and his colleagues studied the IQs of children exposed to lead and by happenstance discovered that the examiner's attitude and demeanor had a greater impact on IQ than the lead level in the child's blood (Gregory, Lehman, & Mohan, 1976). The researchers noticed that one of the five graduate student examiners came up with relatively low scores for the children tested (average IQ of 90), and another consistently produced inflated scores (average IQ of 104). The first examiner "was very formal, precise, cold, and hurried," while the second offered "support and encouragement that bordered on leading the subjects to the correct answer" (Gregory, 1999, p. 89).

Error seems to come out every which way during an IQ test. So, if you can't eliminate it, then give it a name, understand just how much error there is in each test score, and take it into account when interpreting the scores. It sounds simple. But some people still think of the obtained IQ score as something hallowed, a number etched in blood. Why is a developmentally disabled adult who finally breaks the 70 barrier—after years of earning IQs and adaptive behavior scores in the 60s—suddenly declared ineligible to continue in a federally funded sheltered workshop for adults with intellectual disabilities? A different day or test or tester and the results may be reversed. Why, for almost 30 years, were IQs blindly plugged into statistical formulas to diagnose children with specific learning disabilities before this flawed approach was finally challenged by a key law known as IDEA 2004? (See chapter 9.) Formulas and rigid thinking ignore the built-in imperfections of IQ tests.

Standard Error of Measurement

The error in a test is called its *standard error of measurement (SEm)*, and it is expressed in IQ points. Most good IQ tests have SEms of about 3 points. Translation: The odds are about 2 out of 3 that the person's IQ obtained on the test is within 3 points of his or her *true IQ*. True IQ is a figment of some statistician's imagination; it's the average IQ a person would earn if given the same exact test over and over and over again, and if there were no such things as fatigue, boredom, practice, and dislike of psychologists who give IQ tests. It may be a figment, but it's valuable. If a person could be tested thousands of times, the test scores would form a normal curve. The mean of that normal distribution of scores is the person's true score. The standard deviation is the standard error of measurement.

The best way to deal with the SEm is to band every IQ with error. Thus, instead of an IQ of 97, the person earns an IQ of 97 ± 3. The IQ range of 94 to 100, referred to as a *confidence interval,* has about a two-thirds chance of including the true IQ. Two-thirds probability? That doesn't provide much confidence. I wouldn't cross a busy intersection if I had only a 65% to 70% probability of making it to the other side.

A better band of error is one that gives 90% or 95% confidence. For most individually administered IQ tests, that would be about ±4 to ±6 points. For the WISC-IV, a range of about ±5 points around a child's Full Scale IQ offers 95% confidence

(The Psychological Corporation, 2003, pp. 37–38). That same approximate value is the 95% confidence interval for the Fluid-Crystallized Index (FCI) on the KABC-II (Kaufman & Kaufman, 2004a); an impressive ±4 points characterizes the WAIS-IV Full Scale IQ (The Psychological Corporation, 2008) and the Binet-5 Full Scale IQ (Binet-5; Roid, 2003). So, for example, if you find out that your daughter's WISC-IV Full Scale IQ is 114, the first thing you ought to do is think of the IQ as being somewhere (anywhere) in the IQ range from about 109 to 119. An IQ of 114 is in the middle of the high average category, once called bright normal (see Table 4.2). So your daughter may be bright, or she may even be in the superior category (IQs of 120–129). However, error works both ways; you have to be bright enough to recognize that your daughter's IQ of 114 may just as easily be in the average range of 90 to 109. And remember, this is the WISC-IV Full Scale IQ. Your child's IQ on a different IQ test, such as the WJ III (Woodcock et al., 2001) or KABC-II, or RIAS (Reynolds & Kamphaus, 2003) or Binet-5, will undoubtedly be different—maybe higher, maybe lower.

We've been talking about your child's IQ, but we could just as well be talking about your own IQ. Confidence intervals on the adult portion of the WJ III and the Binet-5, or on Wechsler's adult scales, such as the recently published WAIS-IV, are virtually identical to the values for children's tests.

Bands of error surrounding an IQ are so important that test publishers now routinely provide confidence intervals directly in the norms tables themselves. When examiners enter the IQ conversion norms table to translate the sums of the person's scores on the different subtests into an IQ, they not only read off the IQ but they also read off the percentile rank and the confidence intervals that band that particular IQ with error. Norms tables typically provide both the 90% and 95% confidence intervals, and examiners choose whichever interval they prefer. These confidence intervals are often presented as being symmetrical, but not always. Although it is easiest to think of the band of error as a symmetrical confidence interval around the *obtained* IQ (e.g.,

75 ± 5), the interval, in theory, is placed around the person's true IQ. And even though we can never know the person's true IQ, formulas can easily estimate that value. So, for example, on the WISC-IV, the 95% confidence interval given for a Full Scale IQ of 60 is 57–65; on the Binet-5, the 95% confidence interval for a Full Scale IQ of 132 is 127–135. Note that these intervals are not symmetrical. For example, the range of 127 to 135 is 5 points below the obtained IQ and only 3 points above it. The further away the person's IQ is from the overall mean IQ of 100, the more asymmetrical the confidence interval. The asymmetry occurs because of a statistical phenomenon known as regression to the mean. (Galton's original term, when used to describe the inheritance of height, was regression to mediocrity.) And, technically, these asymmetrical bands are formed using the standard error of estimate, not the standard error of measurement. But these statistical details are just that—details. They are not important. What is vital is to internalize the reality that we don't earn a specific IQ—we actually earn a *range of IQs* that most likely includes our true IQ. When examiners select the 90% confidence interval, then the chances are 9 out of 10 that the person's true IQ on that particular test is somewhere within the interval. When using the 95% confidence interval, the odds increase to 19 out of 20.

WILL ALL GOOD IQ TESTS YIELD ABOUT THE SAME IQ FOR THE SAME PERSON?

The SEm of an IQ test means that a person's score on the *same* IQ test will be different from one time to another. The 95% confidence interval of about ± 5 points means that we can safely narrow down a person's IQ to a reasonably small range of, say, 62 to 72. That's not as precise as a single IQ point, but it is still a pretty good indication of how a child or adult is functioning intellectually. But what about *different* IQ tests? Does the IQ range from one test transfer to another one? If a 17-year-old boy earns a Fluid-Crystallized Index of 87 on the KABC-II, does the corresponding range of 82 to 92 also include the boy's "true" Full Scale IQ on the WISC-IV or WAIS-IV or Binet-5? What about on the OLSAT 8, a *group*-administered IQ test?

Group Versus Individual Tests

Tests given in one-on-one fashion often yield IQs that differ, sometimes substantially, from IQs earned on group tests. Not because group tests are ambiguous or poorly constructed or demand luck rather than skill. Many group tests are excellent and straightforward and have no items—not one—ending with "None of the Above." Some manage to measure both verbal and nonverbal skills, and most group IQ tests put out by well-known test publishers have excellent standardization samples—groups of people that are so large that they dwarf the normative samples for individually administered tests. Why? Because it's a lot cheaper and easier for an examiner with limited formal training in testing to give a group IQ test to 100 people at once than for a highly specialized examiner to spend 1 or 2 hours with a single person.

Because individual IQ tests are different from group IQ tests, they will invariably yield different IQs for the same person. Think about taking a multiple-choice test with a group of people. Someone stands in front of a room and reads the instructions to you. She says "Start" while you're still figuring out what you're supposed to do, and "Stop" just when you've finally figured it out. Or maybe she just hands out the exam, and you've got to read the directions yourself. Either way, there's no one there to calm you down if you get anxious or to get you to focus on the test questions if you start daydreaming or paying too much attention to the chatter or laughter barely audible in the street or just outside the testing room. And suppose you're a poor reader. You might not be able to understand the printed directions. Or even if you do, you may have difficulty with certain words in some questions. Or your slow reading may make it impossible for you to finish even a fraction of the items before the examiner booms out, "Stop! Put your pencils down. Now go on to the section on page 24."

When IQ tests are given individually, the examiner first tries to build rapport with you by putting you at ease, making sure you know why you're being tested, learning a bit about your interests and anxieties, and generally making the 90 minutes or so as enjoyable as possible. If you become agitated or bored or distracted during the IQ test, the examiner will deal with these problems as they occur and will try to make sure that he asks you questions or presents materials to be manipulated only when you are interested and attentive. Sometimes a second session has to be arranged to ensure that your IQ is as valid as possible. Poor readers aren't penalized on individual IQ tests, because reading is required for few, if any, items; when it is required, alternate procedures are usually permitted for children or adults with reading problems. And guessing doesn't play a large role in individual IQ tests. In most cases, you have to respond to open-ended questions or assemble some type of puzzle or design. It's only an occasional individual IQ test that allows you to close your eyes and pick out one of four or five responses.

Even though the format is different (multiple-choice versus open-ended verbal and nonverbal responding), many of the tasks that appear on group tests are extremely similar to the subtests that comprise individual, clinical IQ tests. As shown in chapter 2, Wechsler took three of his familiar verbal subtests (Arithmetic, Comprehension, Information) and two of his nonverbal subtests (Picture Completion, Digit Symbol) directly from the group-administered Army Alpha and Army Beta. But group and individual tests might still produce very different IQs for the same person even if they are composed of highly similar tasks, even identical items. And there's not always a blueprint for who is likely to score higher on one type or the other. Poor readers have a better chance of doing better when tested individually than when they have to read the directions and questions on a group test. Very shy people, however, may earn higher IQs when tested anonymously as part of a group. Distractible, anxious, or poorly motivated people may benefit from the individual attention of a clinically trained examiner, but others may feel self-conscious and judged in such an intimidating situation. When you take a group test, the right answer is usually right there in front of you, camouflaged by tempting wrong responses. With individual exams you have to generate the answers from the cobwebbed corners of your brain.

Both kinds of tests do a pretty good job of measuring mental ability; they just do it differently. For some people, it makes no difference what type of test they take. They'll score about equally well whether they're tested individually, in a classroom of 25, or in a stadium filled with thousands. For others, the difference can be dramatic, even 30 or 40 points. Your IQ is 144? What about errors of measurement? Were you given a group test or an individual test? And just what test was it? Sure, 144 sounds nice. Take a different kind of test and next time you may even earn an IQ of 160. But it may also dip to 125. Or 110.

Different IQs on Different Individual IQ Tests

What about when the same person is tested on two different *individual* IQ tests? Will the IQs be about the same? When an IQ test is administered individually by a trained clinical examiner, the odds are that a valid score will result even if the child or adult is anxious, can't read, tends to daydream, or hates IQ tests. Sure, there are errors of measurement, differences in how well examiners establish trust with the client, and clerical errors when the clinician is a dolt as a clerk. Still, competent psychologists are skilled at giving IQ tests, and most will swear by the validity of their results. But that doesn't mean that all individual IQ tests will come up with the same range of IQs for a given person—even if you could magically hold constant every source of measurement error.

Tests differ, sometimes substantially. The old Stanford-Binet (the one that was used for 70 years before it was replaced by the fourth edition in the mid-1980s) was extremely verbal for every age level between Year VI and Superior Adult III. Nonverbal intelligence simply didn't enter into a person's Binet IQ. Yet, as soon as Wechsler introduced the Wechsler-Bellevue in 1939, nonverbal ability constituted about half of a person's overall IQ. If you had limited verbal ability but were great at puzzles and had superior visual-motor coordination, you might still earn a respectable IQ on Wechsler's scales. But you'd be wiped out by the old Binet.

When the K-ABC came along, as discussed in chapter 3, Nadeen and I abandoned both the Binet and Wechsler IQ traditions by excluding from the K-ABC's intelligence scale the kinds of fact-oriented language tasks that appear in abundance in Wechsler's scales and in all Binets from the original 1905 Binet-Simon to the Binet-5 (Roid, 2003). And with all of the theory-based test development that has occurred in the last decade or so, IQ tests now come in a variety of flavors. And even though most tests have a close tie to CHC theory, each one is distinct (see Tables 3.2 to 3.6). The CAS, like the original K-ABC, is based on neuropsychological processing theory and excludes language tasks. The Binet-5 is the only test to include a Quantitative Reasoning scale; the WJ III and KABC-II are the only tests with a scale that measures the ability to learn new material; only the WJ III includes an auditory processing (*Ga*) scale; the DAS-II measures several abilities, but only *Gf, Gc,* and *Gv* are included in the total score; and so forth.

The bottom line? Different IQ tests measure different sets of abilities. The diverse intelligence tests used in schools, clinics, and hospitals throughout the United States are likely to come up with different IQs for the same person, and occasionally these differences will be substantial. This difference in the IQs yielded by one test versus another has existed as long as IQ tests themselves, and it is just as true today as it was in the 1930s when the Wechsler-Bellevue (Wechsler, 1939) joined the Stanford-Binet (Terman & Merrill, 1937) on the clinical assessment scene.

I will demonstrate these discrepancies using data from two research studies showing that the same kinds of IQ differences emerge from one generation (early 1980s) to the next (early 2000s) and occur for the old traditional tests as well as the current high-tech, sophisticated, theory-based instruments that dominate the contemporary assessment scene.

IQs Earned by Young Children Tested Twice on the K-ABC and Stanford-Binet-IV

About 20 years ago, Emily Krohn and Robert Lamp, psychology professors at Southern Illinois University at Edwardsville, tested 89 low-income 4-year-old Head Start children on several tests, including the K-ABC and the fourth edition of the Stanford-Binet (Binet-IV; Thorndike et al., 1986). They then hunted down as many of these children as possible 2 years later and gave the 71 children they found every darned test once more at the end of first grade (Lamp & Krohn, 1990). Their study provides an opportunity to illustrate how IQs vary for the same children—not just from test to test, but also from one age to another. Emily and Bob kindly shared their data, sending me the IQs earned by 10 African American children and 10 White children that they selected randomly from their larger sample. I arbitrarily chose 8 children from each ethnic group to include in Table 5.1; this table shows the IQs that these children earned on the K-ABC and Binet-IV at age 4 and again at age 6. Since Bob and Emily didn't indicate each child's gender (and I didn't want to bother them again), I have referred to the 16 children by number rather than assigning them fictitious names and inadvertently altering someone's gender.

Some children performed remarkably the same each time. Child 7 scored around 105 and Child 12 scored around 90, and it didn't matter which test was given or how old they were when tested. Others varied greatly in their IQs: At age 6, Child 3 scored perilously close to the range associated with intellectual disability on the Binet-IV but was plum average on the K-ABC; the reverse pattern held for Child 1 at age 4. An occasional child seemed

TABLE 5.1 IQs EARNED BY YOUNG CHILDREN WHO WERE TESTED ON THE K-ABC AND THE STANFORD-BINET FOURTH EDITION AT AGE 4 AND AGAIN AT AGE 6

African American Children								
	Child 1		Child 2		Child 3		Child 4	
	Age 4	Age 6	Age 4	Age 6	Age 4	Age 6	Age 4	Age 6
K-ABC	80	83	100	104	89	97	80	87
Binet-IV	99	89	86	105	75	73	74	70
	Child 5		Child 6		Child 7		Child 8	
	Age 4	Age 6	Age 4	Age 6	Age 4	Age 6	Age 4	Age 6
K-ABC	118	105	89	87	104	105	94	103
Binet-IV	116	109	93	74	106	103	96	98
White Children								
	Child 9		Child 10		Child 11		Child 12	
	Age 4	Age 6	Age 4	Age 6	Age 4	Age 6	Age 4	Age 6
K-ABC	80	90	106	87	109	103	91	89
Binet-IV	72	79	88	84	92	98	91	90
	Child 13		Child 14		Child 15		Child 16	
	Age 4	Age 6	Age 4	Age 6	Age 4	Age 6	Age 4	Age 6
K-ABC	100	112	100	100	82	95	91	107
Binet-IV	97	108	84	99	90	99	91	88

Note. Data are from "Stability of the Stanford-Binet Fourth Edition and K-ABC for young black and white children from low income families," by R. E. Lamp and E. J. Krohn, 1990. *Journal of Psychoeducational Assesment, 8,* 139–149. Data used with permission of the authors.

to lose IQ points over the 2-year period, while others gathered mental steam. Child 5, for example, went from bright to average on both tests; Child 9, Child 13, and Child 15 blossomed as they passed from Head Start to kindergarten to first grade.

For most of the children, however, the IQ fluctuations seem random and unexplainable. Child 16 scored identical 91s on the K-ABC and Binet-IV at age 4 but earned quite different IQs as a 6-year-old. Child 2, Child 6, and Child 14 each had one maverick IQ to spoil an otherwise consistent picture. And look at Child 6. If only the Binet-IV had been given at age 4 and age 6, you'd look at the plunging IQs (93 to 74) and wonder, "What happened?" Someone, somewhere, would quickly blame the parents for getting divorced or not taking the kid to museums or not providing nourishing breakfasts. The parents might blame the terrible schools. But if the K-ABC had been given twice, no one would blink twice at IQs of 89 and 87. For Child 10, the K-ABC, which dropped dramatically from 106 to 87, would have led to insinuations and accusations, while the Binet-IV would have produced a ho-hum reaction.

Overall for the 16 children illustrated in Table 5.1, the K-ABC and the Binet-IV differed by an average of about 8 IQ points—in either direction—when the children were tested at age 4. The difference at age 6? Again, about 8 points. How about the average difference just on the Binet-IV for the same children retested after 2 years? Eight IQ points. And the average difference on the K-ABC at ages 4 and 6? Yep, 8 points. Change the test, and you change the IQs. Keep the test constant, but wait a couple of years, and the IQs will vary. Some children will really get brighter, and others will truly perform less well on IQ tests. But mostly it's just a matter of chance, good luck or bad luck, on a given day for a given child in a given mood with a given examiner.

The IQ fluctuations occurred in similar fashion for the African American children and White children; ethnicity didn't matter. Are the IQ differences due to the fact that the children were so young? Isn't it true that preschool children are especially variable in their behavior? Well, very young children are a bit erratic in how they behave with an adult in the testing situation, but that doesn't explain why the IQs jump around (they also jump around for children who are well past their preschool years, as I demonstrate in the following section). Could the IQ changes from age 4 to age 6 be due to the impact of the Head Start program? Did it work and lead to generally higher IQs for most children? Actually, that wasn't even an issue, because when they were tested the first time, at age 4, they had already virtually completed their entire year of Head Start. Also, about the same number of children lost IQ points over the 2 years as gained them.

IQs Earned By Preadolescents Tested on Three Modern-Day Tests

So what about IQ tests with older children? To answer that question I examined the scores of 86 children who were tested on the WISC-III (Wechsler, 1991), the KABC-II (Kaufman & Kaufman, 2004a), and the WJ III (Woodcock et al., 2001) in 2002–2003 as part of the validation of the KABC-II (Kaufman & Kaufman, 2004a) when it was first published. (Whenever a new or revised IQ test is published, the test authors must demonstrate that the test is *valid,* that is to say, it measures the construct of intelligence. One common way of supporting a new test's validity is to correlate it with existing IQ tests that are known to be valid and to show that it correlates substantially with these other tests.)

Because young children are shown in Table 5.1, I limited my analysis of IQs to the older portion of the 2002–2003 sample, the 29 preadolescents aged 12–13. (Thanks are due to Dr. Mark Daniel of Pearson Assessments for providing the data for this analysis.) I divided these 29 children into three socioeconomic categories, using parents' education as the estimate of socioeconomic status (SES): (a) graduated from college or continued in graduate school postcollege, (b) attended 1–3 years of college, and (c) either graduated from high school or dropped out of high school (i.e., had 9 to 12 years of formal schooling). Figure 5.1 presents the IQs on the three more modern tests for 12 of these children. To select this dozen, I made sure that exactly two boys and two girls were chosen for each SES category, but the exact preadolescents selected for the table were picked randomly and represent the group well.

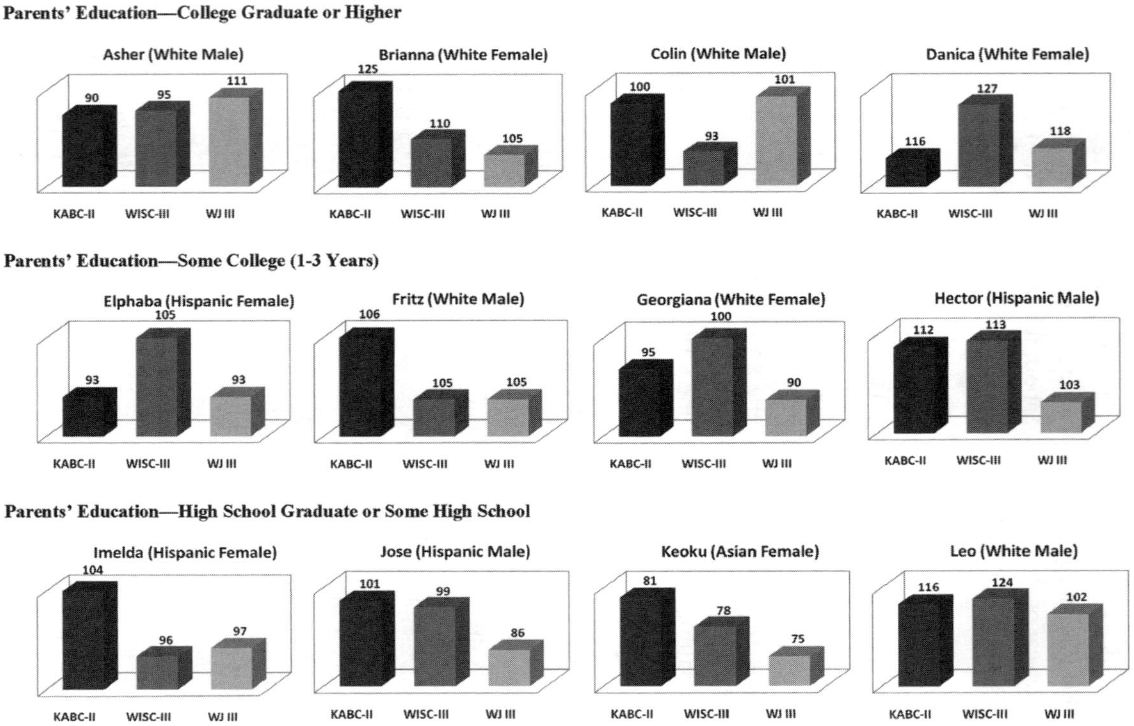

FIGURE 5.1 IQs earned by preadolescents (ages 12–13) who were given three different IQ tests in the early 2000s, grouped by socioeconomic status

Preadolescents—like preschool and school-age children—earn different IQs on different tests. When subtracting each child's lowest IQ from the highest, the differences for the dozen children range from 1 to 22 points, with an average difference of 12 points. Brianna (not her real name) would be classified as average (WJ III), high average (WISC-III), or superior (KABC-II) depending on the test she was given, and the same is true for Leo, who scored highest on the WISC-III.

The fluctuations for these 12 preadolescents are neither larger nor smaller than the fluctuations for the whole group of thrice-tested children. They typify what happens to normal children (or adults) when they are given different IQ tests, and, as with the preschool children in Figure 5.1, what happens is rather dramatic. Leo earned IQs that ranged from 102 on the WJ III to 124 on the WISC-III. Asher had the opposite pattern, scoring higher on the WJ III (111) than on either the WISC-III (95) or KABC-II (90). If Brianna had been tested for entry into a gifted program (with IQ = 125 as the cutoff point), only her score on the KABC-II would have gained her entry. But Danica and Leo would have been more likely to be chosen for the gifted program if tested on the WISC-III than on the KABC-II or WJ III.

And which children demonstrate average or "normal" intelligence, sometimes an entrance criterion for private schools? Suppose Jose and Fritz applied to a private school that used the traditional 90–109 range to denote average ability (see Table 4.3). Jose would have shown normal intelligence on the WISC-III and KABC-II, as he scored about 100 on each test. But he would have fallen short with his 86 on the WJ III. Fritz, by contrast, showed remarkably consistent scores (105–106) on all three tests. Not only do IQs vary as a function of the IQ test chosen—so do the educational placements of many children.

Thus, even for tests that measure similar CHC constructs and that represent the most sophisticated, high-quality IQ tests ever available at any point in time, IQs differ.

So What Does It All Mean?

The children in Table 5.1 and Figure 5.1 lead to an inescapable conclusion: We just don't have "an" IQ. Not even close. But does that sobering thought mean that we should simply abandon IQ tests because they are just not accurate enough? My answer is a decisive "No!" I've been looking at the test scores in the three tables with the goal of explaining why it's wrong to believe that we each have one and only one IQ. Clearly, we don't. I've been playing the devil's advocate to make my case rock solid. But statistics can be looked at in many ways. When discussing Figure 5.1, for example, I focused on children like Brianna and Leo, whose IQs fell into different categories on each of the three tests. But everyone else earned three IQs that either placed them in the same IQ category or in adjacent categories. Colin, Elphaba, Fritz, Georgiana, and Imelda were average, no matter what test they were given. Asher and Hector were average to high average; Danica was high average to superior; Keoku scored 75 to 81, regardless of the test; and so forth. The IQ tests did a good job of conveying each person's approximate level of mental ability. In addition, the preadolescents in Figure 5.1 were grouped by SES. As I showed in chapter 4, individuals exposed to greater opportunities for learning (high SES) tend to score higher on IQ tests than those from lower SES backgrounds. The test scores on all three IQ tests follow this predicted relationship. When averaging the 12 IQs for the group with the highest SES (i.e., 3 IQs for each of the 4 preadolescents whose parents graduated from college), the mean is 107.6. In contrast, the mean for those whose parents had some college is 101.3, and the mean for the lowest SES group (parents with 9–12 years of schooling) is 96.6. Simply put, the IQs tend to be valid even though they vary as to whether the person is given one, two, or three tests.

And Table 5.1 tells the same story. Even though the 16 children were tested on two IQ tests (K-ABC and Binet-IV) at two points in time (age 4 and age 6), 3 children (nos. 7, 8, 11) scored in the same category (average) each of the four times they were tested; and an additional 10 scored in adjacent categories. Of the remaining 3 children whose IQs were more varied, 2 scored consistently higher on the K-ABC than the Binet-IV (nos. 3 and 9). The two tests are different: The K-ABC minimizes the importance of language and academic skills for earning high scores, whereas the Binet-IV includes verbal and math scales. Child 3 and Child 9 likely had some difficulties in language and math, penalizing them on the Binet-IV but not on the K-ABC.

Child 6 is the only one with a maverick score—a Binet-IV IQ of 74 at age 6, compared to IQs of 87 to 93 on the other three test administrations. The most likely explanation is that the child wasn't trying very hard on the Binet-IV at age 6, or was distractible, or was bored, or tired. But a good examiner will figure that out during the test session and realize that the score is not valid. Examiners are trained to be perceptive clinicians, and that leads us to the next main strength of individually administered IQ tests: They are clinical instruments, not just statistical tools.

I learned this lesson as a graduate student, when I was fascinated by the ingenious mental tasks developed by the great Swiss developmental psychologist Jean Piaget. I constructed an intelligence test based on Piaget's theory as part of my doctoral dissertation, and while making this test, I found out that when you test someone, especially a young child, you aren't always measuring what you think you are. A case in point is Bonnie, a 5-year-old kindergartener who was a subject in a pilot study I was conducting on Piaget's notion of *animism*. Young children believe that inanimate objects are alive, especially if they are in motion, like a bicycle, or if they move spontaneously, like the wind.

Testing preschool children is never easy. Anyone who has ever done so knows that you could be blackmailed for life if anyone spied you down on the floor with a young child—saying the most ridiculous things, assuming the most unflattering positions, and contorting your face in ways such that your own IQ and sanity would be open to question—all in the name of keeping a human bobsled interested in your test questions while you try to maintain the standardized, technically correct way to administer every test item.

Well, unlike most others in her class, Bonnie was easy to test. She was polite and calm, and answered "I'm not really sure" to most questions: "Does the ball feel pain when I drop it on the floor?" "Does the bike know you're riding it?" I scored her test and classified her intelligence in one of Piaget's developmental stages (Piaget scored his tasks *qualitatively*, eschewing the *quantitative* approach of IQ tests). I felt sure the test I administered to Bonnie was valid. Until I spoke to her teacher the next day.

"Bonnie was crying and upset after you left," the teacher told me. "Bonnie said that she kept saying 'I don't know' when you asked her if teddy bears could really love her or if cars and trucks felt pain." "Yes," I agreed, "Bonnie was clearly in Piaget's transitional Stage IIB of thought." Not quite.

Her teacher continued: "I said to Bonnie, 'But you know that toys aren't alive, they can't feel or think.' Holding back tears, Bonnie replied, 'Of course I know that. *I wasn't sure if Mr. Kaufman knew.*'" I had developed a poor test of animism, but a good test of children's sensitivity!

Here was an instance where an intelligence test failed to yield a valid score *because* of an individual's personality. But usually IQ tests provide valid scores as well as insight into the person's way of behaving and interacting with the world. As I discussed in chapter 2, Wechsler's main reason for challenging the Binet one-IQ tradition 70 years ago was his desire to develop a test that helped psychologists better understand a person's total personality.

IQ TESTS AS CLINICAL TOOLS

Ultimately, IQ tests are not about numbers; they're about people. A person's score is important in Wechsler's Block Design (see Figure 2.1) or the KABC-II Triangles or the DAS-II Pattern

Construction subtests, all of which are direct descendants of Kohs's (1923) original 4-color Block Design test. That score might demonstrate a child's or adult's uncanny ability to copy abstract designs with blocks (a scaled score of 17, for example, is better than 996 out of 1,000 people; see Table 4.1) or a person's inadequate visual-spatial, simultaneous processing, and *Gv* skills (a scaled score of 3 exceeds only 1 out of 100). In addition to the score, the clinical observations that may help explain an unusually high or low score are of great benefit. A good clinician asks thousands of subvocal questions while watching a child or adult take an intelligence test. Block Design and its variants on other IQ tests are worth a 100 or so: Did the person use a trial-and-error or a systematic, insightful problem-solving approach? What about the person's visual-motor coordination when moving the blocks around, speed of responding, compulsiveness in seeing that the edges of the blocks are aligned, emotional response to the stopwatch, tolerance of frustration in the face of failure, ability to apply strategies learned on the easier items to the harder items, and on and on?

People who are given an IQ test are evaluated for a reason. Maybe they're not learning in school, or they are disrupting their classroom, or they are floundering in an assistant manager training program at the local fast-food chain. Maybe they've recently suffered a stroke, or are suspected of Alzheimer's-type dementia, or were thrown off their motorcycle during a collision with a truck. Possibly they're seeking a career change or someone thinks they might benefit from placement in a gifted program or in a class for students with reading disabilities. No one has ever been referred for testing because of terminal niceness or because someone said, "This person is so incredibly normal—you've just got to test her." When there's a test, there's usually a real-life question to be answered, sometimes a dilemma, which demands attention and intervention.

Whatever the nature of the problem, whether it's something good like giftedness or (much more frequently) something bad like learning problems or suspected brain damage, it can't be solved by computing a global IQ. The clinical observations that surround a person's approach to the test questions can help explain the obtained scores and lead to practical suggestions. IQs, or even scores on separate ability scales (discussed in the next section of this chapter), in isolation, are sterile. Would-be psychologists are trained to be exceptional clinical observers, as I've said, as well as test-givers, to practice an intelligent testing approach to IQ assessment (Kaufman, 1979b; Kaufman & Lichtenberger, 2006). An intelligent, aware, knowledgeable clinician is an even more important tool than the test itself—an astute observer who treats the global IQs as often the least important outcomes of the evaluation.

Consider Wechsler's Block Design, which I discussed earlier (a sample design is shown in Figure 2.1). Observations of test performance not only give insight into behaviors like impulsivity and frustration tolerance; they also may have neurological implications. Block Design has long been known to be sensitive to brain damage in both hemispheres (Lezak, 1995), most notably "to posterior lesions in the right hemisphere, especially the parietal lobes" (Kaufman & Lichtenberger, 2006, p. 402). Lezak (1995) explains how clinical observations of a person's approach to solving Block Design items sometimes give insight into the location of the brain lesion:

- Patients with *right-hemisphere* damage do best on designs that can be analyzed through *verbalization*; their errors are likely to be "disorientation, design distortions, and misperceptions... [and they may] lose sight of the squared or self-contained format of the design altogether" (p. 592). in contrast,
- Patients with *left-hemisphere* damage are able to maintain the square shape of the design but may make smaller errors in details, such as the orientation of a single block; they "tend to show confusion, simplification, and concrete handling of the design" (p. 592).
- Patients with either *left-hemisphere* damage or *right-hemisphere* damage "make many more errors on the side of the design

contralateral to the side of the lesion" (p. 592). That is to say, patients with *left* damage tend to make most of their errors on the *right* half of the design and vice versa.

And Block Design isn't the only Wechsler subtest with a long neuropsychological history. Picture Completion, for example, tends to be resilient in the face of brain damage and sometimes provides a good estimate of the person's IQ before the brain damage occurred (known as *premorbid* IQ, a pretty morbid term). Picture Completion provides an exceptionally good estimate of premorbid IQ for patients with damage to the left hemisphere with limited "ability to formulate the kinds of complex spoken responses needed for tests calling for a verbal response" (Lezak, 1995, p. 636). And the list goes on and on for other Wechsler subtests and for tasks from other tests as well (Kaufman & Lichtenberger, 2006).

In fact, many of today's tests have clinical observations built right into the administration, scoring, and interpretation of the IQ test. The WISC-IV and WAIS-IV include *process scores,* based on Edith Kaplan's (1988) Boston process approach, which focus "on the various processes an individual might use to correctly solve a problem and the processes that might lead to the failure to solve a problem" (Hebben, 2009, p. 237). On the WISC-IV, these process scores offer a more in-depth look at the person's test performance on Block Design, Digit Span, and the supplemental Cancellation subtest (a measure of processing speed). On the WAIS-IV, the process scores relate to Block Design, Digit Span, and Letter-Number Sequencing. Though these process scores are quantitative in nature, a companion to the WISC-IV called the WISC-IV Integrated (The Psychological Corporation, 2004) provides a more qualitative evaluation of the child's responses (and also includes additional subtests, such as Vocabulary in a multiple-choice format) to better understand the child's neuropsychological processes when solving problems. Kaplan's process approach (e.g., Kaplan, Fein, Morris, Kramer, & Delis, 1991) has supplied an important bridge between the quantitative scores yielded by IQ tests and the qualitative observations that help uncover the neuropsychological processes that underlie success or failure on the specific subtests that make up the comprehensive test batteries.

The KABC-II (Kaufman & Kaufman, 2004a) offers qualitative indicators (QIs) to guide an examiner's observations of the children and adolescents during the testing session. The specific observations are grouped into one of two categories, either *disruptive* or *enhancing* with regard to test performance. These QIs (a clever flip of IQ that was coined by Nadeen) were developed in collaboration with our friend, the exceptional neuropsychologist Elaine Fletcher-Janzen. QIs are specific to the demands of each subtest. For example, the QIs for the subtest Story Completion—which requires the child to select pictures that will best complete an incomplete story (see Figure 3.8)—include the following specific observations: (a) *enhancing* (perseveres, tries out options, unusually focused, verbalizes story ideas, works quickly but carefully), and (b) *disruptive* (does not monitor accuracy, fails to sustain attention, impulsively responds incorrectly, reluctant to commit to a response, reluctant to respond when uncertain, worries about time limits). These observations become especially important when they are observed in a variety of tasks. For example, if a child is "reluctant to respond when uncertain" on Story Completion, that, by itself, is not too important; but it becomes noteworthy if that same observation is noted for other subtests as well, such as Rebus (see Figure 3.5) and Gestalt Closure (see Figure 3.1) (Kaufman, Lichtenberger, Fletcher-Janzen, & Kaufman, 2005, chapter 4). That basic principle of gathering multiple sources of data and observations also applies to the process approach for interpreting Wechsler's children's and adult scales.

And the clinical aspect of IQ tests does not apply only to test *interpretation*. It also pertains to test *development*, an important lesson I learned by working closely with Dr. Dorothea McCarthy during the development and standardization of the McCarthy Scales of Children's Abilities (McCarthy, 1972), a child-oriented preschool test that, disappointingly, was never revised or restandardized. I explained in an invited address how even the sequencing of subtests on an IQ test must be guided by clinical considerations (Kaufman, 2005a, 2005b).

Dr. McCarthy understood young children, and she taught me so much about how they think and about how to construct a test from the perspective of the young child. She had taken a task like the old Knox Cubes—a boring test in which the examiner taps four wooden cubes in various sequences that the child has to copy—and converted it into a child-oriented game. She turned the stimulus material from a set of wooden cubes to a toy-like xylophone. Dr. McCarthy had an amazing instinct and insight for clinical assessment, and she was a wonderful mentor. I remember her explaining carefully how she sequenced the subtests in the McCarthy Scales of Children's Abilities. Though the McCarthy was geared to children aged 2½ to 8½ years, she targeted everything to the shy, nonverbal preschool child. "We begin with Block Building," she explained, "because it is entirely nonverbal and is fairly easy, even for 2½ year-olds. It involves imitation rather than problem solving and will get even the shy child involved in the test. Next, we administer Puzzle Solving. It involves reasoning, but the child remains involved because the pictures are so colorful and there is still no talking. But what child can resist talking spontaneously when putting together a puzzle?" Dr. McCarthy continued to explain how her choice of test sequence would gradually get shy children to respond easily when verbal responses were needed—and how the gross motor subtests, which were placed right in the middle of the test sequence, provided a built-in break that allowed them to stretch and move about the testing room. She had conquered my psychometric soul. I was mesmerized.[1]

The important lessons here are that IQ tests are built based on clinical considerations, they offer far more to the skilled

---

1. Copyright 2005 by the National Association of School Psychologists. Bethesda, MD. Adapted with the permission of the publisher. www.nasponline.org

examiner than a bunch of test scores, and a psychologist's experience with a test is an invaluable commodity that cannot be overlooked. A new test may have great promise as a measure of intelligence steeped in a solid theoretical foundation, but you just can't bypass the time factor—the time it takes for examiners to get a clinical "feel" for specific subtests and test items, and the time that must go by to allow research studies to accumulate.

The clinical lessons that I learned by working with McCarthy and Wechsler, and that Nadeen learned during her graduate training in one of the first psycho-educational clinics in the world, at Columbia University, shaped many of the decisions that we made when developing our own tests. Consider our Word Order subtest: The examiner names common objects ("horn—kite—tree—ship") and then shows pictures of these objects; the child has to point to the pictures in the order in which they were named. For more difficult items, the child has to rapidly name pictures of colors before being allowed to point to the objects that were named. This color interference task shows whether the child can recall things despite distraction. It's even difficult for adults. I learned that when our son James (then age 6, and called Jamie) spontaneously administered some Word Order items to me while I was working at my desk. Though I said, "Jamie, leave me alone, I'm busy," he persisted and soon had me rapidly naming colors while I groped to remember the lists of objects he had named. Now I understood exactly what the standardization examiners meant when they complained that the color-naming task frustrated a lot of children and confused some, and was absolutely demonic for rigid individuals who had trouble adapting to a sudden change in tasks.

Nadeen and I had been contemplating getting rid of the color interference task and finding another way to construct difficult Word Order items—until Jamie gave me the test. That experience immediately reminded me of Wechsler's admonition that IQ tests must be clinically sensitive. Nadeen and I agreed right then and there to keep the colors and not rob examiners of the built-in chance to observe a child's flexibility versus rigidity, and a child's ability to cope with frustration and to quickly understand the rules of a "game" when they are suddenly changed. The ability to learn new information despite distraction has real-life applications: Do you need absolute quiet when studying for an exam? If you stop while in your car and ask someone for driving directions, do you remember the correct route even after telling your noisy children to stop fighting in the back seat? I still get a kick watching a videotape of me administering Word Order to the late Fred Briggs, a wonderful NBC news journalist, during a segment of the Tom Brokaw News that was aired in the mid-1980s. Briggs was so flustered by having to name colors for a few seconds that he was only able to point, with good-humored embarrassment, to one of the two pictures I had named. Then I was told to administer the same item again, and once more he got it wrong. And again, and again, and again, and each time he made the exact same mistake. I'd say "tree—hand," and he'd point to the hand. As I was wondering about Fred's IQ, I suddenly realized that it was *my* intelligence that was in question. The film producers liked the sequence so much that they wanted to film it from several angles. Naturally, Fred had to make the same mistake over and over from every possible angle. I was definitely relieved when I finally figured out what was going on in the film studio.

THE BOTTOM LINE IS MULTIPLE ABILITIES, NOT GLOBAL IQ

The clinical aspects of IQ tests are important, but they are not the most important argument in favor of IQ tests. That distinction goes to the multiple abilities and processes that are measured by every major IQ test in use today for assessing children, adolescents, and adults. It's no longer about *g* and it hasn't been for two decades. IQ tests measure important theory-based cognitive abilities and processes (see Tables 3.2 to 3.6) that have crucial importance for understanding the strong and weak abilities of every person evaluated and that are essential for the identification of children with learning disabilities (a topic I return to in chapter 9).

The importance of a person's profile is axiomatic to clinicians who routinely assess children and adults referred for clinical assessment. To give a flavor of this importance, I will again rely on actual data. This time I am looking at 59 children, aged 7 to 16 years, who were tested on both the KABC-II (Kaufman & Kaufman, 2004a) and the WISC-IV (Wechsler, 2003) as part of the validation of the KABC-II (data were provided by Dr. Mark Daniel of Pearson Assessments). I looked at only the most global score yielded by each IQ test, the KABC-II Fluid-Crystallized Index (FCI) and the WISC-IV Full Scale IQ (FS-IQ). I selected three children of varying ability who earned almost identical global scores on both the KABC-II and the WISC-IV; I was looking for one child who scored about 80, one who scored about 100, and one who scored about 120. This search led me to three children (these are not their real names):

- **Mei-I,** a bilingual Asian American female, aged 12 years 9 months, living in the West, whose parents dropped out of high school (FS-IQ = 81 and FCI = 82)
- **Lizzy,** a White female, aged 12 years 5 months, living in the Northeast, whose parents had 1 to 3 years of college (FS-IQ = 99 and FCI = 100)
- **Jason,** a White male, aged 13 years 7 months, living in the Northeast, whose parents graduated from high school (FS-IQ = 124 and FCI = 122)

Table 5.2 describes the four scales (Factor Indexes) that comprise the WISC-IV and Table 5.3 describes the KABC-II's five scales.

As shown at the bottom of Table 5.3, the KABC-II offers two global scores: (a) the FCI, which includes all five scales and is based on the CHC model; and (b) the Luria-based Mental Processing Index (MPI), which includes four of the scales,

TABLE 5.2 DESCRIPTION OF THE WISC-IV FACTOR INDEXES FOR AGES 6–16

Verbal Comprehension Index (VCI)—Solving verbal problems, understanding verbal concepts, expressing one's thoughts in words, and demonstrating the breadth and depth of knowledge acquired from one's culture (Crystallized Knowledge or *Gc*). (Illustrative tasks: See Vocabulary, Similarities, Comprehension, and Information subtests in Figure 2.1.)

Perceptual Reasoning Index (PRI)—Solving novel nonverbal problems that depend on Visual Processing (*Gv*), Fluid Reasoning (*Gf*), or both. (Illustrative tasks: See Block Design, Object Assembly, and Picture Completion in Figure 2.1 and Matrix Reasoning in Figure 4.2; also see matrices items in Figure 3.6 and Figure 4.3.)

Working Memory Index (WMI)—Taking in and temporarily retaining information in memory, holding information, performing some operation or manipulation with it, and producing a result. The items measure working memory (a person's mental scratch pad) and require arranging of the input in sequential order. (Illustrative tasks: See Digit Span and Arithmetic in Figure 2.1 and Letter-Number Sequencing in Figure 5.3.)

Processing Speed Index (PSI)—Fluently and automatically performing cognitive tasks (scanning, sequencing, or discriminating visual information) while under pressure to maintain focused attention and concentration. (Illustrative tasks: See Digit Symbol/Coding in Figure 2.1 and Symbol Search in Figure 3.10).

Global Score

Full Scale IQ (FS-IQ). A composite score made up of the 10 core subtests that make up the four indexes.

but specifically excludes the Knowledge/*Gc* scale. The manual (Kaufman & Kaufman, 2004a) states, "The CHC model should generally be the model of choice" (p. 4), but the Luria model is preferred whenever the examiner believes that the child has not had adequate opportunity to acquire knowledge from the mainstream culture. When I selected the three cases, I specifically used the KABC-II FCI, because that is the global score that is most comparable to the WISC-IV FS-IQ.

TABLE 5.3 DESCRIPTION OF THE KABC-II SCALES FOR SCHOOL-AGE CHILDREN (AGES 7–18)

Sequential/Gsm—Taking in and holding information, and then using it, within a few seconds. The items involve arranging the input in sequential or serial order to solve a problem. (Illustrative task: Word Order—pointing to pictures named by the examiner in the order in which they were named.)

Simultaneous/Gv—Perceiving, storing, manipulating, and thinking with visual patterns. The input has to be integrated and synthesized simultaneously (holistically), usually spatially. (Illustrative tasks: See Block Counting in Figure 3.12, Gestalt Closure in Figure 3.1, and Face Recognition in Figure 3.11.)

Planning/Gf—Solving novel problems by using reasoning abilities such as induction and deduction. Measures the high-level executive processes of decision making and planning. (Illustrative task: See Story Completion in Figure 3.8.)

Learning/Gv—Storing and efficiently retrieving newly learned, or previously learned, information. (Illustrative task: See KAIT Rebus Learning in Figure 3.5.)

Knowledge/Gc—Demonstrating verbal concepts and the breadth and depth of knowledge acquired from one's culture, and also solving verbal problems. (Illustrative tasks: See Expressive Vocabulary in Figure 3.9; also Riddles, in which the child solves a verbal riddle—e.g., What has many contests, cowboys, and horses? What is made of nylon, is carefully folded, and is needed for skydiving?)

Global Scores

CHC Model—Fluid-Crystallized Index (FCI). Includes scores on all five scales.

Luria Model—Mental Processing Index (MPI). Includes scores on the first four scales; excludes Knowledge/Gc. Intended primarily for children from bilingual backgrounds or nonmainstream cultures, and children with known or suspected language disorders.

Descriptions of scales are from *Essentials of KABC-II Assessment,* by A. S. Kaufman, E. O. Lichtenberger, E. Fletcher-Janzen, & N. L. Kaufman, 2005, Hoboken, NJ: Wiley. Rapid Reference 1.6.

Figure 5.2 shows graphically the three children's scores on the five KABC-II scales and the four WISC-IV factor indexes.

Though Jason earned global IQs in the 120s, his standard scores on the KABC-II ranged from 102 on Planning/*Gf* to 134 on Simultaneous/*Gv*, and he had about an equally large range in his cognitive abilities on the WISC-IV (104 on WMI [Working Memory Index] to 133 on PRI). On both tests, he displayed his exceptional visual-spatial processing with scores in the very superior range (above 130), which contrasted with his average level of performance on Planning/*Gf* and WMI. Fluid reasoning is dependent on the executive process of working memory—people must maintain access to all pertinent aspects of a complex problem on their mental scratch-pads long enough to solve the problem correctly. Jason was relatively weak in both areas of cognitive functioning. This is not a surprising finding in view of research that has shown the close relationship between reasoning and working memory; indeed, Kyllonen and Cristal (1990) titled a seminal research article, "Reasoning Ability Is (Little More Than) Working Memory Capacity?!" Jason also scored remarkably consistently on both tests in his crystallized and verbal abilities (Knowledge/*Gc* = 115; VCI = 114). Working memory is illustrated

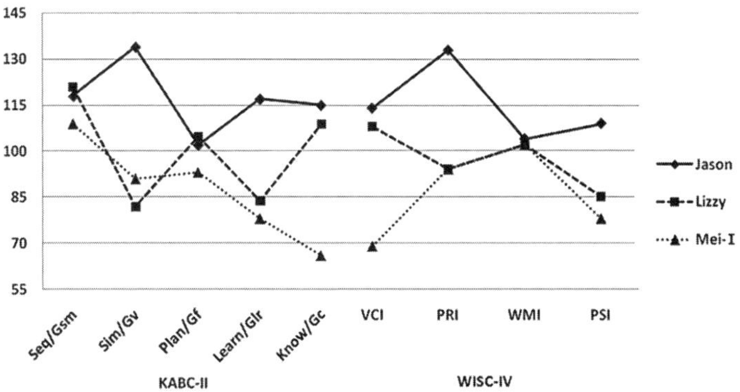

FIGURE 5.2 Standard scores earned by Jason (IQs about 120), Lizzy (IQs about 100), and Mei-I (IQs about 80) on the WISC-IV factor indexes and the KABC-II scales.

by Wechsler's Letter-Number Sequencing subtest in Figure 5.3. The person is read a sequence of alternating numbers and letters and has to repeat the numbers in ascending order and the letters in alphabetical order. The longer sequences (8 stimuli) require an exceptional working memory for success.

The results of the KABC-II and WISC-IV present a consistent picture of a 13½-year-old boy with some exceptional skills (G*v*), some high average abilities (*Gc*, learning ability), and some average abilities (working memory, *Gf*, and processing speed). He performed especially well on *Gv* tests, such as KABC-II's Block Counting (see Figure 3.12), which depend on visual-spatial skills, but not nearly as well on measures of *Gf* that depend on abstract reasoning ability (such as KABC-II Story Completion, illustrated in Figure 3.8).

Taken as a whole, this cognitive profile helps us understand Jason's relative strengths and weaknesses, giving us a full picture

Letter-Number Sequencing

Item	Response
Q-3	3-Q
T-9-1	1-9-T
M-3-P-6	3-6-M-P
F-7-K-2-8	2-7-8-F-K
5-J-4-A-1-S	1-4-5-A-J-S
C-6-4-W-O-7-D	4-6-7-C-D-O-W

FIGURE 5.3 Illustration of a working memory test (Wechsler's Letter-Number Sequencing).

Note. Wechsler Adult Intelligence Scale—Third Edition (WAIS-III), by D. Wechsler, 1997, San Antonio, TX: The Psychological Corporation.

of what school subjects he might have the most difficulty with (e.g., aspects of science that depend on the scientific method), and what instructional methods might work best for him (i.e., approaches that capitalize his visual-spatial processing and make use of concrete materials). None of these insights is possible from a simple IQ of 122 or 124 that masks both his highly developed and his less developed skills and provides little more than an overview of his overall functioning.

Like Jason, Lizzy has a wide variation among her scores on both tests. On the KABC-II, her scores ranged all the way from low average on visual processing (82) and learning ability (84) to superior (121) on short-term memory. On the WISC-IV, she ranged from low average on the Processing Speed Index (84) to an index between average and high average in Verbal Comprehension (108). Once again, Lizzy's average IQs of 99–100 fail to tell an accurate story of how she displays her intelligence.

And Mei-I also cannot be effectively summarized by a simple number in the low 80s. She scored below 70 on the two scales that measure language skills and acquired knowledge (66 on Knowledge/*Gc* and 69 on VCI). She scored in the average range in short-term memory (109 on KABC-II), working memory (102 on WISC-IV), planning ability (93 on KABC-II), and visual processing (91 on KABC-II, 94 on WISC-IV)—and in the "borderline" range in learning ability (78 on KABC-II) and processing speed (78 on WISC-IV). Though she earned IQs at the low end of low average, not one of her standard scores on the separate KABC-II or WISC-IV scales was in the 80s! And her scores in the 60s on language skills and knowledge undoubtedly reflect her bilingual background and do not reflect limited verbal intelligence or *Gc*.

An astute KABC-II examiner would have opted to administer to Mei I the Luria model, which excludes the Knowledge/*Gc* scale from its global score. Instead of a global score of 82, Mei-I would have earned an MPI of 89. That score still does not replace the benefits derived from a profile of scores in diverse areas of functioning, but at least it does not unfairly penalize her for her limited opportunities to learn mainstream U.S. language and culture, and it is on the "average" end of low average, not the "borderline" end. The WISC-IV does not offer this option.

When looking at the graph of the three children's scores in Figure 5.2, it is interesting to note that "average" Lizzy scored lower than "low average" Mei-I on one KABC-II scale (Simultaneous/*Gv*) and higher than "superior" Jason on two other KABC-II scales (Sequential/*Gsm* and Planning/*Gf*). And despite the wide disparity in the three children's FS-IQs, they all scored virtually the same on the WISC-IV Working Memory scale (102–104).

When it comes to IQ tests, the global IQs are nothing more than the tip of the iceberg. They remind me of the claim that a person whose head is in a freezer and feet are on fire is at normal body temperature. To use an IQ test properly, it is essential to examine the person's profile of scores on important research-based and theory-based cognitive abilities and processes. Only then is it truly possible for the IQ tests to serve a useful function: helping to answer the referral questions that led to the child or adult being evaluated in the first place.

6

Hot Topic: Is IQ Genetic?

The hottest of hot topics about IQ tests concerns the importance of heredity versus the importance of environment in determining our IQs. Debates abound, heated debates, that are often more emotional than scientific. Leon Kamin (1974) is at one extreme of the continuum, insisting that, "there exists no data which should lead a prudent man to accept the hypothesis that IQ test scores are in any way heritable" (p. 1), where *heritable* refers to the degree to which any trait is genetic in origin. Kamin, in fact, has been critical of the entire field of behavior genetics (Horgan, 1993; Lewontin, Rose, & Kamin, 1984), a field devoted to the scientific study of the degree to which traits are heritable. At the opposite end of the scale is the late William Shockley, a Nobel prize winner in physics who coinvented the transistor and later became a self-proclaimed expert on the genetics of IQ. Shockley (1987) maintained that IQ was largely genetic and accounted for racial differences in mean

IQs, an opinion shared to some extent by Herrnstein and Murray (1994) in their controversial book *The Bell Curve.*

Herrnstein and Murray argued that low IQ—independent of socioeconomic variables—lies at the root of many intractable social problems, such as out-of-wedlock births and unemployment, and that a "cognitive elite" has emerged. They discussed problems with policies such as affirmative action in education and the workplace and recommended broad-scale change in public policy: "Return to the assumption that in America the government has no business getting in people's way except for the most compelling reason, with 'compelling' required to meet a stiff definition" (p. 542).

Shockley was blunter—he wanted people with low IQs to be sterilized (Pearson, 1992).

This chapter is not about the social implications of heredity versus environment, and it is not about any association between genetics and ethnic differences on IQ tests. It is about *data*—derived from empirical studies by behavioral geneticists—that directly address the interrelated roles of heredity and environment in determining a person's IQ. After key statistical concepts for understanding the results of pertinent research investigations are explained, the data are organized as follows:

Kinship and Adoption Studies

- Kinship studies of identical twins, fraternal twins, non-twin siblings, and others with a known genetic relationship
- A "virtual" twin study—children who were raised as twins from infancy in the same family, but who were not biologically related
- Adoption studies, to compare the children's IQs with the IQs of their biological versus adoptive parents

The Heritability of IQ

- Studies that examine heritability separately by (a) type of cognitive ability, (b) social class, (c) ethnicity (but *not* White—African American), and (d) age

Maternal Environment (the First Environment, the Womb)

- Statistical modeling studies that show the impact of the earliest environment on children's IQs
- Placentation studies showing the intriguing results of investigations that examined identical twins who either shared one placenta or had separate placentas

Home Environment and IQ

- Home environment studies that measured the relationship of various aspects of parenting to children's IQs

The sum total of the data on genetic and environmental factors clearly refutes Kamin's bold antigenetic statements about the IQ, while it also provides empirical support for the key role played by a young child's environment. The data from these studies do not relate at all to issues of race differences, because the studies were in no way designed to answer those kinds of questions. The available data *cannot* answer those questions.

In fact, Whites earn higher IQs, on average, than African Americans. The difference has typically been about 15 IQ points on Wechsler's scales (Kaufman & Lichtenberger, 2006) and about half that on the K-ABC and KABC-II (Kaufman & Kaufman, 1983, 2004a). When the two ethnic groups are equated on SES, the differences are 9 points on the WISC-IV (Prifitera et al., 2005) and 5 points on the KABC-II Mental Processing Index (Kaufman & Kaufman, 2004a, Tables 8.7 and 8.8). But there is no evidence that this IQ difference relates to genetics at all. As Neisser et al. (1996) appropriately conclude regarding the observed race differences in IQ, based on an extensive review of pertinent research, "Several culturally-based explanations of the [African American]/White IQ differential have been proposed; some are plausible, but so far none has been conclusively supported. There is even less empirical support for a genetic interpretation. In short, no adequate explanation of the differential between the IQ means of [African Americans] and Whites is presently available" (p. 97).

Importantly, SES is a far more potent variable than ethnicity. Weiss et al. (2006) conducted an innovative set of statistical analyses using WISC-IV data to demonstrate the degree to which SES variables are responsible for the variance on IQ differences often attributed to race. They showed, for example, that parental education alone accounted for 18.8% of the variance in IQ between African American and White samples, compared to 4.7% for race alone. And controlling for parental education *and* household income reduced the value to 1.6%.

I have been intrigued to discover that differences between Whites and African Americans on mental tasks are sometimes simply a function of how the task is administered, making the question of heredity versus environment irrelevant. As I wrote some time ago (Kaufman, 1994) about a subtest on the original K-ABC's Achievement Scale,

> The K-ABC's Faces & Places is the most culture-loaded task on the battery, the kind of task that produces large African-American/white discrepancies on Wechsler's scales.... This subtest assesses general information in visual format [identifying the names of pictures of famous people or places from history] instead of the auditory format for Wechsler's Information subtest. Faces & Places is just a turn of the kaleidoscope from Information. Yet, unlike Information, Faces & Places produced very small race differences; African-American children averaged about 96 [without equating on SES], close to the normative mean of 100. (p. 12)

As I've indicated, laypeople and professionals alike have long argued about whether IQ is determined almost exclusively by genetics or by environment, and these arguments are often emotional and sometimes nasty. But the question, at its core, has nothing to do with the race differences in IQ. The scientific issues involved are complex and the answers are not simple, but large amounts of objective data do exist to address the questions in a straightforward and objective way. That is what I'll try to do.

SOME BASIC STATISTICAL CONCEPTS FOR UNDERSTANDING HEREDITY-ENVIRONMENT RESEARCH

The most prevalent kind of behavioral genetics study examines the relationship between the IQs earned by members of the same family who share some degree of common genetic background, such as parent-child and brother-sister. And adoption studies also abound. But before looking at the results of these studies, two statistical concepts need to be internalized: the *coefficient of correlation* and the notion of *broad heritability.*

The Coefficient of Correlation

The coefficient of correlation is a statistic that conveys the degree to which two variables are related. A perfect correlation is 1.00, which indicates perfect agreement between two variables; as one variable increases, so does the other in precisely the same manner. A correlation of .00 indicates no relationship at all between two variables, whereas a value of −1.00 denotes perfect disagreement. Correlations in the .30s, .40s, and .50s generally reflect a substantial degree of overlap between two variables, and are noteworthy. It is rare to find perfect correlations of 1.00, because the measurement of virtually anything (not just IQ) has some error. So a correlation of .90 or .95 definitely catches our attention as being an amazingly high relationship. What might correlate that high? Consider identical twins. They have exactly the same genetic makeup. Therefore, you would expect the heights of identical twins to correlate highly, and they do: .94 (Garfinkle, 1982). Or you might expect the IQs earned by a person who was tested twice on the same IQ test to correlate highly and, again, they do. On Wechsler's scales, for example, the average correlation between test 1 and test 2 is .91 for ages 2½ to 7 years, .93 for ages 6 to 16 years, and .96 for ages 16 to 90 years (The Psychological Corporation, 1997, 2002, 2003, 2008; Wechsler, 1991). Despite the errors of measurement that I went on and on about in chapter 5, the test-retest reliability or stability of the IQ nonetheless reflects almost as close an agreement between two variables as is obtainable in the real world.

What about correlations of about .00, depicting no relationship at all? Those kinds of coefficients emerge when correlating a group of third-graders' shoe sizes with their IQs. Or correlating the number of inches of rain in different communities with the average income of adults in the communities. Or correlating the distance teenagers can kick a soccer ball or toss a football with their fluid or crystallized intelligence.

And negative coefficients? On a math test in school, the number of mistakes a student makes will correlate close to −1.00 with the student's grade on the test. That is to say, as the number of errors goes up, the grade goes down. Negative correlations denote inverse relationships. But don't confuse "positive" or "negative" correlations with positive or negative outcomes. Sometimes, as demonstrated by the example of math test errors, a negative correlation is a good thing (the fewer the errors, the higher the grade).

Here are some additional examples of different magnitudes of correlation (the values shown are approximate):

- .90 = correlation between WISC-IV Full Scale IQ and Full Scale IQs on a *different* Wechsler test for normal children or adolescents (e.g., a 6-year-old tested on both the WISC-IV and WPPSI-III or a 16-year-old tested on the WISC-IV and WAIS-IV; Flanagan & Kaufman, 2004, p. 39; The Psychological Corporation, 2008, Table 5.9)
- .80 = correlation between Wechsler's Full Scale IQ and KABC-II's Fluid-Crystallized Index (FCI) (Kaufman & Kaufman, 2004a, Tables 8.17–8.20)
- .70 = correlation between IQ and achievement, as measured by individually administered tests of both variables (Naglieri & Bornstein, 2003)
- .60 = correlation between adult Verbal IQ and years of formal education (Kaufman & Lichtenberger, 2006, Table 4.6)

- .50 = correlation between IQ and success in job training programs (Jensen, 1980)
- .45 = correlation between adult Performance IQ (nonverbal ability) and years of formal education (Kaufman & Lichtenberger, 2006, Table 4.6)
- .30 = correlation between father's or mother's education with their biological child's IQ (Bouchard & Segal, 1985)
- .25 = correlation between IQ and job performance (Jensen, 1980)

Broad Heritability

The broad heritability of a trait, such as intelligence or creativity or extraversion, is the proportion of the variance that is due to heredity (Vandenberg & Vogler, 1985). The total amount of variance for any trait always equals 100%—the sum total of any and all variables that might affect why a person has more or less of a particular trait. So, if the broad heritability of a trait equals 35%, that means that genetics is responsible for 35% of the variability in that trait, leaving 65% for other factors, such as home environment, schooling, health, and so forth. There are various formulas for computing heritability, many of them complex (Plomin & Petrill, 1997), but Falconer (1960) provided a simple formula that closely approximates the estimates of broad heritability yielded by the intricate mathematical formulas. Falconer's formula compares the correlations obtained for identical twins (100% genetic relatedness) to the correlations for fraternal twins (50% genetic relatedness). Fraternal twins are no different from any pair of siblings—regardless of the difference in their ages—when it comes to genetic similarity. The assumption is that identical twins will have a common environment, as will fraternal twins, by virtue of being raised in the same home at the same time by the same caregivers. Therefore, any difference in the correlations is presumed to be genetic in origin. Of course, it is not that simple (one twin might be favored over the other), but, in general, it is a reasonable assumption.

Falconer (1960) subtracts the correlation for fraternal twins from the correlation for identical twins (a specific kind of correlation known as *intra-class*) and multiplies that value by 2 to yield the heritability percentage. Earlier, I used the height of identical twins to illustrate a very high correlation (.94). The comparable value for fraternal twins is .54; subtracting .54 from .94 = .4. Multiply that value by 2 = .8, which means that the broad heritability for height is 80%—that is to say, environmental factors (such as nutrition, illness, or exercise) as well as plain old chance error account for the remaining 20% of the variability in height. For weight, the intra-class correlations for identical twins and fraternal twins are .91 and .67, respectively, leading to a much lower broad heritability of 48% (Garfinkle, 1982). Intuitively, many factors other than genetics affect a person's weight, more so than height.

Whenever broad heritability estimates are computed, they refer "to a particular population at a particular time" (Plomin & Petrill, 1997, p. 57). They are not immutable or eternal. They are likely to differ from one culture or population to another, from subculture to subculture, and from one generation to the next (Scarr & Carter-Saltzman, 1982).

Before going into the details and statistics of the more important kinship and adoption studies, I'll give you the headline: Probably the best overall estimate of the heritability of IQ is 50%, a value proposed as the most sensible summary of the results from the diversity of behavioral genetic research (Plomin & Petrill, 1997). The heritability value of 50% is similar to the value for weight, but not nearly as high as the value for height.

I believe that the comparison between IQ and weight is a good one. In general, overweight people have a genetic predisposition for a large frame, big bones, and a metabolism that promotes weight gain, whereas extremely thin people have the opposite predispositions. But for any given individual, lifestyle and disease can have a substantial effect on how much he or she weighs—eating habits, exercising, dieting, and so forth. Probably the notion of genetics contributing about 50% to IQ and environment contributing about 50% to IQ is as close as we are going to come within science to estimating the relative role of each in a person's IQ. And, of course, genetics and environment interact with each other in determining a child's IQ because it is not possible to separate them. People with a genetic overlap (parents, siblings) also tend to share a common environment. In addition, parents with high intelligence engaged in high status occupations are likely, in general, to provide more enriching environments to their children than are parents of low intelligence who are employed as unskilled workers. Once again, the point is that genetics and environment are not independent of each other but are mutually dependent and interact in complex ways that are not easily pulled apart.

KINSHIP AND ADOPTION STUDIES

The main way in which scientists have studied the relative roles of genetics and environment in determining IQ (and other variables such as personality traits) has been to investigate individuals who differ in their degree of blood relationship. For example, if genetics plays a role in IQ, then identical twins should have IQs that correlate more highly than the IQs of fraternal twins or non-twin siblings. In adoption studies, the main question is whose IQs do the children's IQs most resemble—those of their birth parents (genetics) or those of their adoptive parents (environment).

Twins, Siblings, and Parents-Children—Living Together and Living Apart

Table 6.1 presents the average correlation coefficient among relatives with differing degrees of genetic relationship, based on data accumulated from numerous studies during the past century (data are from Kaufman & Lichtenberger, 2006, Table 2.1, and Sattler, 2008, Table 8–1). Table 6.1 shows IQ relationships

TABLE 6.1 AVERAGE CORRELATIONS BETWEEN THE IQs OF TWINS, SIBLINGS, AND PARENT-CHILD—REARED/LIVING TOGETHER AND APART

Relation	Correlation
Same person (tested twice)	.95
Identical twins—Reared together	.86
Identical twins—Reared apart	.76
Fraternal twins—Reared together	.55
Fraternal twins—Reared apart	.35
Biological siblings—Reared together	.47
Biological siblings—Reared apart	.24
Unrelated children—Reared together	.30
Parent-child—Living together	.42
Parent-child—Living apart	.22
Adoptive parent-child—Living together	.19

for siblings (including identical and fraternal twins) reared together and reared apart, and for parents and their children. The first correlation in Table 6.1 (which shows the stability of an IQ for individuals tested twice) provides a benchmark for comparison.

Certain aspects of the table demonstrate the importance of *genetics* in influencing one's IQ:

1. Identical twins have IQs that are considerably more similar than those of fraternal twins (.86 versus .55).
2. Identical twins separated at birth and reared in different environments have IQs that are more similar than those of fraternal twins who were reared together (.76 versus .55).
3. The IQs of biological parents living with their children correlate substantially more highly (.42) than the IQs of adoptive parents and their adopted children (.19).

Certain aspects of Table 6.1 support the role of *environment* in determining IQ:

1. The IQs of fraternal twins correlate more highly than the IQs of biological siblings of different ages (.55 versus .47), even though all siblings (including fraternal twins) have the same degree of genetic similarity.
2. In all instances, biological siblings living together and raised together have IQs that are more similar than those of biological siblings raised in separate environments (biological siblings refers to identical twins, fraternal twins, and siblings of different ages).
3. The parent-child IQ relationship is much higher when parents and children are living together (.42) than when they are living apart (.22).
4. The correlation between an adoptive parent and child living together (.19) is virtually the same as the correlation between a biological parent and child living apart (.22).
5. The correlation of unrelated children reared together (.30) is higher than the correlation of biological siblings reared apart (.24).

The statistics for identical twins are powerful arguments that heredity plays a key role in determining a person's IQ, contrary to the naysayers like Kamin (1974). The value of .86 for identical twins raised together is unusually high, not much lower than the reliability of the best IQ tests when a single person is tested twice. Further, the high coefficient for identical twins raised together has been resistant to change over time. Even more noteworthy is the coefficient in the .70s for identical twins reared apart, although this unusually high relationship between the IQs of individuals raised in different environments has been the subject of past controversy. Initially, data were derived from three studies conducted between 1937 and 1980 based on a total of 65 pairs of identical twins reared apart. The correlation of .72 for that initial group was criticized as bogus by Kamin (1974) and others because of reasons such as contact between the twins and placement of the twins in similar types of homes. However, two more recent studies, conducted in the 1990s, based on a total of 93 twin pairs reared apart, yielded virtually identical IQ correlations in the .70s (Bouchard, 1996), and, importantly, these newer studies addressed the criticisms of the previous investigations. Neither the criticism regarding the degree of contact (which was measured) nor the criticism that the similarity in home placements inflated the correlations was borne out. The big picture that emerges is that genetics plays an important role in how individuals perform on conventional IQ tests, a conclusion that is supported by Nancy Segal's intriguing research on "virtual twins."

Virtual Twins

Segal (1997, 1999, 2000) investigated the IQs of *virtual twins*—that is, unrelated children of the same age who are reared together from early infancy. She studied 90 of these unique sibling pairs, which mimic "twinness" (at an average age of 8 when tested) but without genetic relatedness (65 pairs included two adopted children and 25 included one adopted and one biological child). Though Segal found a significant correlation of .26 between the IQs of the virtual twins, supporting the environmental contribution, this value is not nearly as high as the coefficients obtained for identical twins (.86), fraternal twins (.55), or even siblings of different ages (.47) (see Table 6.1). Segal (2000) concluded that her results with virtual twins "support explanatory models of intelligence that include genetic factors, demonstrating that shared environments have modest effects on intellectual development" (p. 442). She also presented the interesting data shown in Table 6.2 regarding the average difference in IQs earned by different groups of people (Segal, 1997). These data, which show, for example, that the IQs of identical twins differ by an average of 6 points compared to 14 points for siblings in general, provides an interesting way to translate the meaning of correlations into something more concrete—namely, IQ points.

TABLE 6.2 MEAN IQ DIFFERENCES BETWEEN TWINS, SIBLINGS, AND RANDOM INDIVIDUALS

• Identical twins	6
• Fraternal twins	10
• Siblings, raised together	14
• Virtual twins	15.4
• Individuals selected at random	17

Note. Based on Segal's (1997) virtual twins study.

Adoption Studies—Birth Parent Versus Adoptive Parent

Adoption studies have been key to our understanding of the relative roles of genetics and environment in determining children's IQs. Interestingly, one adoption study conducted by Scarr and Weinberg (1976) has been widely interpreted as supporting the importance of environment on IQ, whereas a second adoption study by the same investigators (Scarr & Weinberg, 1978) supports the role of heredity.

In the 1976 investigation, 130 African American and interracial children adopted at an average age of 18 months by socially advantaged White families in Minnesota earned an average Binet or Wechsler IQ of 106, about 15 points higher than the typical mean IQ earned by African American children from the North Central region of the United States (Scarr & Weinberg, 1976). These exciting findings are tempered to some extent by the finding that the natural children of the adoptive parents scored about 10 points higher than the adopted African American children, but they underscore the powerful role that environment plays in IQ.

Scarr and Weinberg's (1978) second adoption study examined the role of environmental variables in predicting adolescents' IQs in 120 biological and 104 adoptive families (average age at adoption was 2–3 months). An abbreviated, but reliable, version of the WAIS was administered to both parents and teenagers. The researchers tried to predict the adolescents' IQs based on information about the birth parents and adoptive parents (e.g., their IQs and educational attainment). Variables like parental education and income produced a much higher multiple correlation for biological families (.33) than for adoptive families (.14). (The magnitude of a multiple correlation is interpreted in essentially the same way as any correlation; multiple correlations are computed when several variables are combined to predict a single outcome.) The one variable that raised the multiple correlation most for the adoptive families was the *natural* mother's educational attainment. The results of this second adoptive study by Scarr and Weinberg were more supportive of genetic than environmental hypotheses, but the complexity of the issues precludes simple answers.

The Texas Adoption Study (Horn, Loehlin, & Willerman, 1979; Loehlin, Horn, & Willerman, 1994, 1997) is probably the best designed investigation of its type. The project began with 300 Texas families that adopted children a few days after birth, mostly in the 1960s, through a church-related home for unwed mothers. Both birth and adoptive families were mostly White and middle class. Birth mothers were typically tested on the Revised Beta (the nonverbal paper-and-pencil IQ test originally developed during World War I) but occasionally on a Wechsler scale. Adoptive parents were administered both the Revised Beta and the WAIS; preschool children were tested on the old Stanford-Binet, and those aged 5 and above were given the WISC (average age at the original testing was about 8 years, with a range of 3 to 14 years). About 10 years later, the children from 181 families were retested, this time on the WISC-R or WAIS-R (some families had more than one adopted child, so more than 240 children were tested during the follow-up).

Table 6.3 summarizes the correlational data from the Texas Adoption Study, showing results that are both provocative and interesting. The correlation of .02 between the IQs of adoptive mothers and the IQs of their children when the children were

TABLE 6.3 RESULTS OF TEXAS ADOPTION PROJECT

Correlations Between Child IQ and Parent IQ at Two Points in Time		
Adoptive Father and Adoptive Child	Adoptive Mother and Adoptive Child	Birth Mother and Adoptive Child
	When Tested at About Age 8	
.14	.12	.32
	When Tested at About Age 18	
.10	.02	.48

Note. Data are from "Heredity, Environment, and IQ in the Texas Adoption Project," by J. C. Loehlin, J. M. Horn, & L. Willerman, 1997, pp. 105–125. In R. J. Sternberg & E. Grigorenko (Eds.), *Intelligence, Heredity, and Environment,* New York: Cambridge University Press.

about 18 years of age is essentially zero, denoting no relationship at all. The correlations with the birth mother are substantially higher than the correlations with the adoptive parents, suggesting a greater contribution of genetics than environment to the children's IQs. These findings are especially noteworthy because, "These birth mothers had no contact with their children after the first few days of life; in fact, many of the infants went directly from the hospital to their adoptive families" (Loehlin et al., 1997, p. 113). Interestingly, the difference between the correlations for the birth mother versus the adoptive parents was substantially larger at the second testing, when the children were 10 years older. That finding relates to the changing role of genetics with increasing age, which is discussed later in this chapter.

THE HERITABILITY OF IQ

Based on Falconer's (1960) simple formula for determining heritability, the correlations for identical versus fraternal twins reared together (.86 and .55, respectively; see Table 6.1) computes to

62%. However, the value of 50% that I mentioned earlier is still the best estimate when adoption studies are added to the equation and more complex formulas are used: The well-respected behavior geneticists Plomin and Petrill (1997) state that the value of 50% derives from "Model-fitting analyses that simultaneously analyze all of the family, adoption, and twin data . . . , suggesting that about half of the variance of IQ scores in these populations can be attributed to genetic differences among individuals" (p. 59).

However, the overall broad heritability estimate of 50% for IQ represents an overview of values derived from different types of studies and for different kinds of populations. These estimates are a function of numerous variables, such as the ones summarized briefly in the following sections.

Heritability and Type of Cognitive Ability

Different cognitive abilities have different heritabilities. Wechsler's Verbal IQ has consistently been shown to have a higher heritability than Performance IQ for 8-year-olds (Scarr & Carter-Saltzman, 1982, Table 13.5), 11- and 12-year-olds (McGue, Bouchard, Iacono, & Lykken, 1993), and adults (McGue et al., 1993). That consistent finding is counterintuitive and argues against the common misperception that *Gf* is primarily genetic and *Gc* is mainly environmental. However, the results for Wechsler's verbal and nonverbal abilities do not generalize directly to fluid reasoning (*Gf*) and crystallized knowledge (*Gc*) from CHC theory. (Remember, from chapter 3, that Wechsler's Performance Scale measures *Gv* or visual processing, *Gs* or processing speed, and visual-motor coordination, in addition to *Gf*.) Nonetheless, even when fairly "pure" measures of *Gf* and *Gc* are studied (Horn, 1985), there is no support at all for the notion that *Gf* tends to be genetic and *Gc* is mostly environmental.

Bouchard (1998, Table 2) compiled data from the Swedish Adoption/Twin Study of Aging, and reported heritabilities for this adult sample of 58% for both verbal ability and perceptual speed, 46% for spatial ability, and 38% for memory. Perhaps the most extensive compilation of heritabilities was obtained from 34 samples of identical twins reared together (a total of 4,672 pairs) and 41 samples of fraternal twins reared together (a total of 5,546 pairs) (Bouchard & McGue, 1981; Vandenberg & Vogler, 1985). Vandenberg and Vogler (1985) reported the following heritabilities for specific abilities:

Reasoning	48%
Spatial visualization	46%
Clerical speed and accuracy	46%
Verbal comprehension	38%
Number	38%
Memory	32%
Verbal fluency	30%
Divergent thinking	22%

Of considerable interest is the fact that the lowest heritabilities are for verbal fluency and divergent thinking (divergent production), both of which are associated with creativity. Therefore, it is plausible that the heritability value for creativity, at least as it is measured by traditional tests of creativity, is only about half as large as the value for IQ.

Heritability and Social Class

Fischbein (1980), in a study of twins, divided his samples into three social class groupings and found that heritability estimates increased with increasing social class: 78% for the highest social class grouping, but only 30% for the lowest. Extremely similar results were obtained from a large-scale study of almost 2,000 non-Hispanic Whites and African American sibling pairs (identical twins, fraternal twins, full and half siblings, cousins in the same household, and biologically unrelated siblings), from the National Longitudinal Study of Adolescent Health, who were tested on Wechsler's Vocabulary subtest (Rowe, Jacobson, & Van den Oord, 1999). When categorized by parental education, the heritability for the most highly educated families averaged 74%, versus 26% for the less well-educated families (Rowe et al., 1999).

In a twin study conducted in Russia, Grigorenko and Carter (1996) evaluated the *parenting styles* of the mothers of identical and fraternal twins and analyzed these relationships as a function of the family's social class. They found parenting styles to differ for the two types of twins (e.g., mothers of identical twins tended to infantilize identical twins more than did mothers of fraternal twins, and to be more authoritarian). Parenting styles also differed by social class. Grigorenko and Carter (1996) found that Russian mothers with less education and lower occupational status were more likely than their more educated, higher-status counterparts to use authoritarian approaches, to view their children's behavior less positively, and to infantilize their twins' behavior. The styles associated with lower social classes also tended to be associated with lower children's IQs. These findings are especially important because they challenge the basic assumption that identical twins are raised in exactly the same way as fraternal twins, and they remind us that heritability of IQ should not be interpreted in a vacuum but ideally needs to be interpreted within the context of social class and parenting styles.

Heritability and Ethnicity

Fischbein's (1980) study included African Americans and Whites, but his emphasis was on social class, and he administered only one subtest (Vocabulary), not a complete IQ test, so we know little about heritability for Whites versus African Americans. However, heritability seems to be a function of ethnicity. Scarr and Carter-Saltzman (1982, Figure 13.12) demonstrated substantial differences among three ethnic groups in the relationships between the cognitive scores obtained by children and their parents. Correlations between children's scores on cognitive tests and their parents' scores (average of fathers' and mothers' scores) averaged about .70 for Koreans, .50 for Americans of European ancestry living in Hawaii, and .35 for Americans of Japanese ancestry living in Hawaii.

Heritability and Age

Despite occasional disagreement (e.g., Devlin, Daniels, & Roeder, 1997), it has become widely accepted among behavior geneticists that the heritability of IQ is substantially larger in adulthood than in childhood (e.g., Bouchard, 1996, 1998; McGue et al., 1993; Plomin & Petrill, 1997). The greater role of genetics in adulthood than in childhood is evident when comparing the correlations between the IQs of unrelated siblings reared together (adopted/natural or adopted/adopted) when they are tested as children (.28) and when they are tested as adults (.04) (Bouchard, 1998). The same age-related inference can be drawn from Table 6.3 regarding the results of the Texas Adoption Study: The differential between the correlations for the birth mother and those for adoptive parents was substantially greater when the children were older than when they were younger (a difference in coefficients of about .40 at the 10-year follow-up compared to .20 at the original assessments). Furthermore, high heritabilities for Wechsler's Full Scale—in the low- to mid-80s, well above the average of about 50% for studies of children—have been obtained for adult samples, such as the ones tested in twin studies conducted in Norway (Tambs, Sundet, & Magnus, 1984), Sweden (Pederson, Plomin, Nesselroade, & McClearn, 1992), and Minnesota (McGue et al., 1993). All of these findings suggest that the role of genetics increases as children become adolescents and then adults.

These age-related results suggest that a shared home environment has a modest effect on young children's IQ but has little or no effect on IQ when the children grow up. The potentially small role of the shared home environment on older children's and adults' IQs—a notion that has had empirical support for three quarters of a century (Burks, 1928)—is shocking and counterintuitive. As Neisser et al. (1996) observed in their thorough review article, "These findings suggest that differences in the life styles of families—whatever their importance may be for many aspects of children's lives—make little long-term difference for the skills measured by intelligence tests" (p. 88). However, the conclusions reached on heritability and aging by McGue et al. (1993) based on twin studies and by others (e.g., Loehlin et al., 1997) based on adoption studies need to be considered as tentative and inconclusive. As Neisser et al. (1996) emphasize with regard to childhood and adolescent studies: "We should note . . . that low-income and non-White families are poorly represented in existing adoption studies as well as in most twin samples. . . . It remains possible that, across the full range of income and ethnicity, between-family differences have more lasting consequences for psychometric intelligence" (p. 88).

Rowe and colleagues' (1999) study, mentioned previously, which included substantial numbers of African American twin pairs and a variety of income levels, is relevant to this general point, even though it has nothing to do with the age issue. In this study, the percentage of variance for shared home environment was 0 for highly educated families, but it was a substantial 23% for less well-educated families, nearly identical to the heritability value of 26% for the latter families (Rowe et al., 1999). In addition, before reaching firm conclusions about the role of family environment on IQ across the lifespan, it is important for researchers to emulate the methodology of Grigorenko and Carter (1996), who specifically measured parenting styles and examined how these styles interacted with type of twin (identical versus fraternal) and social class.

Maternal Environment (the First Environment, the Womb)

Two interesting lines of research involve what has been termed the *maternal environment,* which refers specifically to the environment in the womb during pregnancy: (a) Devlin et al.'s (1997) statistical, "model-fitting" approach, which gives great credence to the importance of maternal environment for siblings and, especially, for twins; and (b) the interesting findings from genetic research that has distinguished whether identical twins shared a placenta or had separate placentas (e.g., Rose, Uchida, & Christian, 1981).

Statistical Modeling

Devlin et al. (1997) disagree with the common assumption made by genetic researchers that maternal environment effects are trivial. They argue that the mother's womb provides an important early environment, one that witnesses substantial *in utero* brain growth, and that a huge number of perinatal factors, such as the mother's ingestion of alcohol, drugs, or lead, may lower the child's IQ, whereas other factors (e.g., dietary supplements) can raise a child's IQ. Therefore, maternal environmental effects on children's IQs are likely to be rather large for twins and notable for siblings (because mothers' health status and personal habits during pregnancy are likely to be similar but not identical from one pregnancy to another). Devlin et al. (1997) applied sophisticated statistics to large quantities of data (more than 50,000 "pairings"). Their results found a large maternal-environment effect for twins (20%) and a notable effect for siblings (5%).

The important implication of Devlin et al.'s (1997) conclusions is that variance formerly attributed to genetics may actually be attributable to environment (namely, maternal environment). Not every behavior geneticist agrees with Devlin et al.'s conclusions, but even those who disagree concede that "None of the research cited by Devlin et al. (1997) regarding possible *in utero* effects on IQ is unimportant; it simply does not support their narrow argument that maternal effects create excessive similarity in twins" (Bouchard, 1998, p. 270). However, Devlin and colleagues' "narrow" argument has at least some support from the results of placentation research.

Placentation Research

Identical twins either share one placenta (when the zygote divides 4 to 7 days after fertilization) or have separate placentas (when division occurs within 72 hours); about two-thirds of identical twins share one placenta (Rose et al., 1981). This placentation effect relates significantly to identical twins' birth weight, umbilical cord blood cholesterol level, adult personality, and cognition, and it impacts as well on correlations among abilities (Rose et al., 1981). Dramatic placentation differences in the correlations for identical twins were found for Canadian adults (ranging in age from about 20 to 44 years) on the WAIS (Rose et al., 1981) and for French 8- to 12-year-old children on the WISC-R (Spitz et al., 1996). Adult identical twins, regardless of placentation status, correlated at .95 in their scores on WAIS Vocabulary. In great contrast, however, are their correlations on Block Design, as shown in Table 6.4: a value of .92 was obtained for identical twins who shared one placenta (and, hence, had essentially identical maternal environments), but a coefficient of only .48 was obtained for identical twins who had separate placentas. When Falconer's (1960) heritability formula is applied, the values of heritability are markedly different for each type of identical twins (96% for those sharing a placenta and 8% for those with their own placenta). The low heritability for twins with separate placentas reflects the fact that the correlation for those particular identical twins was nearly the same as the value of .44 for fraternal twins.

These findings were replicated by Spitz et al. (1996) for children on the French WISC-R, as shown in Table 6.4. Though the results of the Spitz study are not as dramatic as the Rose findings, they are nonetheless consistent with Rose's results, providing solid support for the specific maternal-environmental effects on Block Design performance. (Like the Rose study, the Spitz study did not find differences in the correlations for Vocabulary.) Whereas American hospitals typically do not systematically record one versus two placentas for identical twins, the fact that

TABLE 6.4 PLACENTATION RESEARCH: CORRELATIONS ON WECHSLER'S BLOCK DESIGN SUBTEST

	Toronto, Canada—WAIS Block Design	Paris, France—WISC-R Block Design
Identical Twins		
One placenta	.92	.84
Two placentas	.48	.61
Fraternal Twins	.44	.51
Heritability		
One placenta	96%	66%
Two placentas	8%	20%

Note. Toronto WAIS data are from "Placentation Effects on Cognitive Resemblance of Adult Monozygotes," by R. J. Rose, I. A. Uchida, & J. C. Christian, 1981. In *Twin Research 3: Intelligence, Personality, and Development*, 35–41. Paris, France. WISC-R data are from "Long-Term Effect of Prenatal Heterogeneity Among Monozygotes," by E. Spitz et al., 1996. *Cahiers de Psychologie Cognitive* [Current Psychology of Cognition], *15*, 283–308.

other countries sometimes note this information meticulously allowed this fascinating research to be conducted.

When the placentation research is interpreted alongside the statistical research, the Devlin hypothesis about the importance of maternal effects takes on added validity. Indeed, Devlin et al. (1997) did not even consider there to be different maternal environments for *fraternal* twins, much less identical twins with one or two placentas. The placentation research suggests that the maternal environment may be even more potent and more subtle than Devlin conceived. If Devlin, Rose, and their colleagues are correct in stressing the maternal environment, then it is possible that a substantial portion of the variance that has routinely been assigned to genetics may actually be due to environmental differences before children are born.

Nonetheless, the conclusions from placentation research are tentative. Bouchard's (1998) intelligent critique of Devlin's methodology provides an alternate explanation of the influence of maternal environment. Also, the sample sizes of both placentation studies are small (across both studies there were 37 pairs of identical twins with one placenta, 39 pairs with two placentas, and 52 pairs of fraternal twins). Also, the results seem fairly specific to Wechsler's Block Design. Spitz et al. (1996) did not obtain the same results with K-ABC subtests, even though K-ABC Triangles measures the same spatial abilities as Block Design.

As I once wrote about the two placentation studies: "Ironically, the greatest effect seems to be on a nonverbal measure of an ability believed to be closely aligned with neurological development, rather than with the verbal, education-dependent *Gc* subtest. The results require additional replication and generalization to be accepted as scientific findings.... The findings are, however, sufficiently provocative to challenge all known heritability estimates pertaining to intelligence and personality because pertinent studies failed to control for the [placentation] effect" (Kaufman, 1999, pp. 627–628).

Home Environment and IQ

Several clever studies of the home environment have been conducted to determine which factors are most related to the development of children's intelligence. One of the first was published by my former professor at Columbia University, Dr. Richard Wolf, who conducted in-depth interviews with the mothers of 60 fifth-grade students. Wolf (1966) was especially interested in the intellectual and language home environment (e.g., quality of available language models, feedback for appropriate language usage, opportunities for enlarging vocabulary). He found high correlations between the overall home environment ratings and IQ (.69) and even higher correlations with scores on achievement tests (.80). One of the special features of the coefficient of correlation that I didn't mention before was that if you square the coefficient, you get the percentage of variance overlap between the two variables. Therefore, a .80 correlation means that the variables being correlated share a 64% overlap (.8 × .8 = .64 = 64%). Figure 6.1 shows the results of Wolf's study graphically. When taken together, the combination of IQ and home environment correlated at .87 with achievement—that is to say, the *combination* of IQ and home environment accounted for a little over three quarters of the variance in children's achievement test scores.

Marjoribanks (1972) also conducted a thorough investigation of the impact of home environment on children's IQs, where home environment was evaluated in terms of parental pressure for their children to achieve, to be active, to follow intellectual pursuits, and to be independent. The sample consisted of 185 11-year-old boys, and the IQ test was the SRA Primary Abilities Test. Figure 6.2 presents the results of Marjoribanks's study using the SRA total score as the measure of IQ. The parental pressures differed in their relationship to IQ, with the pressure for achievement correlating at the highest rate (.69) and the pressure for independence correlating at the lowest (.38); taken together, the multiple correlation of .72 means that the measured parental pressures accounted for 52% of the variance in children's IQs,

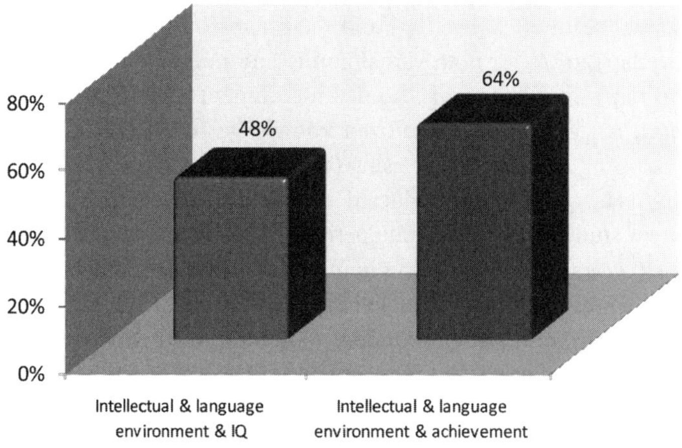

FIGURE 6.1 The relationship of intellectual and language environment at home to overall IQ and school achievement.
Note. From Wolf's (1966) study of 60 fifth-grade girls and boys.

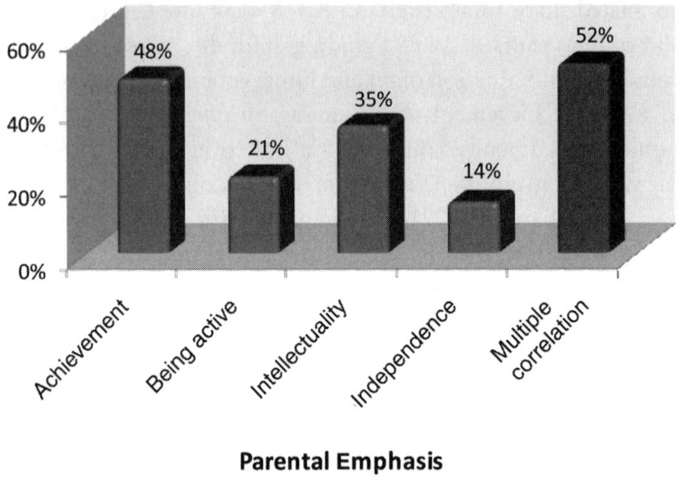

FIGURE 6.2 The relationship of aspects of home environment to overall IQ.
Note. From Marjoribanks's (1972) study of 185 boys, aged 11.

as shown graphically in Figure 6.2. Not shown in the figure is the fact that the multiple correlation differed substantially for the different abilities measured by the SRA, ranging from .26 for spatial ability (7% overlap) and .40 for reasoning ability (16% overlap) to .71 for both verbal ability and number ability (50% overlap). In other words, home environment had a greater impact, in general, on crystallized knowledge (*Gc*) than on fluid reasoning and visual processing (*Gf* and *Gv*).

Hanson (1975) conducted a longitudinal home environment study across three time periods (0–3 years, 4–6 years, and 7–10 years) with 110 predominantly upper-class White boys and girls. Hanson (1975) correlated the "old" Binet IQ with the interesting array of home environment variables shown in Figure 6.3. This summarizes Hanson's results for the two oldest groups (because "infant IQ tests" measure *maturation* more than IQ). The highest correlations were with models of language development (.44) and freedom to engage in verbal expression (.43). Several home environment variables (not shown in Figure 6.3) correlated

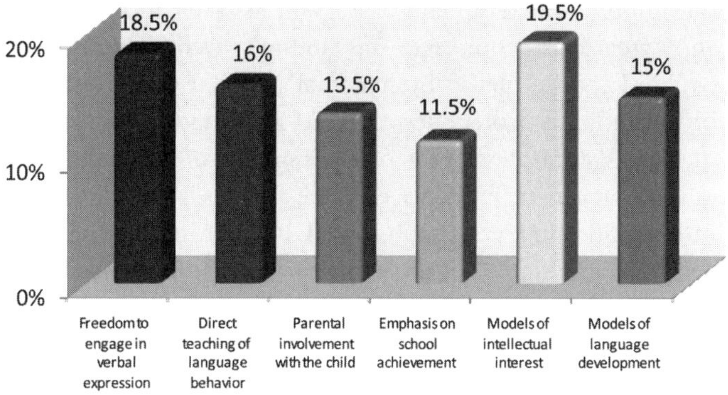

FIGURE 6.3 The relationship of aspects of home environment to overall IQ.
Note. From Hanson's (1975) study of 110 boys and girls aged 4 to 10 years.

poorly with the Binet IQ: These were emphasis on independent performance (.18), freedom to explore the environment (.12), models of task-oriented behavior (.04), and emphasis on female sex role development (–.12).

These illustrative home environment studies demonstrate the positive influence of parenting on children's IQs, especially parental focus on language, intellectual activities, and school achievement. Of lesser importance—at least regarding children's IQs—is parental emphasis on activity and independence. The results of these studies indicate that home environment plays a substantial role in developing children's intelligence, but these results cannot easily be interpreted within the context of heredity versus environment. Parenting styles, and a child's response to those styles, reflect an intricate blend of both genetic and environmental variables.

OVERVIEW OF HEREDITY AND ENVIRONMENT

The bulk of behavior genetics and environmental research, from a diversity of methodologies, converges on the fact that genetics is an important determinant of IQ, and its role conceivably becomes greater as people age. This finding—even in light of the possible key role played by maternal prenatal effects—should not be minimized or underplayed. Plomin and Petrill (1997) stated that "Regardless of the precise estimate of heritability, the point is that genetic influence on IQ test scores is not only statistically significant, it is also substantial. It is rare in the behavioral sciences to explain 5% of the variance. For example, despite the interest in birth order, it accounts for less than 1% of the IQ variance. Finding that heredity accounts for 50% of the variance is a major discovery about intelligence" (p. 59).

Indeed, specific environmental variables, like blood lead level (the hot topic discussed in chapter 9), rarely account for very much variance by themselves. Bouchard and Segal (1985) concluded as follows based on an exhaustive review of myriad environmental variables (anoxia, malnutrition, family income, family configuration, and many more): "The principal finding in this review of environmental effects on IQ is that no single environmental factor appears to have a large influence on IQ. Variables widely believed to be important are usually weak" (p. 452). The environmental-influence update by Neisser et al. (1996) basically agrees with that conclusion, although research findings regarding school attendance are compelling: For example, when children of about the same age go to school a year apart because of admission criteria involving birth dates, *children with the extra year of school score higher on IQ tests.* Neisser et al. (1996) also reported another provocative finding—when one Virginia county closed its schools in the 1960s, preventing most African American children from obtaining formal education, a controlled study indicated that each lost year of school was worth 6 IQ points (Neisser et al., 1996).

The environmental contributions are complex, varying from culture to culture and within subcultures. Despite disappointing results in their evaluation of the impact of environmental variables on IQ when taken one at a time, Bouchard and Segal (1985) recognized "that environmental effects are multifactorial and largely unrelated to each other" (p. 452). When the impact of aggregated cultural or environmental influences on IQ is evaluated (Vandenberg & Vogler, 1985, Table 6), the estimates, on average, are usually of a magnitude similar to the value of 50% for IQ (shown graphically in Figure 9.1, in chapter 9). Some aspects of the environment that contribute to IQ are undoubtedly unknown or difficult to measure. But Flynn (1987) points out that "the fact that the factors are unknown does not mean that when identified, they will prove exotic or unfamiliar" (p. 189).

Weinberg (1989) notes that one needs to accept the role of genes in helping to shape IQ, along with the many environmental and "organic" factors (e.g., a mother's taking drugs or being exposed to excessive radiation during pregnancy), in such a way that acceptance of our "genetic heritage... need not be pessimistic nor bode evil for social and educational policy" (p. 102).

About two decades ago, Plomin (1989) wisely cautioned: "As the pendulum swings from environmentalism, it is important that the pendulum be caught midswing before its momentum carries it to biological determinism" (p. 110). More recently, Plomin and Petrill (1997) continued this metaphor: "The reason for hoping that the pendulum is coming to rest at a point between nature and nurture is not merely that we want everyone to be happy. It is what genetic research on intelligence tells us" (p. 55).

The chapter title asked "Is IQ genetic?" The short answer is no. But heredity plays a strong role in determining a person's IQ, no less than the role of the environment.

7

Hot Topic: Are Our IQs "Fixed" or Are They "Malleable"?

Chapter 6 asks, and tries to answer, tough questions about the roles of heredity and environment on IQ. This chapter addresses the related issue of whether our IQs are fixed and unchangeable or whether they are malleable.

William Angoff (1988) argued that the wrong question has continually been asked by those trying to determine the relative influences of heredity and environment on IQ variability: "*The real issue is whether intelligence can be changed, an issue that does not at all go hand in hand with the issue of heritability*" (p. 713, emphasis in original). "Whatever the 'true' heritability coefficient for intelligence is . . . , the essential point is that in the context of group differences and what these differences connote, its numerical value is irrelevant. What is relevant is whether these group differences can be changed, with what means, and with what effect" (p. 716).

Even though behavior geneticists argue against the notion that high heritability means that a person's IQ is "fixed" (e.g., Plomin, 1983), popular beliefs often die hard. Angoff (1988) argued that intelligence is "thought by many to be largely innate... and to a considerable extent inherited, and therefore unchangeable both within a given lifetime and across generations" (p. 713). That generalization seems to correspond to Herrnstein and Murray's (1994) conclusions in *The Bell Curve.*

Angoff (1988) demonstrated his point with a simple but powerful illustration of how a variable with high heritability (height) has changed markedly from generation to generation: Adolescents in the United States and Great Britain gained about 6 inches in average height in the course of a century (Tanner, 1962), and adult males in Japan grew 3 to 4 inches taller from the mid-1940s to the early 1980s. Angoff also supports the malleability of highly heritable traits with research results that showed American-born Japanese children to be taller, heavier, and more advanced in skeletal development than their contemporaries born and raised in Japan.

In this chapter, I focus on two lines of research that demonstrate the malleability of intelligence: (a) Flynn's (1987, 1998a, 2007) investigations of generational gains in IQs, known as the *Flynn Effect*; and (b) the results of various early intervention studies, especially the highly successful Abecedarian Project (Campbell & Ramey, 1995).

THE FLYNN EFFECT

James Flynn (1984) made the intriguing discovery that the IQs of Americans increased, on average, by 3 points per decade. Children and adults in the United States performed better on IQ tests from generation to generation at a steady, predictable rate. Flynn's initial study evaluated IQ test scores in the United States between 1932 and 1978, and the rate of increase was a steady

3 points per decade. That same rate of gain has held true into the 1980s (Kaufman & Kaufman, 1983), the 1990s (Flynn, 1998c), and the first decade of the 21st century (Zhou & Zhu, 2007).

One consequence of this shift in the average intelligence of the whole country is that the norms for IQ tests become more out of date with each passing year. After 10 years, the norms for an IQ test are 3 points out of date, and after two decades the outdatedness reaches a hefty 6 points. The Flynn Effect is evident whenever a group of children or adults is tested on two different tests. Their mean scores will differ by a predictable number of points based on the year in which each test was standardized. For example, the K-ABC was standardized in the early 1980s and the WISC-R was standardized in the early 1970s. The mean IQs on the two tests should differ by about 3 points, reflecting the decade between the dates when each test's standardization data were obtained.

A glance at the K-ABC manual reveals that the mean IQs differed by 3.1 points for 182 "normal" children tested on both tests (Kaufman & Kaufman, 1983, Table 4.19). The group scored lower on the K-ABC (the newer of the two tests) than on the WISC-R, which was 10 years old at the time. Similarly, a quick look at the new WAIS-IV manual (The Psychological Corporation, 2008, Table 5.5) indicates that a sample of 238 normal individuals scored 2.9 points lower on the WAIS-IV—again, the newer test. These outcomes seem paradoxical. If people are getting smarter (or, at least, scoring higher on IQ tests), shouldn't their IQs be higher on the newer tests? The answer is no. The newer set of norms is based on the smarter group of people just tested, so the new norms are *steep*. In contrast, the norms for the older test are based on a group tested some time ago, and those outdated norms are *soft*. Remember from chapter 4 that IQs are relative scores, always compared to the performance of the normative sample. The new test has steeper norms, so a person's IQs will be lower on the newer test, with new norms, than on the old test, which has an outdated (not as smart) reference group. (This pattern is analogous to that of athletic records. A time or distance that would have won a national collegiate track-meet event 20 years ago would barely qualify for an invitation to the meet today.) The 3-point IQ difference illustrates the power of the Flynn Effect. And it raises a number of questions that I will answer below.

DOES THE 3-POINTS-PER-DECADE FLYNN EFFECT APPLY WORLDWIDE?

In an ambitious undertaking designed to study IQ gains over time in developing nations, Flynn (1987) contacted 165 scholars in 35 countries who were known to be interested in IQ trends. He applied rigorous standards to each data set he received (a) to determine whether the samples were sufficiently comprehensive and representative of each nation, and not biased in some way (e.g., the people had to be "typical" as opposed to, for example, applicants for medical school); and (b) to ensure that the tests administered at two points in a person's life were basically unaltered. It was also desirable for at least some of the test data to be based on measures of *Gf*, like Raven's Matrices, so as to measure skills that are less affected by a specific culture than are *Gc* tests of acquired knowledge. And ideally the samples were at least partially to be based on adults who had reached their "peak" test performance.

Flynn used the quality of the samples and the continuity of the tests to categorize each data set into four statuses: 1 = verified evidence of IQ gains; 2 = probable evidence; 3 = tentative evidence; and 4 = speculative evidence. He presented the amount of gain per year and per generation (30 years), but I prefer to discuss gains per decade. Flynn organized his results by type of test (e.g., verbal, nonverbal), and he kept samples separate if they differed in age range or geographic location. For simplicity, I will present averages across samples to provide gains for each country as a whole—with one exception: When data for a country differed in status, I will present only the data with the highest status (e.g., the data for Canada reflect the verified data from Edmonton, not the probable/tentative data from Saskatchewan).

Each of the 14 nations showed gains in IQ from one generation to the next, and some of these gains are large (Kaufman & Lichtenberger, 2006, Figure 2.1). Japan joined six Western European countries in gaining more than 5 points per decade. Five nations reported Status 1, or verified, data with the following gains in IQ points per decade:

- Netherlands 6.7
- Belgium 5.8
- Canada 4.6
- Norway 3.2
- New Zealand 2.4

As impressive as the 3-point gain per decade for Americans has seemed ever since Flynn's (1984) article, the United States actually outgained only two of the 14 nations studied by Flynn (1987)—New Zealand and Great Britain. And in a subsequent study of Great Britain (Raven, Raven, & Court, 1993), adults were found to have gained 5.4 points per decade from 1942 to 1992 on Raven's Matrices, the test used in Flynn's (1987) study. In contrast, a recent U.S. study (Zhou & Zhu, 2007) showed that the 3-point gain per decade originally identified by Flynn (1984) has been maintained—neither increasing nor decreasing—through the early years of the 21st century.

So, to answer the question that I posed earlier, IQ gains are, indeed, worldwide. And we are not nearly the best in the world.

Does the Flynn Effect Apply Equally Well to Measures of Fluid Reasoning (*Gf*) and Crystallized Knowledge (*Gc*)?

Flynn (1987) pointed out that gains on tests of *Gf*, like Raven's Matrices or some of Wechsler's Performance subtests, have a deeper and more pervasive meaning than gains on crystallized, verbal tests such as Wechsler's Information. Gains in *Gf* imply true improvement in the ability to process information and solve new problems. In contrast, gains in *Gc* may simply reflect an accumulation of acquired knowledge due to the greater availability of information in schools, on TV, and on the Internet. As Flynn (1987) reminds us: "The average person today would outscore Aristotle or Archimedes on general information, but this hardly shows greater intelligence" (p. 184).

In fact, Flynn (1987) showed fairly consistently that gains were greater on fluid tests than on crystallized tests, indicating a true increase in problem-solving ability. For the nations studied by Flynn, the mean gain on the Raven and related *Gf* tests was 7.3 points per decade, compared to 3.3 points per decade on verbal *Gc* tests (see Kaufman & Lichtenberger, 2006, Table 2.4; data are from France, Belgium, and Norway). When Wechsler's scales were used to evaluate gains in five countries (including the United States), for the post-1950 generation, a similar finding emerged: The mean Performance IQ gain was 7.1 points versus 4.2 Verbal IQ points (see Kaufman & Lichtenberger, 2006, Table 2.5).

Gf, or the ability to use abstract reasoning to solve novel problems that are not taught in school, provides a useful index of intelligence and a valuable tool for evaluating worldwide gains across generations. The items are typically abstract analogies that do not become dated over time and are not specific to a culture. *Gf* skills have traditionally not been dependent on either acculturation or school learning, although that may be changing a bit. My colleague John Willis (personal communication, November 2, 2008) points out that "Modern kindergarten and primary math curricula include a lot of patterning activities that look very much like *Gf* tasks."

Gc is also a useful index for measuring IQ gains, but it is more culture specific, dependent on formal schooling, and easily subject to the influences of an increasing array of information available to all societies and to most subcultures within societies. Increases in *Gc* over time are to be expected; increases in *Gf* are not. The fact that the gains tend to be substantially larger on tests of *Gf* than *Gc* is a clue (but not proof) that people are, indeed, becoming smarter as time goes by.

What Causes the Gain in IQ From Generation to Generation?

When Flynn (1984) first published his then-startling findings that Americans gained 3 IQ points per decade, I thought the explanation was intuitive. Most of the pretests were before or just after World War II and the posttests were in the 1970s. The explanations of what would become known as the Flynn Effect seemed simple enough. The 1930s and 1940s preceded the power of TV and the mass media to enable people in the most rural communities to access information during the 1960s and 1970s. Also, studies of the drastic effects of being raised in nonstimulating "sterile-white" orphanages on children's IQs began to be publicized (Hunt, 1961), changing parenting styles forever in terms of the importance of providing cognitive stimulation in infancy.

But those easy explanations would not have predicted such a differential in IQ gain from country to country, nor would they have predicted that the gains (at least in the United States) would remain a steady, indeed a near-constant, 3 points per decade, into the 21st century. And those explanations cannot account for such steady growth on measures of *Gf*, much less *greater* gains in *Gf* than in *Gc*.

Flynn (1998b), who continued to gather data on worldwide IQ gains after his breakthrough 1987 paper on 14 developed countries, concluded: "Data from twenty nations show not a single exception to massive IQ gains over time. The escalation of whatever skills are involved probably began no later than the onset of the industrial revolution" (p. 106). Why the gains? Certainly the increasing reach of the mass media to all corners of the world via TV and the Internet is involved to some extent. So are the contemporary attitudes toward infant stimulation just mentioned; the proliferation of educational TV shows, toys, and software; improved health care; and the health consciousness of pregnant women who have become aware of the dangers of smoking, alcohol, and drugs to the developing fetus. (Regarding educational TV, the pioneering *Sesame Street* show long ago taught not only *Gc* skills and knowledge but *Gf* processing as well—"One of these things is not like the other.")

Some researchers have emphasized the importance of nutrition (e.g., Colom, Lluis-Font, & Andres-Pueyo, 2005), environment in general (e.g., Dickens & Flynn, 2001), education (e.g., Teasdale & Owen, 2005), methodological issues that might cloud the meaningfulness of the Flynn Effect (Rodgers, 1998), and other factors as well (Zhou & Zhu, 2007). *The Rising Curve,* edited by Ulric Neisser (1998), offers a multifaceted look at possible explanations and analyses of generational gains in IQ and related measures such as academic achievement, and Flynn (2007) also explores these issues in *What Is Intelligence?* Flynn (2007) emphasizes changes in the *social environment* since the Industrial Revolution, changes that led to "the spread of the scientific worldview" (p. 40). The end result, according to Flynn (2007), is a greater capability for each new generation to go beyond the concrete when solving problems and to deal more easily with abstractions. However, Flynn's explanation is derived mainly from questionable interpretation of data on Wechsler's subtests and remains nothing more than a hypothesis (A. S. Kaufman, 2009).

Attempts to understand the nature of the Flynn Effect are often referred to as getting inside the "black box" that is behind it (Zhou & Zhu, 2007). Regardless of what is ultimately found to live inside the black box, the gains seem clearly related to cultural and environmental factors, not genetics or evolutionary variables, and reflect the malleability of intelligence. Some researchers have written about the role of genetics in explaining the Flynn Effect (e.g., Rodgers & Wanstrom, 2007), but I tend to agree with Flynn's (1987) comment: "Massive IQ gains cannot be due to genetic factors. Reproductive differentials between social classes would have to be impossibly large to raise the mean IQ even 1 point in a single generation" (p. 188). Even Herrnstein and Murray (1994) concede that "Given their size and speed, the shifts in time necessarily have been due more to changes in the environment than to changes in the genes" (p. 308). More recently, Flynn (2007) has emphasized the *interaction* between genetics and environment in his hypothesized explanation of the Flynn Effect. He speculates: "One child is born with a slightly better brain than another. Which of them will tend to like school, be encouraged, start haunting the library, get into top-stream classes, and attend university?" (Flynn, 2007, p. 39).

For an interesting, more comprehensive discussion of what might be in the black box, and for an interpretation of the Flynn Effect from the perspective of contemporary theories of intelligence, consult Jonathan Plucker's (in press) book, *Intelligence 101*.

Does the Flynn Effect Apply About Equally to All Ages and Ability Levels?

Flynn's (1987) verified data (Status 1) on *Gf* tests for Belgium, the Netherlands, and Norway suggested that childhood IQ gains persist to maturity. In the United States, Flynn (1987) reported gains per decade of about 3 points for children and adolescents, 2 points for adults below age 35, and 3½ points for adults ages 35–75. Flynn (1987) concluded from these results that "American gains on Wechsler tests appear to persist into late adulthood" (p. 186).

And, when synthesizing the results of an increasing array of studies a decade later, Flynn (1998a) stated definitively, "More often than not, gains are similar at all IQ levels... and they certainly persist into adulthood" (p. 61).

Large-scale studies of draftees in the Netherlands disagree with Flynn's assertion about the similarity of gains across IQ levels; Teasdale and Owen (1989) found that virtually all of the malleability in the IQs of the Dutch population occurred for the adults scoring in the *lower half* of the distribution. Spitz (1989) accumulated studies that compared WAIS and WAIS-R Full Scale IQ change across the broad 50–130 IQ range. He not only verified that adults with below average IQs showed the greatest IQ gain; he also found a *reverse* Flynn Effect for adults with above average IQs (they lost IQ points).

More recently, Zhou and Zhu (2007) made the same discovery as Spitz for young children through older adults on Wechsler's Performance IQ. The researchers evaluated the gains for 173 preschool and primary-grade children (1989 WPPSI-R and 2002 WPPSI-III), 238 elementary and high school children (1991 WISC-III and 2003 WISC-IV), and 190 adults ranging from those in late adolescence to the elderly (1981 WAIS-R and 1997 WAIS-III). Overall, the researchers verified the 3 points per decade for all age groups—about 2½ points for WPPSI, 3½ points for WISC, and 3 points for WAIS. (Interestingly, Zhu and his colleagues also evaluated the Flynn Effect for infants and toddlers in a separate study of the Bayley Scales and found that it did *not* apply to this very young population; Yang, Zhu, & Pinon, 2006.)

But the 3-point average gain did not come near to telling the full story of their findings. They combined data across all tests and ages and then examined gains by IQ level. The results were intriguing. They found an average gain of 3½ points per decade for people with IQs of 90 to 109, but the gains were about *7 points* for those with IQs in the 70s and 80s. And a reverse Flynn Effect characterized children and adults with IQs of 110 and above (e.g., those with IQs in the 120s lost 2.4 points). The only people who truly displayed the well-known American Flynn Effect of 3 points per decade were the Average Joes, echoing Flynn's (1984) early, prophetic caution that the 3-point American gain may be a reliable estimate only for those who earn IQs between 90 and 110. Zhou and Zhu's results finally made sense of K-ABC data from a quarter-century ago. I did not understand why the studies of the WISC-R and K-ABC produced the expected Flynn Effect of 2 to 4 points for the normal sample and the samples of "learning disabilities referrals," "learning-disabled," and "behaviorally disordered" (all of whom had average IQs above 90)—but produced a whopping 6 points for the group of "educable mentally retarded" (Kaufman & Kaufman, 1983, Table 4.19). Now I understand that the gain is largest for those with the lowest IQs. The new WAIS-IV manual (The Psychological Corporation, 2008, Tables 5.5 and 5.7) shows the same pattern: IQ differences were larger for adults with mild intellectual disability than for normal adults (4.1 vs. 2.9 points).

The striking variability in IQ change based on IQ level was mirrored by a similar amount of variability in the IQ gains or losses *within* each IQ range. Zhou and Zhu (2007) provide a bottom-line caution about their important results: It is risky business to adjust an individual's observed IQ score by a constant value of 3 points per decade when that average value doesn't apply to anywhere near everyone. That same argument will be made in the course of the discussion of lead and IQ in chapter 9, in connection with the tendency of some researchers to use the average IQ loss for groups of children to make estimates of IQ loss for individual children, ignoring individual differences and ignoring other relevant background information about each specific child.

What Are the Practical Implications of the Flynn Effect?

One positive outcome of the Flynn Effect is that it has made test publishers more accountable. Historically, they were lazy about revising and restandardizing a test. The items would become out of date because of cultural changes (e.g., in the 1949 WISC Arithmetic subtest, 3 pencils cost 5 cents while oranges were 30 cents a dozen), but the publishers were still slow to renorm their IQ tests, because they believed that the outdated content would not affect a person's ability to solve most problems. And they were probably right. But the Flynn Effect changed all that. Now there was research evidence that norms become out of date rapidly, and publishers had to respond to the demands of psychologists to make their tests current. The WISC-R was published in 1974, a long quarter-century after the WISC. The WISC-III came out in 1991 (reflecting a 17-year interval), and the WISC-IV followed only 12 years later in 2003. A similar pattern characterizes the WAIS to WAIS-IV trajectory (Wechsler, 1955, 1981, 1997, 2008). The consumer has benefited directly from the Flynn Effect.

Another outcome is that sometimes the Flynn Effect can be the correct explanation of a research finding that is misinterpreted by the investigators. Consider a study of lead and IQ (a hot topic discussed in chapter 9). Bellinger and Needleman (1983) used IQ based on the Peabody Picture Vocabulary Test (PPVT; Dunn, 1965) as the estimate of mother's IQ (normed in 1959) and the WISC-R, normed in 1972, to measure the children's IQ. Mother's IQ was used to predict the child's "expected" IQ. But based on the Flynn Effect, the mothers' PPVT IQs would be spuriously inflated by 4 points relative to the children's IQs. Therefore, the mother's IQs should have been adjusted by 4 points to make them comparable to the WISC-R IQs of their children. Bellinger and Needleman found that the children with elevated lead levels had IQs that were 3.94 points lower than expected, based on maternal IQs. They attributed the loss of 4 points to the blood lead. But most likely this revealed nothing but the Flynn Effect in action.

And not long ago I served as a consultant on a law case in which a man with a low IQ was convicted of brutal murders. The law says that a person with mental retardation (intellectual disability) cannot be put to death, as discussed in depth by Flynn (2007). So that was the question: Did this man score in the so-called mentally retarded IQ range (below 70) on the IQ tests he was given several times in his life? In 1996 (a year before the WAIS-III was published), he was tested on the WAIS-R, which was standardized in 1978. That means that he was given the test when the norms were about 18 years (i.e., about 5 points) out of date. His Full Scale IQ was 72 (*above* the cut-off), but the Flynn Effect suggests that he received about a 5-point boost from the outdated WAIS-R norms. Therefore, the defense argued, his real IQ was 67—and he should *not* be executed. The answer wasn't simple because of the role of errors of measurement (chapter 5), adaptive behavior (chapter 4), and the fact that he was tested nine times between ages 9 and 39. Interestingly, Zhou and Zhu's

(2007) study suggests that the Flynn Effect for adults with IQs in the 70s is likely to be much greater than 3 points per decade. But that study was not conducted prior to the court case. The important point: The Flynn Effect entered the legal domain and was instrumental in deciding a convicted killer's fate (he was not executed). Talk about high-stakes testing!

But there is one final caution about the Flynn Effect, namely that it may have already ended in some developed nations. Data on the WAIS-III and WAIS-IV suggest that the Flynn Effect is alive and well in the United States in the 21st century (The Psychological Corporation, 2008). However, post-2000 data from Norway and Denmark suggest that the Flynn Effect has stopped occurring in those countries and that there may even be a reverse Flynn Effect (i.e., decline in IQ) taking place, especially in Denmark (Teasdale & Owen, 2005, 2008).

EARLY INTERVENTION STUDIES

The malleability of IQ based on direct interventions has traditionally produced conflicting and often controversial results. Positive findings emerged in several studies from the 1940s (e.g., Honzik, Macfarlane, & Allen, 1948; Tuddenham, 1948), and optimism was rampant in the 1950s and early 1960s about the power of interventions. Hunt (1964) made powerful statements, based mostly on anecdotal information, concerning a follow-up of 13 infants, from Skeels and Dye's (1939) study, who were transferred from an orphanage to a school for the mentally retarded, compared to the 12 infants who were left behind in the orphanage. The 13 infants and toddlers (aged 7–30 months) who were transferred to the school had an average IQ of 64 (really a developmental quotient). At the school, the older and brighter girls became attached to them and played with them frequently. The 12 who stayed behind (aged 12–22 months, mean IQ = 87) continued to be raised in virtual isolation in the orphanage. All the infants and toddlers were retested a few years later. The transferred children had increased dramatically in IQ and the ones who remained in the orphanage showed precipitous drops in IQ. Even more shocking was the follow-up 21 years after the original Skeels and Dye (1939) study, as described by J. McV. Hunt (1964), a leading developmental psychologist of the era:

> The findings are startling. Of the 13 in the group transferred from the orphanage to the school for the mentally retarded: all are self-supporting; none is a ward of any institution, public or private; 11 of the 13 are married, and nine of these have had children. On the other hand, of the 12 children, originally higher in IQ, who were kept in the orphanage: one died in adolescence following continuous residence in a state institution for the mentally retarded; five are still wards of state institutions . . . ; of the six no longer wards of state institutions, only two have been married and one of these is divorced. . . . For the 13 transferred . . . , the median grade completed is the twelfth (*i.e.*, graduation from high school); four have gone on for one or more years of college work. (p. xxii)

The optimism was gone by the end of the 1960s. Much better empirical research had been conducted. The Skeels and Dye orphanage study was more a matter of happenstance than of design. Even if the intervention that featured mothering by intellectually disabled adolescent girls produced such astounding effects, no real conclusions can be drawn from that study because there are too many confounding variables to count (e.g., What unknown factors determined which infants were transferred out of the orphanage and which infants were left behind? Is it really possible to measure IQs in infants?). And, anyway, interventions that might be effective when deprivation is so severe do not generalize to more traditional interventions with at-risk children.

Reviews from 40 years ago (Jensen, 1969) and even a generation ago (Brody, 1985) were quite pessimistic. Jensen's (1969) proclamation that programs like Head Start were a failure caused a public outcry, partly because of the implication that intelligence is more fixed by genetics than most people believed, and mostly because of the racial overtones. Less passionate and pointed but equally pessimistic were the conclusions that (a) studies to raise the IQs of retarded children (Spitz, 1986) generated "the dismal conclusion that they have been uniformly failures" (Angoff, 1988, p. 718); and that (b) "there is little evidence that short-term interventions will lead to enduring changes in intelligence" (Brody, 1985, p. 371).

Barnett's Reviews of Head Start and Other Early Intervention Programs

However, the doom-and-gloom conclusions reached by some past reviewers have been tempered by more recent evaluations of intervention research. Barnett (1995) concluded from a review of 15 well-designed early childhood intervention studies that most could boast positive gains years after the treatment ended. IQ gains were observed a couple of years after the intervention programs but were not long-lasting. However, academic gains in school achievement not only occurred initially (Bryant & Maxwell, 1997) but sometimes lasted into middle childhood (Johnson & Walker, 1991) or mid-adolescence (Berrueta-Clement, Schweinhart, Barnett, Epstein, & Weikart, 1984). And long-lasting *behavioral* gains occurred in the school setting (Lally, Mangione, & Honig, 1988).

More recently, Barnett (2004; Barnett & Husted, 2005) thoroughly evaluated the Head Start literature to determine the effectiveness of "our nation's foremost federally funded provider of educational services to young children in poverty" (p. 16). Head Start, in operation since 1965, has focused mostly on children aged 3–5 years and has provided not only educational intervention but also "social, health, and nutritional services to children and their low-income parents" (Barnett & Husted, 2005, p. 16). The age range was supposed to be extended to birth to age 3 when Early Head Start was established in 1994, but the federal budget has never allowed that promise to become a reality.

After a thorough review of the best Head Start intervention studies, Barnett reached the following conclusions:

- When evaluating benefits on a short-term basis, "Studies have generally shown that programs for children at risk, including Head Start, result in increases of [about 7½ points] in IQ and achievement" (Barnett & Husted, 2005, p. 17).
- Unfortunately, these initial gains fade out over time (Barnett, 2004).
- "The long-term benefits of Head Start rarely have been studied, and never with sufficiently strong research designs" (Barnett & Husted, 2005, p. 21).
- The strongest evidence for large long-term benefits comes from studies of *other* preschool programs, not Head Start, such as the Abecedarian Project (Campbell & Ramey, 1995), "one of the most notable studies of a model program to provide high-quality early education services to at-risk children" (Barnett & Husted, 2005, p. 18).

THE CAROLINA ABECEDARIAN PROJECT

The Carolina Abecedarian Project (Campbell, Pungello, Miller-Johnson, Burchinal, & Ramey, 2001; Ramey & Campbell, 1984) is unquestionably the best intervention study ever conducted. The substantial long-term IQ gains for the children in that study illustrate the amazing malleability of children's intelligence as long as the intervention is brilliantly conceived and implemented and the program begins when the children are infants.

Description of the Program

The Abecedarian Project was a true experiment in every sense of the word, as 57 infants were randomly assigned to the treatment group and 54 were randomly assigned to the control group. The infants (98% African American, all from low-income families) were on average 4½ months of age when they began attending a particular child care center in the early to mid 1970s. All 111 infants were identified as "high risk" based on maternal education (10th grade, on average), family income, and other factors. The treatment program, developed especially for the Abecedarian Project, was targeted to promote cognitive, language, perceptual-motor, and social development.

- The child care center was open 8 hours per day, 5 days per week, and 50 weeks per year, and the treatment was maintained for 5 years.
- Teacher-child ratios were low (ranging from 1:3 for infants to 1:6 for children age 5).
- For preschool children, the clear focus of the curriculum was language development and preliteracy skills.

And what about the infants who were randomly assigned to the control group? They received enhanced nutrition until they were 15 months old to ensure that any IQ gains observed for the treatment group weren't a function of better nutrition. Also, the control group's families benefited from social work services and received disposable diapers until their child was toilet trained, as an incentive for participation. Many control children did, in fact, attend other child care centers, some starting in infancy and others in the preschool years (Campbell et al., 2001).

The following IQ tests were administered: Stanford Binet (Terman & Merrill, 1973) at ages 3–4; WPPSI (Wechsler, 1967) at age 5; WISC-R at ages 6½, 8, 12, and 15 years; and WAIS-R at age 21. Reading and math were measured with the Woodcock-Johnson achievement battery, at ages 8, 12, and 15 years (WJ; Woodcock & Johnson, 1977) and at age 21 years (WJ-R; Woodcock & Johnson, 1989). The sample size varied at each age due to normal attrition, but even at age 21 the sample included 93.7% of the original sample of infants (53 treatment and 51 control).

In the name of science, it was essential for the control children not to participate in the special Abecedarian intervention program. No one really had a clue, based on previous intervention research, that these children would miss out on the opportunity of a lifetime.

IQ and Achievement Gains Through Age 21

Campbell et al. (2001) reported IQ gains from age 3 to 21 years, and achievement gains from age 8 to 21 years, for both the children who participated in the experimental intervention program and those in the control group. The results are fantastic. During the preschool years, the treatment group outscored the controls by about 16½ points (age 3), 12½ points (age 4) and 7½ points (age 5). The gains during elementary and high school on the WISC-R were smaller than the shorter-term gains but still substantial (4 points at age 8, and 6 points at ages 6.5, 12, and 15). At age 21, the gain was still a significant 4½ points, with the treatment group earning an average WAIS-R Full Scale IQ of 89.7 versus 85.2 for the controls. The gains on the achievement tests were even larger than the IQ gains. At age 8, the gain in reading was almost 9 points, leveling off to about a constant 6 points for ages 12, 15, and 21. For math, the gains were about 5 points at ages 8, 12, and 21, and nearly 7 points at age 15. In addition, there were other long-term benefits of the early intervention: The treatment group was significantly more likely to be engaged in skilled occupations (Campbell, Ramey, Pungello, Sparling, & Miller-Johnson, 2002), less likely to have used marijuana in the last month (Campbell et al., 2002), and less likely to display symptoms of depression (McLaughlin, Campbell, Pungello, & Skinner, 2007).

The Abecedarian intervention program was more complicated than I have indicated here (Campbell et al., 2002). In fact, some children were given the interventions during both the preschool and the school-age years; some received only the preschool intervention; and some of the control sample received only the school-age intervention. I've simplified the presentation of the results because the bottom line is that the original group of infants randomly selected as the treatment sample has consistently outperformed the infants placed in the control group, regardless of participation in the school-age program.

The very large IQ gains at ages 3 and 4 may have been artificially high, because the old Stanford-Binet was highly verbal and the intervention program specifically stressed language development. But the persistent long-term gains of about 4 to 6 IQ points on the WISC-R and WAIS-R and about 5 to 7 standard-score points on the Woodcock-Johnson reading and math "are a testimony to the maintained intellectual and academic gains that resulted from an intensive and carefully-conceived early childhood intervention program. And, more importantly, they illustrate the malleability of cognitive ability" (Kaufman & Lichtenberger, 2006, p. 44).

However, the authors of the study advised caution about inferences from their results (Campbell et al., 2002): "Because the study sample was 98% African American, the findings generalize to that segment of the population, and the group comparisons made here reflect differences among African Americans, born into low-income families, who either did or did not experience the Abecedarian early childhood program" (p. 52).

The remarkable benefits of the Abecedarian intervention into early adulthood were not matched by other excellent intervention programs, most notably the Early Training Project (Gray, Ramsey, & Klaus, 1982) and the Perry Preschool Project (Berrueta-Clement et al., 1984). Campbell et al. (2001) believe the success of the Abecedarian Project, relative to other fine programs, was likely due to such reasons as the following:

- Starting treatment in early infancy rather than at ages 3 or 4 years
- Providing five years of treatment instead of the typical 1 to 2 years
- Offering an intensive year-round 8-hour-a-day program instead of half-day programs that were in operation for part of a year

It is conceivable that the programs that did not show enduring gains, such as the Early Training Project and the Perry Preschool Project, provided too little too late. Their failure to show enduring gains was *not* because of a lack of malleability in intellectual development.

Recently, Nisbett (2009) has summarized an array of intervention studies that have shown short-term gains in intelligence and achievement, especially for African American students in middle and high school. These gains have often been based on "small" treatments, such as telling the students that their intelligence is under their own control or providing them with exercises in life planning (e.g., having the students talk about what kind of future they'd like to have, what obstacles they anticipate). In addition, Nisbett (2009) discusses programs that are more intensive, such as a middle-school intervention that provides an innovative curriculum and requires long school days and 3 extra weeks of instruction. However, virtually all of the interventions discussed by Nisbett (2009) produced short-term gains, not unlike the Head Start program. Ultimately, successful interventions must be demonstrated to produce gains that last long after the interventions have ended.

OVERVIEW OF MALLEABILITY OF IQ

For *groups,* IQ has been shown to be fairly constant from early childhood through adulthood (Conley, 1984; Pinneau, 1961; Sattler, 2008):

- IQs at age 5 have been shown to correlate at .50–.60 with IQ at age 40, and IQs at age 9 to correlate at about .70 (McCall, 1977).
- IQs at age 11 correlated at .66 at age 80 for a large Scottish sample (Deary, Whiteman, Starr, Whalley, & Fox, 2004), with higher correlations for women (.69) than for men (.62).

- The average of children's IQs at ages 10 to 12 predict average IQs at ages 17 and 18 ridiculously well, at .96 (Pinneau, 1961).
- A group of 101 intellectually disabled children tested four times on Form L-M of the Stanford-Binet, with 1-year intervals between assessments, obtained rather constant IQs, producing a median correlation of .85 (Silverstein, 1982).

But these are group data, which obscure individual differences, a point that is raised again in chapter 9 on the misuse of group findings on the relationship between lead level and IQ loss to make inferences about specific individuals. Group results do not take into account the malleability of the IQ for infants who are given early intensive intervention, as in the Abecedarian Project. Anastasi and Urbina (1997) point out that "Studies of individuals... may reveal large upward or downward shifts in test scores" (p. 326).

And the Flynn Effect, though itself a result of group data, not only differs from nation to nation (Flynn, 1987) but also from individual to individual and from IQ level to IQ level (Zhou & Zhu, 2007). More research is needed to help isolate the specific environmental variables that are most associated with the largest gains in intelligence. The average IQ of Americans (and, even more, that of Europeans and Asians) is increasing at a steady, measurable, and substantial rate, suggesting that good scientists will be able to answer these crucial questions—providing answers that might be a precursor to the development of successful interventions to reduce group differences across social classes (Flynn, 1998a; Neisser, 1998).

As I have written elsewhere (Kaufman & Lichtenberger, 2006),

> Angoff (1988) has argued that researchers and other professionals should focus more on the IQ's changeability than on dividing its variance into genetic and environmental components. As he pointed out, the prevalent focus has led to controversy, unscientific

> arguments and assertions about a scientific issue, name-calling, and claims that intelligence tests are invalid or useless. (p. 46)[1]

The Flynn Effect, which has persisted over time and across cultures, and the success of the Abecedarian Project both call out for scientists to be innovative in their research on environmental variables that impact the development and enhancement of intelligence and encourage much optimism regarding the malleability of IQ.

1. Quoted with permission of the publisher, John Wiley & Sons.

8

Hot Topic—IQ and Aging: Do We Get Smarter or Dumber as We Reach Old Age?

We all know the stereotypes about what happens to our intelligence as we move from young adulthood to old age. We get wiser. We lose our memories. We get slower. But what is urban legend and what is truth? What does the research tell us?

CROSS-SECTIONAL STUDIES

Cross-sectional studies constitute one common type of research investigation on aging and IQ. This approach examines a cross-section of the adult population at a single point in time. Suppose we look at the IQs of adults in different age groups who were tested on the same test in about the same year. How do their scores differ from one another? Data of that sort were available back in the late 1930s, when Wechsler (1939) first standardized the Wechsler-Bellevue through age 64. Normative data are among the best possible data to use to examine age differences, because substantial numbers of adults in every age group are systematically tested under standardized conditions. And the adults selected are matched with the U.S. Census to ensure that they are representative in terms of important background variables such as socioeconomic status, geographic region, and gender.

Comparing mean IQs can't be done simply or directly, because, by definition, a person's IQ is always relative to that of other people the same age. Therefore, a simple comparison of mean IQs for different age groups tells us nothing, because the mean IQ for every age group always equals 100. That is the way the IQ scale is constructed, to yield an average IQ of 100 for every age group. So to compare mean IQs for different adult age groups, the scores for each age group need to be based on a common yardstick—that is, everyone needs to be compared to the same adult norms. It doesn't matter which norms are used as the yardstick, so long as the same norms are used for everyone. I've chosen the norms for ages 20–34 years—young adulthood—as the common reference group to permit comparisons of an array of age groups between 20–24 and old age.

Table 8.1 illustrates age differences in mean IQ using WAIS-III data (Kaufman, 2001c), and the results aren't pretty. Mean Verbal IQs (based on the norms for ages 20–34) maintain, and sometimes increase, into the 50s before declining. The peak WAIS-III Verbal IQ (104 for people around age 50) is 14 points higher—almost 1 standard deviation—than the mean for adults in their late 80s. And the results for Performance IQ (again, based on the norms for ages 20–34) dwarf the age-related declines in mean Verbal IQs. On the Performance Scale—which measures fluid reasoning (*Gf*), spatial ability (*Gv*), and speed (*Gs*)—the decline in mean scores is rapid and dramatic. It begins in the mid-20s and

TABLE 8.1 WAIS-III VERBAL AND PERFORMANCE IQs FROM AGES 20 TO 89 YEARS (BASED ON NORMS FOR AGES 20–34)

Age Group	Mean Verbal IQ	Mean Performance IQ
20–24	97	101
25–34	100	99
35–44	102	97
45–54	104	92
55–64	99	86
65–69	98	81
70–74	97	79
75–79	96	76
80–84	91	73
85–89	90	70

From "WAIS-III IQs, Horn's Theory, and Generational Changes From Young Adulthood to Old Age," by A. S. Kaufman, 2001c. *Intelligence, 29*, 131–167.

continues steadily until it reaches more than 30 points in the late 80s (a peak of 101 at 20–24 versus 70 in old age). And though I've used WAIS-III data to illustrate what Botwinick (1977) called the "classic intellectual aging pattern," the same results have emerged for every Wechsler adult scale, starting with the Wechsler-Bellevue. Wechsler (1958) was concerned a half-century ago, when he concluded, "What is definitely established is . . . that the abilities by which intelligence is measured do in fact decline with age; and . . . that this decline is systematic and after age 30 more or less linear" (p. 142).

But Wechsler's conclusions were premature and overgeneralized. There are powerful *cohort* (generational) differences that make it impossible to compare the IQs of different age groups who are tested at a single point in time. Consider people tested in the mid-1990s on the WAIS-III, when that test was standardized. Adults of about 20 were children of the Watergate era and the 1980s, quite a different experience from being children raised during the days of the Vietnam War and Woodstock, or during the Korean War and *Happy Days* era, or while World War II was raging, or during the Depression of the 1930s. The last-mentioned sample includes much of the elderly population whose mean scores are depicted in Table 8.1. Cohort differences relate closely to how well a person scores on an IQ test. In each generation, numerous aspects of society greatly impact test performance, for example, the emphasis on education, the availability of information via the media, the economy, social customs, catastrophic events, issues pertaining to health and childcare—in short, the same kinds of variables that probably produce the Flynn Effect (see chapter 7). Cross-sectional differences must be controlled, at least to some extent, in order to interpret the mean IQs earned by different age groups at the same point in time.

In fact, one major cohort variable that totally distorts the interpretation of the apparent decline in IQ with increasing age that seems so evident in Table 8.1 is generational differences in educational attainment. Intuitively, we know many more people graduate from college today than in times gone by, and that at one time graduating from high school was not all that common. The age groups that differed so greatly in IQ in Table 8.1 differed just as much in their educational attainment, as shown in Table 8.2. Well, education and IQ go hand-in-hand (Table 4.3). No inferences about IQ decline, even tentative inferences, can be made from cross-sectional data without first controlling for cohort differences. Let's see what happens when one key cohort variable (educational attainment) is controlled.

When mean IQs are adjusted for age differences in education, the decline in mean Verbal IQs disappears almost completely, but the steep decline in mean Performance IQs remains. This dramatically different pattern of age-related differences in mean IQs for the Verbal versus the Performance Scale, even when education is controlled, was found for the WAIS (Birren & Morrison,

TABLE 8.2 PERCENTAGES OF THE WAIS-III STANDARDIZATION SAMPLE WITH DIFFERENT YEARS OF SCHOOLING

Age Group	0–8 Years	13 or More Years
20–44	4%	53%
45–64	11%	42%
65–79	18%	29%
80–89	32%	22%

1961) and the WAIS-R (Kaufman et al., 1989) and is depicted pictorially for the WAIS-III in Figure 8.1 (data are from Kaufman, 2001c; and Kaufman & Lichtenberger, 1999). Education-adjusted Verbal IQs (using the norms for ages 20–34) ranged from 98 to 104 for each age group between 20–24 and 80–84. Only for the oldest age group (85–89) was the adjusted Verbal IQ as low as 96 (values for ages 16–19 are not adjusted for education because most of those in this group were still in school).

Performance IQs received about the same boost as did Verbal IQs when education was controlled (about 3 to 6 IQ points for each adult age group 55–64 and older), but that little increase was not enough to change the steep decline in mean Performance IQ between early adulthood and very old age. The dramatically different age-related changes on Wechsler's IQs mirror precisely the distinction that Horn and Cattell (1967) long ago identified for crystallized knowledge (*Gc*), a *maintained* ability, versus fluid reasoning (*Gf*), which is *vulnerable* to the effects of aging. Not everyone agrees with Horn's (1989) distinction between maintained and vulnerable abilities—most notably Schaie (1983b) and his colleagues (e.g., Schaie & Labouvie-Vief, 1974), who have argued that all abilities are fairly resilient with regard to the effects of aging. However, cross-sectional data that have been obtained by using individually administered IQ tests have

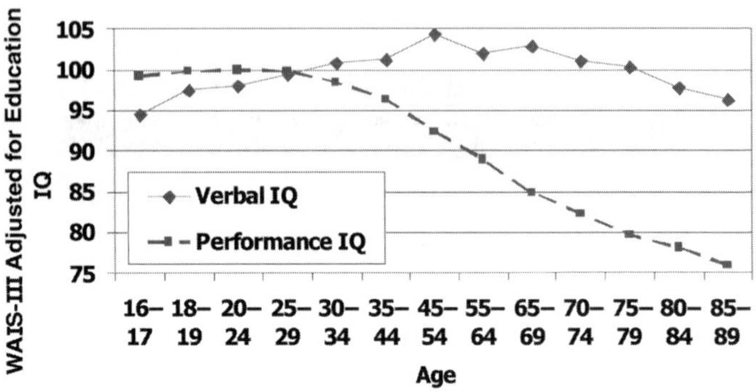

FIGURE 8.1 Age-related changes on the WAIS-III Verbal and Performance IQs for ages 16 to 89 years, adjusted for education.
Note. Mean scores for all ages are based on norms for reference group (ages 20–34). Values for ages 20–89 are adjusted for education; unadjusted values are shown for ages 16–19 because many of these adolescents had not yet completed their education. From *Essentials of WAIS-III Assessment,* by A. S. Kaufman and E. O. Lichtenberger, 1999, New York: Wiley (adapted from Figure 6.1, p. 192). Copyright © 1999, John Wiley & Sons. Adapted with permission.

provided strong support for the vulnerability of *Gf* and the maintenance of *Gc* across the adult life span. This support does not come only from studies of Wechsler's adult scales but also from investigations of the Kaufman Adolescent and Adult Intelligence Test (KAIT) and Woodcock-Johnson III (Kaufman & Horn, 1996; McGrew et al., 2006). And the results generalize to other cultures as well, as the familiar aging patterns for *Gc* versus *Gf* emerged for the German adult sample tested on the German KAIT (Melchers, Schürmann, & Scholten, 2006) and for the Dutch sample on the Dutch KAIT (Mulder, Dekker, & Dekker, 2004).

Nonetheless, even the unanimity in the findings across tests, generations, and nations cannot alter the fact that these are all cross-sectional data. We can make inferences about what seems like a decline in ability with increasing age, but, even then, it is more accurate to speak of *differences in the mean scores* of various age groups, not declines, because educational attainment is but one cohort variable, and so many others (such as physical health) remain uncontrolled.

And what about abilities other than *Gc* and *Gf*? The four WAIS-III Indexes provide a clue to different rates of growth and decline on four distinct abilities, though it is only a clue, because these data, too, are from cross-sections of adults at a single point in time. Verbal IQ comprises two separate components, and Performance IQ comprises three. Verbal IQ is made up of both *Gc* and short-term memory (*Gsm*). Those facets of the Verbal Scale are embodied by the Verbal Comprehension Index (VCI) and Working Memory Index (WMI), respectively. Analogously, the Performance Scale measures *Gf*, visual-spatial processing (*Gv*), and processing speed (*Gs*). *Gf* and *Gv* are measured by the Perceptual Reasoning Index (PRI), and *Gs* is measured by the Processing Speed Index (PSI).

Figure 8.2 presents mean index standard scores for 13 age groups between 16–17 and 85–89 years for the four separate scales. The means are adjusted for education (for ages 20 and above), and each curve is different. The mean VCI (*Gc*) peaks at about age 50 and is maintained through the late 70s; even in the 80s,

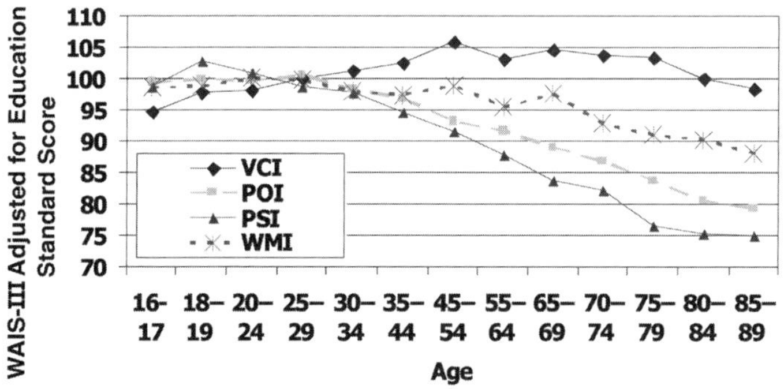

FIGURE 8.2 Age-related changes on the four WAIS-III indexes for ages 16 to 89 years, adjusted for education.

Note. Mean scores for all ages are based on norms for reference group (ages 20–34). Values for ages 20–89 are adjusted for education; unadjusted values are shown for ages 16–19 because many of these adolescents had not yet completed their education. From *Essentials of WAIS-III Assessment*, by A. S. Kaufman and E. O. Lichtenberger, 1999, New York: Wiley (adapted from Figure 6.2, p. 195). Copyright © 1999, John Wiley & Sons. Adapted with permission.

education-adjusted mean standard scores are about 100. The other three abilities display patterns that suggest vulnerability to the effects of aging. Despite the stereotype of memory loss in the elderly, the decline in mean standard scores on tests of short-term memory is mild, as evidenced by the graph for WMI. Memory is maintained through the late 60s before the mean scores begin a gradual decline. However, the decline in mean PRI (a blend of *Gf* and *Gv*) clearly suggests great vulnerability to normal aging, and the most vulnerable of all is processing speed (*Gs*).

The rapid decline of speed with age is well known. This slowing "is not only an acknowledged laboratory result but also of considerable practical importance.... Age-related slowness is evident in tasks of daily living such as zipping a garment, dialing a telephone, picking up coins, unwrapping a band-aid, cutting with a knife, and even putting on a shirt" (Salthouse, 1985, p. 400). Not to mention driving a car.

But the age-related decline in mean scores on tests of novel problem solving, especially those that demand fluid reasoning or spatial visualization, is less well known. Yet that decline has just as many practical and societal consequences, particularly when people who are well past their peak problem-solving years are asked to make high-stakes decisions. Nonetheless, all of the data presented so far are from cross-sectional samples of adults. The apparent vulnerability of abilities such as *Gf* or *Gs* must be verified with more than just one cohort variable (education) controlled. What happens when all cohort variables are controlled simultaneously, at least to the degree that this is possible? That type of research requires *longitudinal* studies, namely, those that test adults from the same cohort at several points in time.

LONGITUDINAL STUDIES

The essence of interpreting decline in ability rests on controlling cohort variables via longitudinal studies, and there has been no shortage of such investigations (Berkowitz & Green, 1963; Kaufman & Lichtenberger, 2006, chapter 5). In the typical study, a Wechsler scale such as the Wechsler-Bellevue or the WAIS was administered at several points in time to the same sample of adults (or, at least, to as many of the adults who were willing and able to participate in the study over time). In a longitudinal study conducted at Duke University, for example, 267 adults from North Carolina (ages 59–94) were initially tested on the WAIS in 1955; by the time the last phase of the study took place, in 1976, the 42 survivors had been given the WAIS as many as 11 times (Siegler & Botwinick, 1979). While that degree of exposure to the same comprehensive IQ test might be considered cruel and unusual punishment in some states, there are other problems to contend with. These include the following:

- *Practice Effects and Progressive Error.* It is well known that Wechsler's Performance IQ has a huge practice effect on children, adolescents, or adults who are tested twice. Administer the test a second time after a few months have gone by, and IQs will go up just from the *practice* of taking the test previously. But the IQ gains are not equal for the Verbal and Performance Scales. On the old WAIS, for example, the average gains were 8 points in Performance IQ and 2 points in Verbal IQ (Matarazzo, Carmody, & Jacobs, 1980). The Performance Scale is designed to measure a person's ability to solve *novel* problems that are not taught in school. Administer the nonverbal subtests a second time and they stop being novel. Administer them 5 or 10 times, even over 20 years, and they are more like old friends than novel problems. In longitudinal research, this type of error is known as *progressive error.* Not surprisingly, Performance IQs have not been found to decline over time in longitudinal studies and do not display the vulnerability that is so striking in cross-sectional studies. Schmitz-Scherzer and Thomae's (1983) longitudinal study tested adults on the German WAIS as many as 5 times and reported either maintenance or increase in nonverbal ability through the first 4 administrations. But just as in the Duke study, the progressive error contaminated the results, making it impossible to reach any conclusions at all about changes in Performance IQ over time. Solving new problems (*Gf*), processing information visually (*Gv*), and handling information rapidly (*Gs*) are measured the 1st time people are tested, and maybe even the 2nd time if only a few years have elapsed. But by the 3rd or 5th or 10th time, the Performance IQ is no longer measuring the abilities that Wechsler intended to measure when he developed his subtests.

- *Selective Attrition.* Another serious problem that affects interpretation of longitudinal data on aging and IQ concerns exactly who keeps coming back to participate in the research studies every few years. When the phone rings, or the letter arrives, or the e-mail pops up in the inbox, who responds? And who ignores the phone call or e-mail or returns the letter unopened? Certainly, over time, some of the adults in the sample move away, fall ill, or die. But research has shown that the adults who drop out of longitudinal studies of aging and IQ are not a random sampling of the group. Instead, the adults who quit after 1 or 2 times earn lower IQs than the ones who keep returning for more (Horn & Donaldson, 1976). This phenomenon, known as *selective attrition,* is demonstrated beautifully by the Duke study, which tested adults 11 times (Siegler & Botwinick, 1979). These investigators asked a simple question about the dwindling sample of adults who showed up time after time: How did these adults perform on the WAIS the very first time they were tested? Table 8.3 shows the fascinating results.

Those who showed up only once averaged an IQ of 98; those who came twice averaged 101; and the mean IQ increased slowly and steadily until it reached 111 for those persistent adults who showed up either 10 or all 11 times. Just as progressive error casts doubt on the validity of the changes in IQ over time (especially Performance IQ), so does selective attrition. How much can one

TABLE 8.3 MEAN WAIS FULL SCALE IQs OF ADULTS (AGES 60–74) THE FIRST TIME THEY WERE TESTED IN THE DUKE LONGITUDINAL STUDY

Number of Times They Participated in the Study	Individuals' Mean IQ the *First* Time They Were Tested
1	98
2	101
3	104
4	107
5	108
6–7	109
8–9	110
10–11	111

Note: Mean WAIS Full Scale IQs are obtained from the norms table for ages 65–69, entering the mean Full Scale scores reported by Siegler and Botwinick (1979).

generalize the findings from the relatively bright adults who keep returning to be tested? And the problem exists even before anyone is invited to come back at all. The people who volunteer for the study in the first place earn higher IQs than those who choose not to participate in the research (Horn & Donaldson, 1976).

The net result? Neither cross-sectional nor longitudinal aging-IQ studies provide easy or unequivocal answers to what happens to our IQs as we age.

Schaie's Cross-Sequential Studies

K. Warner Schaie's (1996) brilliant and creative 21-year Seattle longitudinal cross-sequential study began with the testing of 500 adults, aged 25–67, in 1956 on the group-administered Primary Mental Abilities (PMA) test. Schaie and his colleagues then blended cross-sectional and longitudinal experimental designs to try to come up with definitive answers to the question of how our intellect changes as we grow old. During the course of the Seattle study, three large additional cross-sectional samples (totaling more than 2,300 adults) were tested in 1963 (ages 25–74), 1970 (ages 25–81), and 1977 (ages 25–81). Every 7 years, when Schaie conducted a new cross-sectional study, he also invited back adults from previous cross-sectional studies to participate in longitudinal investigations of aging. So in addition to the four cross-sectional studies, he obtained longitudinal data for three 7-year intervals, two 14-year intervals, and one 21-year interval based on data from 130 of the original 1956 sample of 500.

He was then able to control for cohort effects by grouping adults by their year of birth. He controlled for time-of-measurement effects (the year of testing) by making statistical adjustments to account for the kinds of cultural and societal changes that occur over time (this would later be known as the Flynn Effect). By testing large samples of adults across a wide age span over a 21-year period, and using his clever integration of experimental methodologies (called *cross-sequential*), he was able to pinpoint the extent to which the changes in IQ were due simply to the normal aging process.

Schaie's first cross-sectional study in 1956 showed the same type of decrease in IQs with advancing age that was so evident from analyses of Wechsler's adult scale (see Table 8.1 and Figure 8.1). But when he retested 303 of the 500 adults in 1963, the declines had virtually disappeared (Schaie & Strother, 1968), providing a dramatically different answer to the age-old questions about aging. In Schaie's first longitudinal follow-up, even such nonverbal, Performance-like subtests as Space and Reasoning showed no decline with age.

There was much controversy about whether *Gc* was maintained throughout life while *Gf* fell precipitously (Horn's position), or whether all types of intelligence were maintained into old age (Schaie's position). The arguments were sometimes heated (Baltes & Schaie, 1976; Horn & Donaldson, 1977), with

Horn arguing that factors like selective attrition accounted for an illusory maintenance of reasoning and spatial ability into old age. Schaie and his colleagues were responsive to Horn's criticisms and modified their future analyses accordingly; they even admitted that their original cross-sequential design was ill equipped to evaluate age changes (Schaie & Hertzog, 1983).

In subsequent research, Schaie and his collaborators controlled for selective attrition as well as for cohort and time-of-measurement effects, and they still came to the same conclusion that they had come to earlier, that "most of the adult life span is characterized by an absence of decisive intellectual increments" (Schaie & Labouvie-Vief, 1974, p. 15). But that position was softened a little in Schaie's (1983b) exhaustive analysis of the aging-IQ data his team had collected over a generation. When controlled, as necessary, for confounders such as selective attrition, his accumulated results did indeed show a decline in old age, although the declines in Space (*Gv*) and Reasoning (*Gf*) occurred much later in life (after age 60) than they did in Horn's data and in cross-sectional analyses of Wechsler's adult scales (Birren & Morrison, 1961; Kaufman, 2001c; Kaufman et al., 1989). Verbal Meaning (*Gc*) increased steadily until age 53, but a notable decline occurred between ages 67 and 74. *Gv* peaked earlier (age 46), and didn't really decline until 67–74, but it did decline more dramatically than *Gc*. And *Gf* plunged to an IQ of 73 by age 81.

Ultimately, Horn's vulnerable abilities still proved to be vulnerable in Schaie's investigations. They simply declined much later in life than in Horn's research or in studies of Wechsler's adult scales. But despite the genius of Schaie's work, his research has one nagging flaw that limits its generalizability to IQ as we know it: the PMA is a group-administered test, not an individually administered battery, and it was developed for children and adolescents, not adults. And even though it was used to measure changes in adult IQ through old age in Schaie's research, it was normed only through age 18 years. More importantly, Wechsler's adult tests provide the criteria of what we mean when we speak of adult IQ. They are clinical tests that are administered by highly qualified and trained clinicians. They require adults to express their ideas in words and to manipulate concrete materials to solve novel problems. They are not multiple-choice tests, like the PMA, and, therefore, the PMA data cannot speak for Wechsler's IQ tests. Which means that Schaie's data cannot speak to changes in adult IQ from young adulthood to old age, not in the way in which IQ has been conventionally and traditionally defined since before World War II.

Longitudinal Studies of Wechsler's Scales With Independent Samples

Twenty years ago, while writing the first edition of *Assessing Adolescent and Adult Intelligence* (Kaufman, 1990), I was immersed in cross-sectional research on aging and IQ (Kaufman et al., 1989) and was also studying the array of pertinent literature on the topic. I was writing the chapter on "Age and IQ Across the Adult Life Span" and was feeling disheartened by the results of the many studies. If Horn was right, and the Wechsler cross-sectional data were correct, then my own decline in *Gf* was well underway (I was in my mid-40s then). If Schaie was right, then maybe I had a few good years before the inevitable decline took its swift hold on my brain. Either way, I was concerned, and if Horn was right, then I was wondering if I was smart enough to finish the book intelligently. What I wanted was to see the results of a cross-sequential study with Wechsler's adult scales, not the PMA.

Perhaps it was my desperation, but I suddenly realized that all the data were available for me to conduct exactly the kind of study I wished for. The test manuals of the WAIS and WAIS-R included enough information to enable me to follow the same age groups from one time period (the early-1950s, when the WAIS was standardized) to the next (the late-1970s, when the WAIS-R was standardized). I would not be following exactly the same people over time, because different representative samples of adults were tested for the WAIS and WAIS-R standardizations. But actually that was a good thing. I would be able to compare the abilities of *independent* samples of adults from the same cohorts (e.g., people born between 1904 and 1908) without having to worry about the killer variables of progressive error and selective attrition. The use of independent samples or *cohort substitution* is an excellent research strategy, according to Kausler (1991), so long as the independent samples are truly comparable and random.

I was able to identify the four cohorts of adults shown in Table 8.4 (Kaufman, 1990). Adults born between 1924 and 1933 were in their 20s in 1953 when the WAIS was standardized and about 50 when the WAIS-R was standardized 25 years later. The other cohorts aged from their 30s to about 60; from their early 40s to their late 60s; and from their late 40s to their early 70s. The cohorts were in place, so now I had to make some comparisons and

TABLE 8.4 THE FOUR ADULT AGE COHORTS REPRESENTED IN THE WAIS AND WAIS-R STANDARDIZATION SAMPLES

Cohort (Year of Birth)	Age in 1953 (WAIS Standardization)	Age in 1978 (WAIS-R Standardization)
1924–1933	20–29	45–54
1914–1923	30–39	55–64
1909–1913	40–44	65–69
1904–1908	45–49	70–74

Note. From *Assessing Adolescent and Adult Intelligence* (3rd ed.) by A. S. Kaufman and E. O. Lichtenberger, 2006, Hoboken, NJ: Wiley (adapted from Table 5.11, p. 173). Copyright © 2006, by John Wiley & Sons. Included with permission statistical adjustments. Were the samples comparable in terms of key background variables like SES? The answer was a decided yes. Each cohort from 1953 closely matched its 1978 mate on educational attainment (Kaufman, 1990, Table 7.12). Two different tests were used at the two points in time (the WAIS and WAIS-R), and although the structure of these tests was identical, many of the specific items changed from the WAIS to the WAIS-R and, of course, the two tests had different norms. Based on the data obtained on a group of adults tested on both tests, statistical adjustment for the test administered was simple and straightforward.

That left only one important need—to adjust the data for time-of-measurement or *time lag* effects, that is, the cultural and societal changes that occurred between 1953 and 1978. The huge importance of adjustment for time lag was demonstrated by Owens (1966), whose early longitudinal study of the Army Alpha stimulated "a critical reexamination of the inevitability of intellectual decline in adulthood" (Schaie, 1983c, pp. 13, 15). Owens (1953) administered the Army Alpha to 127 men, aged 50, who had been given the same test at age 19 as freshmen at Iowa State University in 1919 (the freshman class had had 363 members, so Owens did a good job of tracking down the men). Owens (1966) continued the study in 1961 when he tested 96 of the men at age 61. Simple examination of his data indicated that mean scores on the Army Alpha *Gf* test (Relations or Reasoning) *increased* from age 19 to 50 to 61. However, Owens had the insight to test a new random sample of 19-year-old freshmen at Iowa State on the Army Alpha in 1961–62. That told him about the impact of the Flynn-like cultural change from 1919 to 1961. By comparing the 19-year-olds tested in 1919 with the 19-year-olds tested in the early 1960s, Owens could measure the effects of culture, while holding chronological age constant. The age 19 sample tested in 1961–1962 showed a notable gain over the 19-year-olds tested more than 40 years earlier. That gain reflected time lag and had nothing to do with developmental changes over time. This gain from cultural change had to be subtracted from any *Gf* gain the 61-year-olds displayed on the Army Alpha. True changes due to aging could only be assessed by removing the contamination of the Flynn Effect. And when Owens (1966) corrected his data for time lag, his initial finding of increases in *Gf* from age 19 to 61 disappeared. There was no longer an increase with age; instead, *Gf* decreased, although "The losses appear to be small and probably are not of much practical significance until at least age 60" (Cunningham & Owens, 1983, p. 34).

So I applied Owens's exact procedure four times when I compared the IQs of the four cohorts in my Wechsler longitudinal study. Then I was ready to look at the results of the study, heart in hand. I wanted so much for the *Gf* pattern of early and rapid decline that jumped out from the cross-sectional data (Figure 8.1) to disappear, or at least mimic the more encouraging results of Schaie's and Owens's studies, which suggested a decline only after age 60.

But my hopes were dashed when I looked at the results: The decline in Performance IQ from the longitudinal study overlapped almost completely with the pattern of decreasing mean IQs from the cross-sectional study—if anything, as shown in Figure 8.3, the longitudinal data showed an even steeper decline!

When the WAIS-III came out in 1997, I repeated the same longitudinal investigation with independent samples. This time I was able to compare cohorts tested 17 years apart on the WAIS-R (in 1978) and the WAIS-III (in 1995). The cohorts ranged from adults born in 1904–1908 (about age 72 on the WAIS versus age 89 on the WAIS-R) to adults born in 1954–1958 (age 22 versus 39). I made all the appropriate comparisons and statistical corrections, held my breath once more (because I was then in my mid-50s), and examined the results. The same as before! Performance IQ declined early and rapidly and dramatically. Once again, the age-related changes for various cross-sectional and longitudinal studies of Wechsler's Performance IQ were mirrored in the newest data I had obtained (Kaufman, 2001c). And this same pattern reappeared once again when the WAIS-IV was published in 2008. I analyzed data for 11 cohorts tested 12 years apart on the WAIS-III (1995) and the WAIS-IV (2007). This time it was no

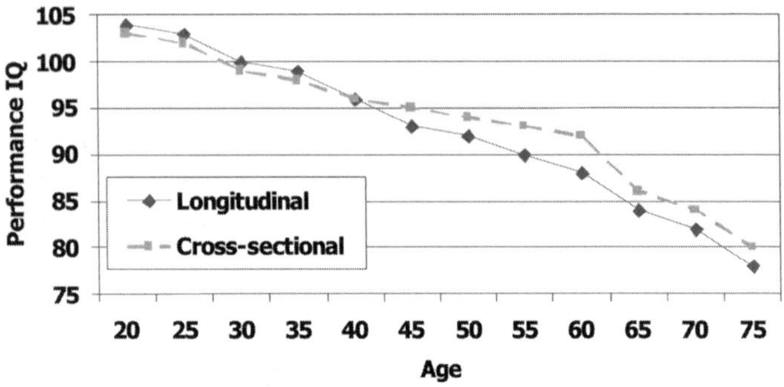

FIGURE 8.3 Changes in Wechsler Performance IQ with chronological age using two different experimental designs: cross-sectional (controlling for education) and longitudinal (controlling for instrument and time-lag effects).

Note. From *Assessing Adolescent and Adult Intelligence* (3rd ed.) by A. S. Kaufman and E. O. Lichtenberger, 2006, Hoboken, NJ: Wiley (adapted from Table 5.18, p. 175). Copyright © 2006, John Wiley & Sons. Included with permission.

surprise at all to find, once again, the inevitable rapid decline in perceptual reasoning and processing speed as we travel the time-worn path from young adulthood to old age (Lichtenberger & Kaufman, 2009).

All of these data were in agreement, as well, with the results of some other recent, well-designed longitudinal studies of aging and IQ (McArdle, Ferrer-Caja, Hamagami, & Woodcock, 2002; Zimprich & Martin, 2002). And all of these results were the spitting image of the vulnerable aging curves that Horn (1989) had repeatedly identified for *Gf* and *Gs* based on his life's work.

OVERVIEW OF AGING-IQ STUDIES

An integration of the diversity of longitudinal, cross-sectional, and cross-sequential studies of aging and IQ, conducted in the United States and throughout the world (e.g., Baltes & Lindenberger,

1997; Rabbitt, 1993; Zimprich & Martin, 2002), leads to the conclusion that *Gf, Gv,* and *Gs* are vulnerable to the effects of normal aging, and that the decline probably begins fairly early in adulthood. In contrast, *Gc* is maintained throughout much of adulthood before declining, sometimes dramatically, after age 75 (Kaufman & Horn, 1996). Horn and Cattell (1967) argued many years ago that there were very different aging patterns for *Gf* and *Gc,* and their initial research has been verified many times over. The main question is what actually declines over time.

Botwinick (1977) interpreted the classic aging pattern in terms of speed, namely, that speeded tasks are vulnerable to aging but nonspeeded tasks are not. Salthouse (1985, 1996) has written much about the key role that speed plays in the decline of adult abilities across the life span. But does problem-solving ability decline as well, or is that an illusion caused by the real culprit—processing speed? Salthouse has consistently stressed that the decline in *Gf* is partly a function of the well-known age-related decline in speed of performance; based on the accumulated data, processing speed probably plays a moderate to substantial role in accounting for the decline in *Gf* across the adult life span (Salthouse, 1996). Often the conclusions about speed depend on the kind of study that is conducted: The results of cross-sectional studies often suggest that processing speed accounts for much of the age-related decline in *Gf* (Verhaeghen & Salthouse, 1997); longitudinal data suggest a much more modest role for processing speed (Zimprich & Martin, 2002).

But even cross-sectional studies provide a wealth of evidence that problem-solving ability (*Gf*) declines even when speed of performance is not a factor. Doppelt and Wallace (1955) allowed a sample of adults, aged 60 and above, an unlimited amount of time to solve even the most highly speeded items on the WAIS Arithmetic subtest and on several WAIS Performance subtests (all of which allot bonus points for quick, perfect performance). Doppelt and Wallace scored the items both ways—the "correct" way, with time limits enforced, and the liberal way, with no time limits at all. The adults improved their performance only slightly on most tasks when time limits were removed, and this finding was repeated by Storandt (1977).

Another illustration: The WAIS-III includes a prototypical *Gf* subtest that wasn't on previous versions of Wechsler's scales (Matrix Reasoning). This subtest includes only untimed items, in contrast to most other WAIS-III Performance subtests, which are not only timed but often give bonus points for speed. Yet, when the mean scores, adjusted for education, were examined, the pattern of rapid, early decline on Matrix Reasoning was virtually identical to the patterns for the other highly speeded Performance subtests like Block Design and Object Assembly (Kaufman, 2000a).

Nonetheless, Salthouse (2004) insists that a decline in processing speed explains virtually all of the IQ decline in old age, even on tests that do not demand a quick response time. And, indeed, these issues are complex because speed interacts with short-term memory, as John Willis (personal communication, November 2, 2008) explains: "I think that the time issue is not the time limit on the test. The issue is not being able to finish the problem before you forget the beginning. In solving *Gf* problems, one can afford to process slowly or have a short memory span, but NOT both. As the Spanish say, 'God gives walnuts to those who no longer have teeth to crack them.' The problem with aging is the combined loss of both *Gs* and *Gsm*. I'll bet that we elderly folk would look better on a *Gf* task normed without time limits, with several practice items with feedback, and the opportunity to work as much as we want with scratch paper."

Bottom line? Speed is important, it clearly declines with advancing age (even more than fluid ability; see Figure 8.2), and it is responsible for some of the age-related decline in *Gf*. However, the loss of problem-solving ability with increasing age is a fact of life. It is real. And it likely manifests itself in many ways, as I learned in a recent study I conducted with colleagues on age changes in mean scores for ages 22–25 through 81–90 on tests of reading, math, and writing (Kaufman et al. 2008).

I was intrigued to find that reading ability did not decline significantly with age, whereas math and writing ability did. Here are the mean education-adjusted standard scores for selected age groups to illustrate these results:

Age Group	Reading	Math	Writing
22–25	102	107	104
46–55	102	102	98
81–90	97	93	91

However, further analysis showed that when the two parts of the reading test were evaluated separately, there was no age-related decline in mean scores on word reading (which measures acquired knowledge, akin to *Gc*), but there was a significant decline in reading comprehension (which requires *Gf* to understand the passages). In addition, when *Gf* was controlled, the entire age-related decrease in mean scores disappeared for math and writing (Kaufman et al., 2008). In other words, the decline in problem-solving ability and reasoning with old age also seems to affect our ability to understand what we read, how well we apply math to real-life problems, and how well we express our ideas in writing.

The degree to which a task requires *Gf* also comes back to haunt our long-term memory. The KAIT has two delayed recall tasks, both of which assess how well people remember things they learned about 30–45 minutes earlier in the testing session. One task requires individuals to remember the words and verbal concepts that were paired with symbols; the other measures their recall of facts from news stories that were "broadcast" to them by a mock newscaster. The first task requires recall of associations taught by the examiner during the Rebus Learning subtest. That subtest—illustrated in Figure 3.5—is on the KAIT *Gf* scale. The second delayed recall task demands recall of news stories heard earlier during the Auditory Comprehension subtest, which is on the KAIT *Gc* scale. Both delayed recall tasks (measures of long-term retrieval or *Glr*) are administered in exactly the same way: The examiner asks the individual, without advance warning, to remember information that was taught to her a bit earlier. When the education-adjusted mean standard scores are examined for an array of age groups between 15 and 94 years, the delayed Rebus task shows the classic vulnerable *Gf* pattern, and the delayed auditory task shows the maintained *Gc* pattern, even though both tasks measure long-term memory (A. S. Kaufman, J. C. Kaufman, Chen, & Kaufman, 1996).

One final thought—Is it possible that the lower IQs earned by older age groups in comparison with those earned by younger age groups on *Gf* tests are mostly a function of the deteriorating health (and possible dementia) of the subjects in the elderly portion standardization sample? The answer is no. The eligibility requirements for standardization samples are strict, in order to ensure that the norms are truly based on normal people. The WAIS-III, for example, excluded individuals with sensory impairments (e.g., hearing loss) or coordination problems; those who took antidepressants or antianxiety medication or had more than occasional drinks of alcohol; and those with known or possible neurological impairment (including those who went to a professional for the treatment of memory problems) (The Psychological Corporation, 1997). The fact that the steep declines in *Gf* and *Gs* (and *Gv)* occur in the face of the stringent exclusionary criteria is a testament to the consistent research results.

CAN THE AGE-RELATED DECLINES BE SLOWED DOWN OR STOPPED?

The steady declines in *Gf* and *Gs* with aging seem pretty inevitable. Aging attacks elderly people equally, whether they are eminent academics or blue-collar workers (Christensen, Henderson, Griffiths, & Levings, 1997). It shows no mercy to Berkeley professors (Shimamura, Berry, Mangels, Rusting & Jurica, 1995). Christensen et al. (1997) concluded that the rate of decline is the same, regardless of how high your IQ is, and that cognitive deterioration on nonverbal IQ tests is universal. Yes, those eminent academics earned substantially higher IQs at all ages than did blue-collar workers. But the rate of decline was the same. And, as with any group finding, there are individual differences in the amount of decline. Yet it is not clear just which lifestyle variables are most important for slowing the decline.

A variety of cross-sectional studies have been conducted, leading to the general conclusion that participation in physical, social, and intellectual activities is associated with higher IQs (Hultsch, Hertzog, Small, & Dixon, 1999). Longitudinal research suggests that the following factors are associated with strong mental functioning in old age: pursuing a great deal of environmental stimulation, continuing formal and informal education throughout the life span, and having stimulating work experiences as a young adult (Schaie, 1984, 1996).

But none of those studies, cross-sectional or longitudinal, demonstrate cause and effect, because the studies tend to be confounded with SES and education. It is just as likely that adults who were brighter initially pursued a stimulating lifestyle, rather than the other way around. Probably the best study for inferring causality is the Victoria Longitudinal Study of 250 middle-aged and older adults who were tested three times in 6 years (when the study began, the sample contained 487 adults, aged 55–86) (Hultsch et al., 1999). The study measured the adults' verbal abilities, memory, and processing speed, and also assessed their lifestyle, namely their degree of participation in activities that emphasized physical fitness, socializing, and intellectual pursuits (e.g., learning a new language, playing bridge, doing crossword puzzles).

The *good news* is as follows:

- The study was well designed and well controlled.
- Engaging in intellectual activities was significantly associated with improved intellectual functioning.

The *bad news* is as follows:

- Engaging in social and physical activities was *not* significantly associated with improved intellectual functioning (unless the social activity was also intellectual, for example, playing scrabble).

- By and large, Hultsch and colleagues' many hypotheses about the potential importance of health, personality, and lifestyle variables for maintaining IQ were *not* supported.
- They failed to include any intellectual measures of *Gf*.
- Subsequent statistical analyses were just as supportive of the hypothesis that intelligent people lead stimulating lives as of the reverse hypothesis, that stimulating lives increase intelligence.

PRACTICAL IMPLICATIONS OF THE AGING-IQ RESEARCH

So where does that leave us? Without research-based guidelines on how to age gracefully. Without evidence that the roller-coaster ride of decreasing *Gf, Gv,* or *Gs* that stalks us as we age can be derailed or slowed down. With evidence that we are likely to improve our knowledge base between adolescence and adulthood, and maintain it through age 75 or so, before *Gc* finally joins *Gf* in a downward spiral. There is evidence from a large-scale longitudinal study in Scotland that childhood intelligence at age 11 predicts functional independence in old age, as well as longevity, frailty, and death from various types of cancer and cardiovascular disease (Deary et al., 2004). We can predict life and death, but not how to avoid declines in IQ as we age.

What should we do? Understand the research so we can anticipate a decline in problem-solving ability in middle age, and probably an even greater decline in old age. Recognize that we do get wiser and more knowledgeable as we age, at least for a time. Seek out activities and challenges that capitalize on *Gc* abilities—for example, writing, reading, attending lectures and workshops, participating in book clubs, digging deeper into topics you know well, doing challenging volunteer work, and using your maintained abilities to learn new and unfamiliar material. But at the same time that you prepare yourself for the decline in solving new problems, you need to recognize that every *group* finding simply describes the average person. There are always *individual* differences, so why can't you be the one whose decline is gradual or nonexistent?

And though the research on how to maintain your IQ is meager, the significant findings have a commonsense validity, even without a definitive causality. If you are middle-aged or elderly, go to lectures, take continuing education courses, engage in intellectually stimulating activities, keep active. Try Sudoku, which depends, at least to some extent, on *Gf*. Continue to try new things, no matter how challenging and different from things you've done in the past. But give yourself a break. If you have difficulty catching on to the new software, or card game, or musical instrument, don't let it damage your ego. Keep at it and allow yourself a little extra time to succeed, even if you've always been a quick study. And if you are young, you won't think it can ever happen to you. But be patient with elderly people—especially your grandparents!—when they have difficulty learning new things, remembering old things, or understanding the simple thing you are trying to teach them.

9

Hot Topic—IQ Tests in the Public Forum: Lead Level, Learning Disabilities, and IQ

IQ tests do not reside only in the domains of psychology and education. They are woven into the fabric of our society and often resonate in the public forum. The Flynn Effect can determine whether a convicted criminal will live or die (see chapter 7), in an outgrowth of the 2002 Supreme Court ruling in the case of *Daryl Adkins v. Virginia* (536 U.S. 304). The Court ruled that the death penalty is unconstitutional for offenders with mental retardation, and the "3-points-per-decade" correction for a test's outdated norms can make all the difference in whether a low-functioning criminal is diagnosed with an intellectual disability.

And the U.S. court system is alive with other public issues that may not be matters of life and death but that surely qualify as hot topics. I have chosen two of these topics to illustrate the role that IQ tests play in our everyday lives. First, does a little bit of lead in a child's blood lead to IQ loss, brain damage, and even delinquency? And second, are IQ tests completely irrelevant to the diagnosis of specific learning disabilities in children and adolescents? The first topic has been the subject of great controversy over what should be considered a safe blood lead level and has been the focus of a huge number of multimillion and even billion dollar lawsuits. The second topic has centered on the law known as IDEA 2004, dealing with the best methods for identifying children with specific learning disabilities, and has brought to the forefront a group of vocal anti–IQ testing professionals and politicians who would love to witness the public execution of IQ tests.

HOW DANGEROUS IS A LITTLE BIT OF LEAD?

Lead is an environmental toxin. A blood lead level at or above 70 micrograms per deciliter (μg/dl) is considered a medical emergency, and there is evidence that acute lead poisoning (>80 μg/dl) can produce damage to brain tissue (Goldstein, 1984). Levels of 45 μg/dl are often the cut-off point for administering a chemical treatment called chelation that is designed to rapidly reduce the body's blood lead level. Clearly, moderately high or high blood lead levels may have neuropsychological consequences. The potential health implications of lead are well known. Fortunately, the environmental sources of lead have been regulated; this has resulted, for example, in the removal of lead from paint in 1978 and the phasing out of lead in gasoline beginning in 1973. The regulatory changes occurred in part due to the level of lead that the

Centers for Disease Control and Prevention (CDC) considered to be dangerous. "Between 1960 and 1990 the blood lead level for individual intervention in children was lowered from 60 µg/dL to 25 µg/dL. In 1991 the CDC recommended lowering the level for individual intervention to 15 µg/dL and implementing community wide primary lead poisoning prevention activities in areas where many children have BLLs >10 µg/dL" (CDC, 2005, p. 2).

What Does the Research Say About Low Levels of Blood Lead?

Since 1991, the CDC has considered 10 µg/dL to be the level of concern, although some recent researchers have claimed that no level is safe (e.g., Canfield et al., 2003; Lanphear et al., 2005). Most of the research since the early 1980s has targeted the so-called low lead levels of 10–20 µg/dL as being particularly harmful to children's intelligence and behaviors, and there is considerable controversy on this topic. What has the research shown? Three meta-analyses have been conducted on the topic of low lead levels and IQ loss, where lead level has been measured in children's teeth, bones, or blood (Needleman & Gatsonis, 1990; Pocock, Smith, & Baghurst, 1994; Schwartz, 1994). The researchers for each meta-analysis first selected the best-designed studies and then aggregated the results from these studies in order to offer an overview of the findings.

What distinguishes the best-designed studies? They are the ones that did the best job of controlling for confounding variables. The early research in the 1970s typically reported substantial IQ loss based on low to moderate lead levels (e.g., Kotok, 1972; Landrigan, Balow, Whitworth, Staeling, & Rosenbloom, 1975), but these findings were suspect because the studies failed to control for important, potentially confounding variables such as socioeconomic status (SES) and parents' IQ. These variables are known to be significantly associated with *both* lead level *and* children's IQs, and, therefore, confound the results of the study if they are not controlled.

We've already seen how markedly SES and parents' IQs relate to children's IQs. But these variables also have been shown to relate to children's lead levels as well (e.g., Ernhart, Morrow-Tlucak, Wolf, Super, & Drotar, 1989); the children of parents with lower education and intelligence have higher blood lead levels, on average, than the children of better-educated and more intelligent parents. The higher lead levels may be related to parenting skills (e.g., better supervision by more intelligent parents), to the greater availability of deteriorated paint in lower socioeconomic homes, or any number of reasons. The important thing is that confounding variables must be controlled, and controlled well, in order to interpret the results of research studies. The finding that blood lead is related to IQ loss, by itself, is not meaningful unless parents' IQs, SES, and other confounding variables (e.g., mothers taking drugs or alcohol while pregnant) are controlled. Otherwise, these other variables might be the culprits that are responsible for the apparent IQ loss, and not lead level at all.

Pocock et al. (1994) concluded from their meta-analysis, "Overall synthesis of this evidence, including a meta-analysis, indicates that a typical doubling of body lead burden (from 10 to 20 mg/dl…) is associated with a mean deficit in full-scale IQ of around 1–2 IQ points" (p. 1189). When factoring in the results of the other two meta-analyses (Needleman & Gatsonis, 1990; Schwartz, 1994), and the findings of well-designed studies conducted in the last 15 years, the most reasonable synthesis is that low lead levels are associated with an IQ loss of about 1 to 3 points. But I am not convinced that the association is causal. And even if it is causal, I don't believe the audacious statements made by some lead researchers about the dangers of a little bit of lead in an infant's blood.

How Do the Lead-Level Researchers Interpret Their Results?

Some of the more outspoken lead researchers not only emphasize an *extreme* loss of IQ but also argue that even low levels of blood lead are likely a direct cause of poor school achievement in high school (Fergusson, Horwood, & Lynskey, 1997), brain damage (Lidsky & Schneider, 2006), ADHD (Braun, Kahn, Froelich, Auinger, & Lanphear, 2006), and juvenile delinquency (Needleman, Riess, Tobin, Biesecker, & Greenhouse, 1996). Hebben (2001) stated that "As a neuropsychologist who is often called upon to evaluate children with low lead levels in the forensic area, I never cease to be surprised by the opinions of the opposing experts. In my experience, I have seen low lead level 'causally' linked to mental retardation (even in the face of serious birth injury), autism, [and] specific arithmetic disability" (p. 355).

Why am I so skeptical? I have carefully reviewed the literature on the relationship of low lead level to IQ loss, ADHD, brain damage, poor school achievement, delinquency, and the like, and even the best studies have serious flaws that compromise their validity (Kaufman, 2001a, 2001b). In addition, like Nancy Hebben, I have entered the forensic arena and have seen neuropsychologists and pediatricians claim—with no research support whatsoever—that a small amount of lead was a "significant contributing factor" (to use the legal vernacular) to brain damage, low intellectual functioning, attention deficits, learning disabilities, emotional disturbance, and delinquency in numerous children and adolescents in countless families who were raised in utter poverty by violent and abusive parents, and who skipped school more often than not.

Weaknesses in the Lead Literature

Let me turn to my review of the lead-IQ literature (Kaufman, 2001a), which served as the centerpiece of a special issue of *Archives of Clinical Neuropsychology* and which was rebutted by leading psychologists, including several who conducted some of the lead-IQ studies reviewed. I was then given the opportunity to respond to the critiques of my article (Kaufman, 2001b). In the initial article, I was targeting the 26 "best" studies, the ones that were included in at least one of the three meta-analyses, but my conclusions apply just as well to the studies conducted in the decade and a half since the meta-analyses were published. Three of these criticisms illustrate my concerns about the quality of the research (Kaufman, 2001a), concerns that I elaborated on in my response article (Kaufman, 2001b):

- *Uncontrolled variables cloud the conclusions drawn from even the best studies.* The studies of lead and IQ were included in the meta-analyses if they controlled for SES and other important variables. As we've seen, parental behaviors differ by social class and even from one identical twin to the other (Grigorenko & Carter, 1996), and they relate directly to their children's IQs (Figures 6.1 to 6.3). Adequate measures of home environment exist, most notably the Home Observation for Measurement of the Environment (HOME) Inventory (Caldwell & Bradley, 1984), which requires an observer to go to the child's home and observe the interaction between the parent and child, ask questions of the parent, and observe the environment (e.g., the number of books in the home). This type of measurement is essential in the effort to control for the confounding variable of SES in the lead-IQ studies. Global measures of SES, such as parental education or occupation, are not sufficient to truly control for the SES. Nonetheless, only 14 of the 26 studies made an effort to obtain any type of specific information about parenting: Nine of the 26 teams of investigators administered the HOME inventory and 5 other teams interviewed the parent in an attempt to obtain information about parent-child interactions, parenting styles, and so forth. The other 12 studies relied on global indexes of SES. In addition, most studies failed to control for a variety of other potential confounding variables, such as the commonplace infant illness of otitis media (ear infections), which has been shown in some studies to relate meaningfully to language ability (Teele, Klein, & Rosner, 1984), intelligence (Teele, Klein, Chase, Menyuk, & Rosner, 1990), and reading ability (Teele et al., 1990; Updike & Thornburg, 1992). Yet only 2 of the 26 studies specifically controlled for persistent otitis media or illnesses affecting sensory function (Ernhart et al., 1989; Hatzakis et al., 1989). Also, of the 26 studies, only 8 either specifically controlled for pregnancy risk factors in general or even controlled for maternal smoking. In short, the failure of most researchers to control for variables such as children's medical problems or prenatal care challenges the validity of the 1–3 IQ points allegedly lost due to low lead levels.

- *Parental IQ is typically measured poorly or not at all.* In view of the known relationship between the parent's IQ and the child's IQ (see Table 6.1), lead researchers have become aware that one of the strongest correlates both of IQ and lead level is parental IQ, a potential confounding variable that must be controlled for in lead-IQ studies. Nevertheless, 8 of the 26 studies failed to measure parental IQ and an additional 8 studies measured it poorly (either with a brief picture vocabulary test or a group-administered test of verbal ability). The most common brief test administered to parents was the Peabody Picture Vocabulary Test—Revised (PPVT-R; Dunn & Dunn, 1981), a one-subtest measure. The test authors state in the test manual that "The PPVT-R is designed primarily to measure a subject's receptive (hearing) vocabulary.... It is not, however, a comprehensive test of general intelligence" (p. 2). In addition, each PPVT-R item is a four-option multiple-choice question, which allows chance guessing to play a potentially large role in a person's obtained score. The range of correlations with global IQ is unusually large for the PPVT-R (Robertson & Eisenberg, 1981, Table 4.4). Correlations with IQ commonly dip below .40 in PPVT-R studies, and sometimes below .20. In addition, the coefficients have tended to be lowest for samples of low SES children, a prototypical sample in the lead-IQ studies. And only a single study systematically tested both fathers and mothers (Lansdown, Yule, Urbanowicz, & Hunter, 1986), although genetic data indicate that children's IQs correlate .42 with one parent's IQ as against .50 with the average of both parents' IQs (Vandenberg & Vogler, 1985). The failure to properly control for at least one parent's IQ in many of the best lead-IQ studies is a serious shortcoming of these investigations, and at least one of the major lead researchers (Gail Wasserman) agrees with me: "Poorly measured parental intelligence results in poor control for this potentially confounding variable; such poor control may spuriously increase the association between lead and IQ" (Wasserman & Factor-Litvak, 2001, p. 346).

- *There is a lack of quality control in measuring children's IQs.* Clinical, individually administered IQ tests such as Wechsler's scales, the Kaufman tests, and the Binet-5 are not like most other kinds of tests used in research investigations. The clinical tests should not be administered by examiners who lack the proper clinical training. Even research assistants who are provided with specific in-depth training prior to the data collection are not qualified to administer tests such as Wechsler's scales. The WISC-III manual (Wechsler, 1991) explains this point as it applies to all clinical IQ tests: "Because of the complexities of test administration, diagnosis, and assessment, examiners who use the WISC-III should have training and experience in the administration and interpretation of standardized, clinical instruments, such as the WISC-R or other Wechsler intelligence scales. They should also have experience in testing children whose ages, linguistic backgrounds, and clinical, cultural, or educational histories are similar to those of the children they will be testing" (p. 10). Unfortunately, from my personal knowledge of large-scale research projects, it is common for inexperienced examiners to be used to collect IQ data in research studies. It is important for any study that uses an individually administered IQ test, such as Wechsler's scales, to indicate the qualifications of the examiners and to incorporate some type of quality control to ensure the accuracy of the data. Yet these procedures are rarely followed, even in the best lead-IQ studies. Winneke, Brockhaus, Ewers, Kramer, and Neuf (1990) used thorough quality assurance procedures "to improve the comparability of the psychological test data" (p. 555), in a notable contrast to the lack of attention given to this crucial validity variable by most other lead-IQ research teams. Of the 26 studies, seven studies failed to demonstrate any type of awareness that individually administered IQ tests demand carefully trained professionals to obtain valid data (in contrast, they often listed pediatricians, nurses, and other health personnel for various medical procedures, even the drawing of blood). Some lead-IQ researchers take issue with my claims (Needleman & Bellinger, 2001): "It would be more accurate to say that the methods used to establish and monitor the quality of these measurements are not fully reported" (p. 365). Others are more willing to agree with me and concede that quality control is a serious issue: "Kaufman correctly points out that many of the studies do not report quality control assessments for key measured variables. This is unfortunately common and inexcusable in clinical epidemiology" (Wasserman & Factor-Litvak, 2001, p. 350).

Research Studies and Public Policy

Despite the methodological shortcomings of even the best lead-IQ studies, these investigations have been used to set public policy, establishing low lead levels as a menace to the neuropsychological development of young children. The guidelines proposed by the Environmental Protection Agency (EPA) on the identification of dangerous lead levels (Federal Register, 1998) read as follows: "EPA assigns risk reduction value to fractional losses of an IQ point—tenths and even hundredths of a point" (p. 30320); and "The computation of IQ point loss is based on an average decrease of 0.257 IQ points per increase of one ug/dL in blood-lead concentration" (p. 30321). Or, from an earlier document: "preventing a one ug/dL increase in a 1 year old child's blood lead level saves $1493 . . . in lifetime earnings" (Federal Register, 1996, p. 29103).

Needleman (1989) argued that low blood lead levels will result "in a fourfold increase in the rate of severe deficit (IQ < 80). . . . [Also,] 5 percent of lead-exposed children are prevented from achieving truly superior function (IQ > 125)" (p. 643). This inevitable downward shift in the IQs of children will have a societal impact (Nation & Gleaves, 2001; Needleman & Bellinger, 2001), burdening society with the need to provide increased special education services for the increased numbers of low-functioning children (Needleman, 1989). The proclamations in federal guidelines and by some researchers often focus on fractions of an IQ point, which are meaningless in view of the errors of measurement inherent in any IQ test (as discussed in detail in chapter 5). Indeed, even the alleged IQ loss of 1–3 points due to low levels of lead, as found in the meta-analyses, is well within the standard error of measurement, rendering the claims of societal impact a little over the top.

Further, global IQs are emphasized, even though the field of clinical assessment has switched to the interpretation of profiles of specific cognitive abilities and processes (chapter 3). And the need for referral to special education services is treated as if diagnosis is based solely on global IQ instead of on a variety of tests (IQ plus adaptive behavior in the case of intellectual disabilities; see chapter 4). Finally, the researchers give little or no credence to methodological arguments that the studies of lead level and IQ have a number of shortcomings that make it uncertain whether there really is a loss of a few IQ points due to low levels of lead (Hebben, 2001; Kaufman, 2001a, 2001b; Phelps, 1999). Nonetheless, I need to add that some respected researchers (Needleman & Bellinger, 2001) strongly disagree with me: "Kaufman takes issue with the thesis that lead at low dose will increase the need for special services.…The shift in [IQ] distribution across the entire range is more than a theoretical concept; it is an empirical fact" (pp. 366–367).

Apart from the possible societal consequences of a couple of points of IQ loss (which I still believe is far-fetched), the height of absurdity comes from interpreting *fractions* of IQ points as meaningful. I once gave a talk before the California Air Resources Board (Kaufman, 1997). At that hearing, there was deep concern about children's diminished cognitive functioning due to the loss of *less than one-tenth of 1 IQ point* because of lead dust in the air: "Applying the mean changes to the cohort of 4.73 million children in California below age 7..., the current ambient concentration of 0.06 μg/dl relates to an average loss of 0.08 IQ points" (Ostro , Mann, Collins, Vance, & Alexeef, 1996, p. 5–10). Or consider the following: "Using this slope coefficient [of 0.245 IQ points per μg/dl], we can estimate that a permanent reduction in blood lead concentrations of 1 μg/dl will produce a net present value benefit of $1300 per child for the cohort turning 6 years of age each year, for a total benefit of $5.06 billion per year" (Schwartz, 1994, p. 114).

Lead Levels That Are Lower Than Low

But all of these arguments pale in comparison to the contemporary emphasis on the alleged dangers of lead levels *below* 10 μg/dl. Several recent research studies have claimed that the loss in IQ points is even *greater* below 10 μg/dl than at the low levels of 10–20 μg/dl or even in the 20s and 30s (Canfield et al., 2003; Lanphear et al., 2005). However, these studies have methodological flaws just as serious as those of the previous body of research. For example, the two main studies in support of the claim are, to a large extent, based on analysis of data from the *same sample,* instead of from completely separate samples (i.e., two thirds of the children with lead levels below 7.5 μg/dl in the Lanphear et al. study were also included in the Canfield et al. study). In addition, the large IQ loss attributed to lead levels below 10 μg/dl was not replicated in some subsequent studies (e.g., Kordas et al., 2006). Even more compelling, the entire relationship between IQ loss and very low lead levels is conceivably nothing more than a statistical artifact of the specific statistical procedure the studies employed, having nothing to do with the relationship of lead level and IQ (Bowers & Beck, 2006).

None of these scientific cautions have prevented some neuropsychologists from making blatantly outlandish claims of the IQ loss that is sure to accompany a tiny amount of blood lead: "there is a loss of 7–8 points in Full Scale IQ as blood lead level increases [from zero] to 10 μg/dl and at least an additional 1–3-point decrement as the blood lead level reaches 20 μg/dl. The magnitude of this loss is substantial, amounting to about two-thirds of a standard deviation" (Lidsky & Schneider, 2006, p. 285).

That is unadulterated scientific baloney. The role of lead level in affecting children's IQ is small relative to the powerful impact of other variables (genetics, home environment, other aspects of SES). According to the CDC, the best estimate of lead level's contribution to children's IQs is 1%–3% (CDC, 2002, p. 83). Figure 9.1 puts that percentage in perspective, something that is lacking in Lidsky and Schneider's "two-thirds of a standard deviation" claim.

Low Lead Levels and Delinquency

Also without basis are the strong claims that low lead levels cause juvenile delinquency (Dietrich, Ris, Succop, Berger, & Bornschein,

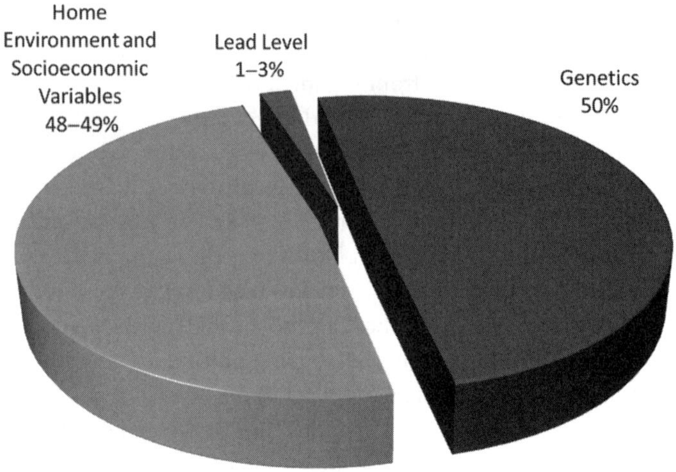

FIGURE 9.1 Heredity, environment, lead level, and IQ.

2001; Needleman et al., 1996). The few studies conducted on the topic of delinquency have even more flaws than the lead-IQ studies. For example, the researchers in the delinquency investigations are content to conclude that low levels of lead cause juvenile delinquency even though they made no attempt to measure or otherwise control for the obvious confounding variable of *parents' antisocial behaviors* (Ernhart, 1996).

Another Toxin That Has Entered the Public Arena—PCBs

And the overstatements by environmental toxin researchers do not begin and end with lead. Another set of toxins that has been widely researched is polychlorinated biphenyls (PCBs), synthetic hydrocarbon compounds once used as insulating materials in electrical transformers and capacitors. Exposure to PCBs comes mainly from mothers eating fish (owing to the dumping of industrial waste in the water) and passing on the PCBs to their infants while pregnant. As with lead, there is no question that PCBs are toxins. And, also as with lead, the main question is whether the small amount of PCBs that goes through the placenta is sufficient to cause IQ loss and other types of neuropsychological deficits. The body of research on PCBs is far weaker than the research on lead level, and the shortcomings of the studies are vast.

My colleagues at Yale University's Child Study Center, Drs. Dom Cicchetti and Sara Sparrow, joined me in writing a careful evaluation of the PCB literature that served as the centerpiece of a special issue of *Psychology in the Schools* (Cicchetti et al., 2004b). PCB researchers and other top scientists wrote responses to our article and we responded to their criticisms (Cicchetti et al., 2004a). This fairly weak set of studies has also been used to set public policy, and, as in the lead literature, the researchers tend to exaggerate the potential dangers of PCBs (e.g., Jacobson & Jacobson, 1996; Vreugdenhil, Lanting, Mulder, Boersma, & Weisglas-Kuperus, 2002).

Bottom Line

Why do I care so much about the claims made by researchers about the neuropsychological effects of small amounts of lead or PCBs in children's blood? Partly because they are bad science. Partly because parents of children with low lead levels, or parents who have eaten too much fish from a "contaminated" lake (like Lake Michigan) can be frightened, or made to feel guilty, when they hear about the evils of small amounts of toxins. Research is based on *group* data, and the results are then applied to *individuals,* a shaky practice at best. Holly Ruff (1999), who has conducted research on the effects of lead, asks, "why do parents, lawyers, and other concerned parties usually think of research results as relevant to individuals?" (p. 43). She also shares my concern about frightening the parents of exposed children, objecting to the way in which research results are sometimes presented to the public, especially with regard to the need to counsel the parents of children with slight lead elevations who have been scared by newspaper reports of the irreversible dangers of low blood lead (Ruff, 1999). And what about the persistent reports of the terrible dangers of lead that we hear about on CNN and read about on the Internet whenever lead is reported to be found in a child's toy or artificial grass or clay pottery or the dust in an old apartment building? Yes, as parents we need to be cautious and make sure that our children and grandchildren are living in as lead-free an environment as possible. But we don't need to panic when we find out that one of our kin may have been exposed to a little bit of lead.

In my response to the psychologists who critiqued my review of the lead literature, I wrote the following, which takes a *common sense* look at the allegedly great dangers of a small amount of lead (Kaufman, 2001b):

> How did all of us who are writing articles for this special issue ever make it successfully into the 21st century in view of the mean BLLs [blood lead levels] in the US that were found to be 58 μg/dL

> in 1935..., around 30 μg/dl from the late 1930s to the mid-1950s...and about 20 μg/dL during the decade of the 1960s...? By way of contrast, the mean BLL in the US for the population ages 1 year and older in 1991–1994...was 2.3 μg/dl, with a mean of 2.7 μg/dl obtained for children ages 1–5 years. (p. 424)

And I wrote that *before* there was any talk about the even greater danger of lead levels below 10 μg/dl!

But common sense is not always followed. Some of the lead-IQ researchers are persuasive speakers and are occasionally almost evangelical in their belief that the results of their studies (which they perceive to be rock-solid) must translate to public policy. The California Environmental Protection Agency (EPA) "proposes a benchmark incremental change in blood lead of 1 μg/dl as a new child-specific health guidance value for lead for use in health risk assessment at school sites.... [It] is not an absolutely safe exposure level, since no safe level has been definitively established.... [It] is estimated to decrease IQ by 1 point" (Carlisle & Dowling, 2007, p. 21). A formula that attributes 1 point of IQ loss for each μg/dl of lead in the blood, starting with 1 μg/dl, would estimate a 20-point IQ loss for a child with a lead level 20 μg/dl. That is a preposterous conclusion from a research base that has supported (via meta-analyses) only a 1–3 point loss as a child's blood lead increases from 10 to 20 μg/dl.

Currently, the most important public policies are based on a sophisticated understanding of the research, including the studies of lead levels below 10 μg/dl. The CDC (2005, 2007) has resisted reducing the level of concern below the value of 10 μg/dl that was set in 1991. The CDC does accept the notion that "Research conducted since 1991 has strengthened the evidence that children's physical and mental development can be affected at BLLs < 10 μg/dL" (CDC, 2007, p. 1). However, the CDC remains cautious in its approach. In contrast to Lidsky and Schneider's (2006) one-size-fits-all bold assertions about IQ loss at levels below 10 μg/dL, the CDC (2005) states that "The adverse health effects associated with elevated BLLs are subtle. Individual variation in response to exposure, and other influences on developmental status, make isolating the effect of lead or predicting the overall magnitude of potential adverse health effects exceedingly difficult" (CDC, 2005, p. 2). Further, the CDC urges clinicians to "understand the laboratory error range for blood lead values" (CDC, 2007, p. 1) because lead levels, like IQs, have a standard error of measurement that is surprisingly large, and also encourages clinicians "to obtain an environmental history on all children they examine" (CDC, 2007, p. 1), acknowledging that "The child's family and personal psychosocial experiences are strongly associated with performance on neurodevelopment measures and account for a greater proportion of the explained variance in these measures than BLLs < 10 μg/dL" (CDC, 2007, p. 4).

The American Academy of Pediatrics (AAP) has likewise been appropriately cautious, recommending the funding of "studies to confirm or refute the finding that blood lead concentrations of less than 10 μg /dL are associated with lower IQ" (AAP, 2005, p. 1044). Although these further studies have not yet been conducted, the AAP may soon change its tune to bring itself into lockstep with the California EPA in declaring lead levels as low as 1 μg/dL to be hazardous to a child's health. At least that is a feasible outcome if the testimony before Congress of Dr. Dana Best, a member of the AAP Committee on Environmental Health (Best, 2007), is heeded—even in the face of a lack of solid scientific support.

ARE IQ TESTS WORTHLESS FOR DIAGNOSING SPECIFIC LEARNING DISABILITIES?

Even if we don't actually realize it, we all know people who have a learning disability. They usually have normal intelligence, sometimes even well above average, but cannot learn to read or write or do math very well. What are learning disabilities and how should they be identified? That's where many of today's professionals diverge to such an extent that opposing political factions are trying to shape the future on a state-by-state basis. The main battlegrounds are state departments of education and school systems throughout the nation. The combatants in this vocal, emotional, energetic "I-know-what's-best-for-children" war are, among other things, arguing over the fate of IQ tests for identifying children as having a learning disability.

The controversy has raged within the educational and psychological literature, the courts of law, and the legislature ever since the passage of the Right to Education for All Handicapped Children's Act of 1975. That landmark law, which safeguarded the right of handicapped children to be educated in the least restrictive environment, also provided the first federal guidelines for diagnosing children with learning disabilities. The law was revised and reauthorized twice in the 1990s, but the provisions for identifying children with learning disabilities remained virtually unchanged. That's no longer true, with the latest reauthorization of the law, known as the Individuals With Disabilities Educational Improvement Act of 2004 (sometimes called IDEIA 2004, but usually referred to as IDEA 2004). The ground rules for diagnosing children with a learning disability were modified dramatically, and the war on the relevance of IQ tests for identifying children with learning disabilities was underway. But before I describe the nature of the artillery on both sides, I want to provide a bit of background information.

Brief History of Learning Disabilities

Accounts of individuals with unexplainable problems in specific academic skills began to appear in the medical literature in Europe more than a century ago. Dejerine (1892) wrote about an adult patient who lost the ability to read following a stroke, even though he could speak and write fluently, remember details, and quickly grasp things that were told to him. Dr. W. Pringle

Morgan's (1896) description of a 14-year-old nonreader, Percy F., hits home to anyone who has had a child or student or friend with a learning disability: "I might add that the boy is bright and of average intelligence in conversation. . . . The schoolmaster who has taught him for some years says that he would be the smartest lad in school if the instruction were entirely oral" (p. 1378). There followed case histories of clear-cut instances of children or adults with learning disabilities specific to reading and writing (e.g., Kerr, 1897) and, later on, specific to arithmetic (Schmitt, 1921).

James Hinshelwood (1895), an ophthalmologist, was initially intrigued by an adult patient who could not read following specific brain injury. However, he soon became even more fascinated by the accounts published by physicians (himself included) of 14 cases in Europe and North America of children and adolescents with reading disorders that were apparently present at birth with no evidence of brain injury (Spreen, 2001). Hinshelwood (1917) published a popular monograph, *Congenital Word Blindness,* that told about these children, for example, a 12-year-old boy who was brought by his mother to have his eyesight checked: "He could barely read by sight more than two or three words, but came to a standstill every second or third word. . . . [But he] read all combinations of figures with the greatest of fluency up to millions" (p. 21).

Samuel Orton (1937) coined the term *strephosymbolia* (twisted symbols) to describe children with reading disorders who had special difficulties, as they reversed letters and words, the kinds of transpositions that suggested to Orton that these children read from right to left. Orton's clinical descriptions of children with *dyslexia* (as the reading disorder came to be known) were thorough and insightful. He was a firm believer in clinical assessment, featuring IQ tests, achievement tests, family histories, and school histories. He observed that many children with dyslexia were male; that most also had speech and coordination problems; that he often treated several members of the same family; and that the academic difficulties were life-long.

To Orton and Hinshelwood, the problem was a developmental disorder in reading or writing or arithmetic (or a combination of these specific academic areas) that was presumed to be caused by some type of brain dysfunction. The specific disabilities appeared in children who had normal intelligence and normal achievement in the nonaffected academic areas. And, for both men, the best type of intervention was to teach the child directly in the weak academic skill—if the problem was in math or writing, then find the best way to teach the child math or writing; if the problem was in reading, then use a phonics approach (using sound-symbol relationships) to remediate the disability.

Perhaps we wouldn't have so many controversies today about identifying students with learning disabilities if the Hinshelwood-Orton history of learning disabilities was *the* history. Then we would think of learning disabilities as developmental disorders in academic skills (like reading, writing, or arithmetic). We would need to identify the child's normal or "spared" abilities. And we would need to determine the best way to capitalize on these normal abilities to teach the child to read, write, or do math—despite the presumed brain dysfunction that led to the learning disability in the first place.

But a second history of specific learning disability (SLD) that developed alongside the first is—in many ways—opposite to the Hinshelwood-Orton approach, even incompatible with it. This second history is rooted firmly in the field of adult brain damage. As I have written elsewhere (Kaufman, 2008),

> The history of SLD is not a linear or chronological one but rather an uneasy amalgam of two traditions that are conceptually distinct and seemingly resistant to integration. The Goldstein-Strauss-Werner history—based initially on Kurt Goldstein's (1942) studies of the perceptual, cognitive, attentional, and mood disorders of soldiers who sustained head injuries—emphasizes disorders of perception, especially visual perception. Indeed, it is the deficit in perceptual processing that is considered the specific learning *disability* (there is

> no room in this model for specific learning *disabilities*) (p. 1).... The Goldstein-Strauss-Werner theory posited that a disorder of visual perception, along with the concomitant attentional problems, impairs learning on tasks that depend on perception and attention. Fix the perceptual disorder of these brain-damaged individuals (in a learning environment that reduces distraction and inattention), and you have fixed the learning problem (pp. 2–3).[1]

Goldstein's student, Alfred Strauss, extended the theory from adults with head injuries to adolescents with the kind of intellectual disability that was known to be caused by brain injury (Strauss & Werner, 1943). Strauss joined with an educator, Laura Lehtinen, to develop methods to remediate the disability through perceptual training (e.g., teaching figure-ground relationships, having people copy squares and diamonds) (Strauss & Lehtinen, 1947). Next, researchers brought the theory from adults and adolescents with brain damage to children with known brain damage (those with cerebral palsy) (Cruickshank, Bice, & Wallen, 1957). The key trigger for the SLD field, though, came when Goldstein's original work with head-injured soldiers was ultimately applied to children who experienced learning and behavior problems but showed no clinical signs of brain damage.

Thus was born the alternate historical root of SLD—children with *minimal brain dysfunction* who demonstrate a processing disorder (usually in visual perception), with problems in school learning and with behavior problems, such as poor attention span, distractibility, and mood disorders. This approach to SLD proliferated in the 1960s, with thousands of children being treated for their learning disability by spending hours each day copying designs, connecting dots, and learning to distinguish the figure from the ground in a design—instead of being directly taught to read, write, or calculate.

1. Quoted with permission of the publisher, John Wiley & Sons.

Unfortunately, subsequent reviews of 81 research studies, encompassing hundreds of statistical comparisons, concluded that "none of the treatments was particularly effective in stimulating cognitive, linguistic, academic, or school readiness abilities and that there was a serious question as to whether the training activities even have value for enhancing visual perception and/or motor skills in children" (Hammill & Bartel, 1978, p. 371). But the negative research results did not stop the perceptual training in the schools for quite some time. Moreover, several influential special educators who have studied SLD history (e.g., Torgesen, 1998) believe that the Goldstein-Strauss-Werner method—more than the Hinshelwood-Orton approach—"influenced the definition of 'specific learning disability' in federal laws and also influenced US public school practices" (Shepherd, 2001, p. 5).

SLD was known variously as dyslexia, learning disorder, perceptual disorder, and minimal brain dysfunction, and bore a variety of other labels, until noted special educator Samuel Kirk attempted to unify the diverse approaches to and definitions of the same disorder (Kaufman, 2008):

> Kirk (1963) coined the term *learning disabilities* when he delivered a speech to a large group of parents whose children were having school difficulties and to a smaller group of professionals with a keen interest in the topic. All were seeking a label for these children that Kirk referred to as having "developmental deficits of one kind or another" (which encompasses developmental disorders of both perception and written language). Kirk's label had a decided educational flavor, focusing on the nature of the problem rather than the hypothesized cause, and it was the precursor for the federal definitions and laws of the late 1960s and 1970s that proclaimed *specific learning disabilities* as a disorder that entitled...anyone with a SLD diagnosis [to special education services]. When reading the text of Kirk's (1963) speech, it is clear that his notion of learning disabilities was more aligned with Hinshelwood-Orton than Goldstein-Strauss-Werner as he referred to "a group of children who have disorders in development in language, speech, reading

and associated communication skills needed for social interaction" (p. 3). However, like the perceptual theorists, Kirk stressed that the disorder involved a processing disorder (Kaufman, 2008, pp. 5–6).[2]

The Federal Definition of SLD

The federal definition of SLD that built upon Kirk's attempt to integrate the field of SLD first appeared in the Children With Specific Learning Disabilities Act of 1969. The definition had three parts:

- The term "specific learning disability" means a disorder in one or more of the basic psychological processes involved in understanding or in using language, spoken or written, which disorder may manifest itself in imperfect ability to listen, think, speak, read, write, spell, or do mathematical calculations.
- DISORDERS INCLUDED—Such term includes such conditions as perceptual disabilities, brain injury, minimal brain dysfunction, dyslexia, and developmental aphasia.
- DISORDERS NOT INCLUDED—Such term does not include a learning problem that is primarily the result of visual, hearing, or motor disabilities, of mental retardation, of emotional disturbance, or of environmental, cultural, or economic disadvantage.

This same definition of SLD reappeared in the Right to Education for All Handicapped Children Act of 1975 and has remained intact with very minor word changes in every subsequent reauthorization of the law, including the most recent one: IDEA 2004. Thus, a remarkably consistent federal definition has lasted for 40 years and is still going strong: (a) *SLD* means a disorder in one or more of the basic psychological processes, (b) it includes conditions that go by various names such as *perceptual disabilities* and

---

2. Quoted with permission of the publisher, John Wiley & Sons.

minimal brain dysfunction, and (c) it excludes learning problems that have a primary, specific, and different known cause such as visual impairment or economic disadvantage.

The definition is an amalgam of the two historical roots of SLD—Goldstein-Strauss-Werner and Orton-Hinshelwood. The processing deficit requirement comes only from the Goldstein approach, as do such terms as perceptual disabilities and minimal brain dysfunction. Dyslexia is in the voice of Orton. Thus, the federal definition of SLD, like its two-pronged historical foundation, is not a simple, unified concept. It is, literally, a definition that was created by a committee. That is part of the reason for the current controversies. But the biggest upheaval and controversy in the SLD field has come from the guidelines for identifying children with SLD, which were changed drastically by Congress in 2004.

Federal Guidelines for Identifying SLD

Starting with the Right to Education for All Handicapped Children Act of 1975, and continuing with IDEA 1990 and IDEA 1997, the following federal guidelines were in effect to aid those who were involved with identifying children with SLD:

- The child does not achieve commensurate with age and ability when provided with appropriate educational experiences.
- The child has a severe discrepancy between levels of ability and achievement in one or more of seven areas that are specifically listed (basic reading skills, reading comprehension, mathematics calculation, mathematics reasoning, oral expression, listening comprehension, and written expression).

The first guideline is intended to ensure that the child's problem with school achievement reflects inadequate *learning* and not inadequate *teaching* (Cohen, 1971). But, the hallmark of these criteria is the second guideline, which stipulates that a child diagnosed with SLD is *expected* to display a severe discrepancy between standard scores on an IQ test—or levels of achievement predicted from standard scores on an IQ test—and on an achievement test (this is also referred to as an aptitude-achievement discrepancy). Different states interpreted "severe discrepancy" differently (e.g., 15 points, 22 points, 22.5 points), and they didn't necessarily agree on which IQ had to be used (some states insisted on a Full Scale IQ, others accepted a less global measure such as Performance IQ). But regardless of how the guideline was interpreted, one thing was uniform: *An IQ test had to be administered* to determine whether the child's actual achievement was sufficiently lower than his or her expected achievement based upon his or her IQ. A severe discrepancy based on IQ was a kind of documentation that the child's school achievement in at least one academic skill was much lower than expected. The IQ could be used to determine that expectation or "aptitude."

The IQ-achievement discrepancy also served a second purpose, one that was tied directly into the definition. The pioneers in the field of SLD had a difficult time figuring out exactly how to define or identify a processing disorder, once the 1969 federal definition stipulated that SLD was a disorder in a basic psychological process. What are the basic processes? How do you measure them? How low must the score in a psychological test be in order to constitute a "disorder"? Margaret Jo Shepherd, Nadeen's mentor at Columbia University, explained the dilemma, and the proposed solution, in a videotaped training program devoted to the "Best Practices" for identifying children with SLD (Flanagan, Kaufman, Kaufman, & Lichtenberger, 2008):

> Dr. Shepherd: We began to realize that what we were saying about the psychological processing deficit on the basis of the tests that we were using didn't make much sense—couldn't really explain the youngster's problem with reading or math, if that was the learning disability. We felt, and rightly so, that the tests that we were using were inadequate for the task in which we were trying to use them. . . . The framers of the [Right to Education for All Handicapped Children Act of 1975] took the default position of saying, "We can't

> find the psychological processing deficit given the tools that we have. And so the only way we can recommend the identification of learning disabled youngsters is by an aptitude-achievement discrepancy," which was the procedure that was coded into the first federal law.[3]

In 2004, all that changed. The guidelines for identifying SLD were modified so much that they became almost unrecognizable from previous guidelines. Specifically, IDEA 2004 requires that each state has to develop criteria for identifying children with SLD that

- MUST NOT REQUIRE the use of a severe discrepancy between IQ and achievement in one or more of *eight* areas (the old laws listed seven areas);
- MUST PERMIT the use of a process based on the child's response to scientific, research-based intervention; and
- MAY PERMIT the use of other alternative research-based procedures (e.g., patterns of strengths and weaknesses on IQ tests).

The first provision represents a major change in the law, eliminating the mandated use of the discrepancy formula to identify children with SLD. In fact, the three guidelines reflect a blend of the original wording in the 2004 law plus modifications to the wording that came from a subsequent federal publication designed to help implement IDEA 2004 (U.S. Department of Education, Office of Special Education and Rehabilitative Services, 2006). The 2004 law included only the seven traditional areas of achievement listed in previous laws and excluded the third guideline

---

3. Quoted from *Agora: The Marketplace of Ideas. Best Practices: Applying Response to Intervention (RTI) and Comprehensive Assessment for the Identification of Specific Learning Disabilities* [DVD]. Copyright © 2008 by NCS Pearson, Inc. Reproduced with permission. All rights reserved. This chapter includes eight quotes—this quote from Dr. Shepherd plus subsequent quotes from Drs. Fuchs, Fletcher (two separate quotes), Mather, Dumont, Reynolds, and Ortiz.

(about alternative procedures). The 2006 publication added an eighth academic area—*reading fluency skills*—to the seven traditional areas, and stipulated that unnamed alternative procedures could be used so long as they were supported by science.

The changes in the law have transformed the field of SLD. They were instituted after a hard-fought battle by professionals within the fields of psychology and education and by lobbyists within the halls of Congress. The anti–IQ testing professionals and politicians had more clout than those who favored cognitive assessment. The mantra of the more powerful faction emphasized the inadequacy of the IQ-achievement discrepancy for identifying children with SLD and the necessity of incorporating response to intervention (RTI) into the diagnostic process. The battle lines thus became drawn—proponents of IQ versus proponents of RTI.

IQ Versus RTI

Why did the changes in the law lead to the taking up of arms? Because once the IQ-achievement discrepancy was removed as a requirement for identifying SLD, the RTI advocates said, in effect, let's go a bit further—let's not only eliminate the use of the discrepancy, but let's also eliminate the IQ tests as well. After all, they reasoned, the IQ tests have *not* been shown by research to translate to educational intervention, so they are useless. In fact, the IQ-achievement discrepancy has *never* made much sense, as I stressed a generation ago (Kaufman, 1979b). Plugging standard scores into formulas is the opposite of intelligent testing and ignores the impact of errors of measurement in *both* the IQ test *and* the achievement test. Good riddance to the discrepancy formula! But getting rid of IQ tests altogether demonstrates a profound lack of insight into the varied ways in which today's theory-based IQ tests can by used by astute clinicians to identify children's strengths and weaknesses and, therefore, make a difference in their lives. And the unyielding claims by RTI advocates that no research studies support the use of IQ tests to develop effective interventions (e.g., Gresham, Restori, & Cook, 2008) blatantly ignore (a) research studies using Luria's neuropsychological model that show significant relationships between planning ability and math and between sequential (as against simultaneous) processing and reading (Naglieri & Kaufman, 2008); and (b) investigations that have shown CHC broad abilities such as *Gf* and narrow abilities such as working memory to relate substantially to school achievement. *Gv*, for example, predicts a student's ability to succeed in higher math subjects like geometry, trigonometry, and calculus. And *Gsm*, especially working memory, predicts math achievement in all areas at all ages (McGrew, 2005).

A second aspect of the law that made the controversy fester is the irrational disconnect in IDEA 2004 between the federal *definition* of SLD and the federal *guidelines* for identifying children with SLD (Hale et al., 2004). The definition has not changed significantly since its inception more than a generation ago; SLD is still defined as a disorder in one or more basic psychological processes. *But the guidelines fail to address this aspect of the definition.* Most advocates of IQ testing believe that psychologists should identify, rather than simply infer, the processing disorder in order to fulfill the true definition of SLD, and that today's theory-based IQ tests are the ideal tools to help identify the processing disorder. The RTI proponents tend not to be concerned by the disconnect and see it as a kind of loophole that permits them to rely solely on the second SLD guideline for identifying SLD, namely, the use of a process based on the child's response to scientific, research-based intervention. These professionals can reasonably be called "RTI-only" (even though they hate that label), because they believe that IDEA 2004 allows them to diagnose SLD based only on RTI (e.g., Gresham, 2002; Gresham et al., 2008). And they constitute a powerful, politically active group that has already made strong inroads in convincing some state departments of education (e.g., Iowa, Florida) to use RTI as the sole method for identifying children with SLD.

Actually, some could argue that the RTI concept is not new at all, as Dr. Ron Dumont, a school psychology professor and trainer, emphasized: "Under the 'old' IDEA guidelines, we had to see if the child was not achieving commensurate with age and ability when *provided with appropriate educational experiences.* Before a child could be determined eligible for Special Education services, there had to be proof that the child 'needed special education.' How would one know that a child needed special education services if one had not exhausted the regular education services by providing logical interventions and monitoring how those interventions worked (RTI)?" (personal communication, October 29, 2008).

Furthermore, introducing RTI into the SLD diagnostic process is a good thing, and that is not at issue here. Addressing how well children respond to scientifically validated educational interventions gets to the heart of one key issue in SLD—that these children experience academic failure, and methods are sorely needed to intervene and help these children learn before they start to experience failure. Here are two capsule perspectives on RTI by two leaders in the field of SLD, Doug Fuchs, a professor of special education, and Jack Fletcher, a clinical child neuropsychologist (quoted in Flanagan et al., 2008):

> Dr. Fuchs: RTI is a strongly behaviorally inspired movement that seeks to strengthen education services for at risk children and also tries to use strong measurement techniques to identify children who are responding to good general education instruction and who are not.

> Dr. Fletcher: RTI is an approach to delivering different kinds of interventions. In reading, for example, people have studied core reading instruction and looked at better ways to provide reading instruction to entire classrooms.

Why can't the professionals who are pro-IQ and those who are RTI-only find a middle ground? Sometimes they can. RTI and cognitive assessment are often thought of as part of a three-tier system, an approach advocated by leading professional organizations, most notably the National Association of School Psychologists (NASP, 2007). At Tier 1, RTI is used as part of regular education, and it translates to high-quality teaching within the classroom. When RTI is found not to be successful for some children, they move to Tier 2 and are given more personalized RTI within the classroom, typically in small groups. Children who are not successful at Tiers 1 or 2 then progress to Tier 3, which means referral for a comprehensive evaluation (typically including IQ tests) to determine whether the child has a specific learning disability and is eligible for special education. Consistent with the three-tier model, many professionals perceive RTI and IQ (usually referred to as cognitive assessment in these debates) to be on a continuum and to be compatible with each other. Nancy Mather, a special educator who studied with Sam Kirk and who is a coauthor of the WJ III, explains this perspective nicely (quoted in Flanagan et al., 2008):

> Dr. Mather: RTI is really being a part of the pre-referral process—a system that's in place in general education to catch any child who is struggling in school and try to provide help immediately rather than waiting until they fail. Whereas the cognitive assessment, that's a piece of a comprehensive evaluation that typically addresses the needs of one child, attempts to determine strengths and weaknesses, why a child is struggling. The two again are part of the system, a continuum of services, but one can't replace the other. They both have different functions, purposes, intents.

The RTI-only people often want to bypass the comprehensive evaluation, especially the IQ testing, and use RTI as the only basis for identification. They would then argue that if RTI did not work at Tier 1 or Tier 2, and that if an extra dose of RTI at Tier 3 was likewise unsuccessful, then the diagnosis of SLD would be complete. Would IQ testing ever be needed? According to some RTI-only professionals, yes, but only if the child's evaluation team had to come to a decision as to whether the child had an intellectual disability.

The controversies within the field and in state departments of education are likely to continue for years, in part because of the flaws built into IDEA 2004, as argued by Ron Dumont (quoted in Flanagan et al., 2008):

> Dr. Dumont: The problem is that they've written a law that nobody can understand and then told you that we in the government don't understand what we meant, so just do what you want.... What is a disorder in a basic psychological process? What are basic psychological processes? And it says that the disorders are manifested in an imperfect ability to read, write, or think. Well, what's imperfect? Does perfect imply just that, perfect, and imperfect is any deviation from that? I think our problem is we're trying to figure out what they meant. And the courts are the ones who are going to figure it out when we go to due process, and we go to hearings.

Is RTI-Only Defensible As the Sole Method for Diagnosing SLD?

The history of SLD, as I explained earlier, has two separate roots, with the two historical approaches at odds with each other on an array of issues ranging from the nature of the disability to the best way to remediate it. But more important than these differences are the similarities. The Goldstein-Strauss-Werner and Hinshelwood-Orton theories of SLD agree on the following:

- The child with SLD has areas of normal functioning and, sometimes, above average or superior functioning—abilities that have been spared—that stand in marked contrast to the areas of disability.
- The cause of the disability is presumed to be neurological in nature.
- The poor academic achievement is demonstrated *not* to be due to other possible causes such as visual impairment or cultural disadvantage.
- Children with SLD represent a distinct category within the field of special education, a category that is not defined merely

by low achievement or failure to respond to intervention and that is qualitatively different from categories such as behavior disorders or emotional disturbance.

All of these unifying characteristics are lost when an RTI-only approach is used and comprehensive evaluations are bypassed or trivialized. Children can fail to respond to intervention for an abundance of reasons, including behavior problems and emotional disorders—not to mention poorly designed or poorly implemented interventions. RTI lumps all of these children together, losing the essence of the SLD classification and ignoring the individual's strengths and weaknesses, which are known by clinicians to be very important in understanding how children think and learn. These patterns of strength and weakness form the essence of pinpointing *why* the child is experiencing academic failure and *how* to best provide educational interventions. For example, children with weaknesses in short-term memory are best served by the following educational accommodations (Mather & Jaffe, 2002):

- Keep oral directions short and simple
- Provide aids to help student compensate (e.g., write directions on the board or paper)
- Keep lessons short
- Allow for overlearning, review, and repetition

Without comprehensive evaluations, especially those that feature cognitive assessment, one cannot (a) rule out possible causes of the academic failure apart from SLD; (b) identify a processing disorder; (c) determine whether the child's cognitive weaknesses are consistent with his or her academic deficits (e.g., low sequential processing is known to relate directly to difficulty decoding words); or (d) adapt the specific RTI approach to each individual child's specific areas of strength and weakness.

Cecil Reynolds, test author and expert in neuropsychology and psychometrics (and my former doctoral student and a one-time pitcher in the New York Mets organization), discusses the importance of IQ tests for SLD identification and treatment (quoted in Flanagan et al., 2008):

> Dr. Reynolds: The same score pattern doesn't mean the same thing for every child who walks into your office. As I tell people, you shouldn't diagnose raccoons with insomnia because they stay up all night. We need to understand the history and context of children.... If we are going to have an intelligent means of modifying that instruction so that it works, we need that comprehensive understanding of that child. And personally I don't know how to develop that comprehensive understanding without having an understanding of their intellectual ability and the interaction of the key intellectual factors in their development. I'm just not bright enough to figure that out.

Four superstars in the field of SLD—the late Ken Kavale, James Kauffman (no relation), Cecil Reynolds, and Sally Shaywitz—criticize the RTI-only model as a means of SLD identification. Kavale, Kauffman, Bachmeier, and LeFever (2008) state that as a diagnostic approach, RTI "is conceptually flawed, practically inadequate, and politically rather than scientifically motivated.... With a model that combines RTI and cognitive assessments, it is possible to provide an identification process that closely aligns with the best current conceptualizations of SLD" (p. 135). Reynolds and Shaywitz (2009) stress that an RTI-only model "*represents a fundamental alteration in the concept of disability and cuts out the very roots basic to the concept of an LD as an unexpected difficulty in learning intrinsic to the child*" (p. 46, emphasis in the original).

RTI-only also falls short in other ways. It won't identify bright or gifted children with learning disabilities because their achievement, though normal or average, won't reflect their high intelligence (Reynolds & Shaywitz, 2009). Also, relying only on RTI for diagnosing SLD will be especially unfair to English language learners and others from diverse cultural backgrounds, as

Samuel Ortiz (an expert in bilingual and bicultural assessment) explains (quoted in Flanagan et al., 2008):

> Dr. Ortiz: It will cause many of these children to fail or to appear that they're failing—to appear that they're not making progress. And what is the end result? Well, if they're not making the progress, we know the research says it should be effective intervention. But it's not being effective, then it must be that the children have learning disabilities. That will only contribute to the problem of overrepresentation of children of diverse ethnic and cultural backgrounds in special education.

Nonetheless, other SLD superstars, such as Dan Reschly, Frank Gresham, Jack Fletcher, and Sharon Vaughn, insist that RTI is a well-researched approach that holds great promise for identifying children with learning disabilities. According to Gresham et al. (2004), "nothing in the current and past versions of the IDEA statute or regulations requires that standardized tests be given to determine a child's eligibility for special education.... RTI along with a problem solving process operationalizes disability.... Disability is conceptualized as (a) *low level* of performance in a relevant domain in relation to peers, (b) slow growth rates compared to peers despite high quality scientifically-based interventions" (pp. 26, 28; emphasis in the original), and other criteria as well. But IQ tests have zero value in their model for identifying or treating children with SLD.

Also, as quoted by Reynolds and Shaywitz (2009): "Fletcher and Vaughn state the primary goal of RTI is 'improved academic and behavioral outcomes for all students' with a 'secondary goal of RTI' to 'provide data for identification of learning disabilities (LDs)'" (p. 44). But, again, the differing opinions of the true experts in the field are evident in Reynolds and Shaywitz's (2009) rebuttal of the Fletcher-Vaughn position: "After carefully reading their article and reviewing the evidence, we conclude that RTI remains an unproven thesis. RTI currently lacks a trustworthy evidence base to indicate that it meets either of these two laudatory goals and remains instead a series of assumptions without validation" (p. 44).

And, as my colleague John Willis (personal communication, October 25, 2008), a practicing assessment specialist and senior lecturer in assessment, notes: "Exclusive reliance on RTI for identification of SLD . . . is almost comparable to assuming that any child who still has difficulty with listening skills in class after interventions should be classified as deaf. What I find difficult to understand is the adamant refusal of some RTI proponents to permit individual cognitive and achievement assessment even for the few children who have not responded to any of the scientifically-based interventions the team has been able to find." Willis adds that "a word-reading problem represents the *beginning,* not the end of understanding the child's learning difficulty and raising the child's achievement. . . . It is essential to understand *why* the child has a word-reading problem" (emphasis added). Ron Dumont (personal communication, October 29, 2008) notes: "The reading problem itself is not the learning disability—it is the result of the learning disability! The definition clearly says that SLD is 'a disorder in one or more of the basic psychological processes.'"

A Final Word on the Irrelevance of IQ Tests for SLD Identification

I have lectured frequently on the topic of the reputed irrelevance of IQ tests for the diagnosis of SLD; for example, in Atlanta a few years ago (Kaufman, 2005a, 2005b), I argued in favor of IQ tests as follows.

In the first decade of the 21st century, debates are raging over the implementation of the new IDEA guidelines for the assessment of SLDs. IQ tests are being ushered out the door by some outspoken critics who favor the diagnosing of SLD based solely on RTI. How odd, and disappointing, now that the IQ-achievement discrepancy is no longer a mandatory part of the diagnostic procedure, that all comprehensive cognitive ability tests are deemed expendable by some. I say odd, because the past 5 years have witnessed the development of undoubtedly the best group of cognitive ability instruments in history in terms of their psychometric and theoretical foundations—the WJ III (2001), WPPSI-III (2002), Stanford-Binet-5 (2003), WISC-IV (2003), KABC-II (2004), and DAS-II (2007). Each of these instruments (as well as others developed in the 1990s such as the CAS) provides an array of 4 to 7 abilities or processes that are either developed from theory or, in the case of Wechsler's scales, easily interpreted using theory. Each one downplays global IQs or standard scores and emphasizes a profile of scores on the specific abilities. Each is state of the art and can easily be used by well-trained professionals to identify a child's processing strengths (for making remedial suggestions) and processing weaknesses (for identifying disorders in basic psychological processes). Though basic disorders in psychological processes remain the crux of the IDEA definition of SLD, and despite the availability of the best IQ tests ever, the RTI activists remain steadfast in their opposition to the assessment of cognitive processing. It makes no rational sense.[4]

Although I remain solidly in the camp that advocates IQ tests for SLD identification in a process that includes RTI at Tiers 1 and 2, I must admit that participating in the development of the DVD-based Agora training program has softened my stance. As I listened to the interviews and lectures of dozens of prominent leaders who represent all points in the RTI-IQ spectrum, read tons of literature on the topic, and discussed the interviews and lectures with Nadeen and with two of our closest friends and colleagues (our coauthors Dawn Flanagan and Liz Lichtenberger), I began to gain more appreciation for the "other side." I am no longer as sure of myself as I was before I began to truly

---

4. Copyright 2005 by the National Association of School Psychologists. Bethesda, MD. Adapted with the permission of the publisher. www.nasponline.org

hear (not just listen to, but *hear*) the alternate viewpoint. I would no longer say "It makes no rational sense," as I said a few years ago. Some of the RTI advocates are quite compelling, articulate, and rational, and none more so than Jack Fletcher (who, along with Sally Shaywitz, has conducted the exciting neuroimaging research that I discuss in chapter 10). Fletcher is not as extreme as some. He is in favor of administering individual tests of achievement (such as the KTEA-II) for SLD diagnosis, even if he sees little use for IQ tests such as the WISC-IV or KABC-II (Flanagan et al., 2008):

> Dr. Fletcher: I'm not saying that psychological processes don't cause learning disabilities; clearly they do—that's why we've done a lot of the research. But what the research tells us is that the things that help us understand the disability don't necessarily contribute to identification or intervention.... Once we know a child has a word reading problem, the value of additional assessments of specific cognitive processes that are tied to or correlated with word recognition is what's questionable.... And so once you've essentially measured achievement domains, there's no value-added information from an assessment of cognitive processes.

I disagree with Dr. Fletcher's conclusions, but I understand them and respect his opinions. The controversy about the value of IQ tests is a real one that has intelligent advocates on both sides. It will not soon disappear from newspapers, journals, and listservs.

How ironic that the two heated public forum topics discussed in this chapter reveal polar opposites regarding the value of IQ tests. The lead level researchers are willing to implicate the loss of a couple of IQ points as the cause of dramatic damage to children's futures, and freely discuss the ominous threats to society. They deify the IQ test, making claims for it that are unsupported by science. In contrast, the RTI-only disciples simply want to follow influential 1920s political commentator and journalist Walter Lippmann, who claimed if the IQ tests "really measure intelligence, that they constitute a sort of last judgment on the child's capacity, that they reveal 'scientifically' his predestined ability, then it would be a thousand times better if all the intelligence testers and all their questionnaires were sunk without warning into the Sargasso Sea."

10

The Future of IQ Tests

In the early 1980s, a few months before the K-ABC was published in the United States, Nadeen and I were being interviewed on one of the morning shows by Diane Sawyer about the new IQ test we had developed that reduced ethnic differences. Near the end of Sawyer's probing, astute interview came the following exchange:

DIANE: Do you think that 10, 20 years from now that we're going to be measuring intelligence in a vastly different way from the way we do now? Maybe even chemically or through computers?

NADEEN: Well, I think it's desirable. The more we find out about how people think and how people can learn, we need to be able to incorporate this new information and create new measures to help us get at what's inside people's brains.

DIANE: (joking) I'm going to go back and take your test. It may change my life. I'll become a nuclear physicist or something. That's what I should have done, of course, all along.[1]

And I think it would have been wonderful if the field of IQ measurement had moved along as fast as Diane Sawyer speculated a quarter of a century ago. But it hasn't. It hasn't even come close. The most impressive advances have come from brain research, but so far that research has remained outside the mainstream of IQ testing.

NEUROIMAGING RESEARCH

The fields of neuropsychology and the neurosciences have flourished since the early 1990s, with advances in brain technology coming at breakneck speed in ways never even imagined a generation ago. Functional magnetic resonance imaging (fMRI) and other sophisticated techniques have been applied while children and adults read, do math, or solve complex problems. These metabolic imaging studies have provided intriguing results based on changes in blood flow while people with and without reading problems perform specific reading tasks such as demonstrating skills in phonological processing and phonics, including decoding nonsense words (Shaywitz, 2003). This type of research produces not only numerical data but also photographic images of brain activity to identify exactly which parts of the brain are active while the person reads a sentence or solves a problem—using the science-fiction-like procedure called neuroimaging.

1. More recently, the results of a vocational interests test known as the Self-Directed Search suggested that Diane's ultimate job match might be bartender (Ahuja, 2008)!

The exciting results of the studies have helped localize the brain areas involved in each aspect of reading and have identified differences (for example) in how typical individuals and those diagnosed with dyslexia process information (and males and females do it differently (Shaywitz, 2003)! From the perspective of IDEA 2004, which puts RTI solidly on the table for SLD diagnosis, the neuroimaging technique allows RTI researchers to determine what parts of children's brains are active during the reading process both before and after reading interventions have been provided (e.g., Shaywitz et al., 2004). Before the interventions, children with reading problems typically use the *wrong* parts of their brain to read, leading to difficulty decoding words or understanding what they are reading. After interventions, several research studies have shown that the same children now use the *correct* parts of the brain while engaged in reading (i.e., the parts of the brain that are used by good readers). The evidence from neuroscience indicates that we can determine scientifically whether children have responded to intervention. That is a wonderful step forward, because it adds a neuropsychological dimension to the RTI component of SLD identification.

The neuroimaging studies are high tech and ingenious (and extremely expensive). They use medical methodologies with magical names such as positron emission tomography (PET), single-photon emission tomography (SPECT), functional magnetic resonance imaging (fMRI), and diffusion tensor imaging (DTI). These approaches tell us whether a person's brain is *functioning* appropriately while performing a school-related or novel task, a great step forward from previous approaches that emphasized *structural* abnormalities in the brains—searching for damaged brain tissue in people diagnosed with dyslexia or other types of brain dysfunction. The structural studies tended to be inconclusive and sometimes contradictory (Bigler, Lajiness-O'Neill, & Howes, 1998; Morgan & Hynd, 1998). More disturbing, they were pessimistic in their outcomes. How do you fix "broken" brain tissue? By contrast, the functional approaches are optimistic, because it is indeed possible to teach young dogs (i.e., children with reading disorders) new tricks.

Yet, how do these new procedures directly affect IQ testing? When we study the pictures of the brain while people read or solve problems, they tell us *what* specific parts of their brains people activate while they are reading or solving problems; and based on which brain areas are activated, they tell us *how* they are processing the stimuli. But they do not tell us *how well* the person has performed on the test. Neuroimaging techniques have not yet allowed us to actually *measure* IQ or achievement. But as I will discuss later in the chapter, I believe that neuroimaging will prove to play a huge role in the IQ testing of the future.

COMPUTERIZED IQ TESTS

Fifteen or so years ago I was certain that individually administered IQ tests would be replaced by computerized tests in a matter of years, if not moments. The world was becoming increasingly dependent on personal computers and the Internet, as laptops, e-mail, e-Bay, Amazon.com, Apple, Bill Gates, and so forth started to dominate everyday conversations. Technology was everywhere, into everything. Within the field of IQ testing, computerized psychological reports—usually impersonal and generic—proliferated, replacing the individualized, highly personalized reports that had become so much a part of the intelligence testing philosophy that I had espoused for decades. Computerized personality tests became widespread. But individual IQ tests survived and thrived (Dumont, Willis, Farr, & McCarthy, 1997).

Nadeen and I pleaded with our test publisher to offer computerized versions of our tests, more than a decade and a half ago, but the idea was always shelved for later. We did not want clinical IQ tests to be replaced by computerized tests; we simply didn't want to be left behind by what we presumed to be the wave of the future. We had always treasured the clinician's role in evaluating children and adults. One of the basic tenets of intelligent testing is that the clinician is just as valuable as the test instrument itself. Another tenet is that IQs or subtest scores in isolation are meaningless. They must be interpreted within the context of the person's specific background and test behaviors, and the behaviors need to be observed and interpreted by astute, qualified clinicians (Kaufman, 1979b, 1994; Kaufman & Kaufman, 1977, 2001; Kaufman & Lichtenberger, 2006). We dreaded the likely loss of the individual assessment of intelligence and the reduced role of the clinician, and we feared the onslaught of technology, especially if it meant that machines won out over humans. We dreaded it and we expected it, but we are about one decade into the 21st century and the Wechsler scales remain the big dogs of IQ testing. Our own tests continue to thrive and be adapted worldwide, Binet's name has not lost any luster after more than a century, Naglieri's PASS model influences educational interventions throughout the United States, and the Woodcock-Johnson has more listserv devotees than can be counted.

Well, we did develop a computerized IQ test after all—the K-CLASSIC (Kaufman & Kaufman, 2007), for ages 6–10 years. The United States wasn't interested, but the French publisher of Wechsler's scales and the Kaufman tests (ECPA, http://ecpa.fr/test/test_resume.asp?ID = 541) asked us to develop a computerized test for French-speaking children. And we said yes, sort of the way Binet did when he was approached by the minister of public instruction in Paris a century earlier. The test was in development for years, as everything that possibly could go wrong did go wrong for a while. But things clicked when we switched programmers (from Minnesotans to Parisians) and the bugs finally disappeared.

Computer technology has some advantages over individual testing (some, but not many) and we built them into the K-CLASSIC. For one thing, it is possible to individualize each subtest for everyone who is tested, a process called *adaptive testing*. First, a "routing" test is given (items that skip quickly from easy to hard) to quickly identify the child's approximate level of ability. Then, every time the child passes or fails an item, that success or failure triggers the very next item administered. Pass the item, and the child is challenged with a more difficult item; fail the item, and the computer program automatically administers an easier item. Adaptive testing saves time and helps the child avoid the frustration of failing many items in a row. You can experience this process at http://www.freerice.com/. Another advantage of computer technology is the ease of building in game-like feedback whenever the child fails an easy item, helping the child understand what is expected of her. And the computer administers and scores the entire test with completely standardized procedures (when a stimulus is supposed to be exposed for 5 seconds, the computer exposes it for *exactly* 5 seconds); it generates the child's scores on all subtests and composites; and it prints out a case report that includes suggestions for intervention.

So am I crazy? A total hypocrite? Well, we built in some safeguards. The K-CLASSIC is a *screening* test, which means it is brief and is intended to get a general idea of the child's attention (separate from the IQ scale), language, and problem-solving ability. It is not meant as a replacement for a comprehensive IQ test. If a child scores low on the test of attention, or earns a low IQ, or has wide variability on the subtests, the first recommendation printed out in the report is for a psychologist to administer a comprehensive IQ test such as the French WISC-IV or the French KABC-II. Also, we stipulate that the K-CLASSIC be administered by a psychologist, not by someone with limited knowledge of IQ testing, and the psychologist is instructed to spend at least 15 minutes sitting with the child to observe the child's behaviors, even though the entire 45-minute test is administered by the voice on the computer. And the examiner must answer questionnaires directly on the computer after the child has completed the test. The examiner provides specific background information about the child (e.g., reason for the testing, SES) and rates the child's facility with the computer as well as test behaviors, such as distractibility, tolerance of frustration, and anxiety. The report generated for each child reflects the examiner's answers to the questions about background and behaviors. Both the interpretation of the child's test scores and the educational recommendations are based just as much on the examiner's questionnaires as on the scores.

Are the safeguards foolproof? Of course not. Psychologists may choose to have an untrained person supervise the administration (which is sometimes done today with Wechsler's scales). Or they may decide to spend less than 15 minutes with the child, or no time at all. And they may ignore the recommendation to administer a clinical IQ test.

Are computerized tests going to replace individually administered IQ tests? Probably not, at least not too soon. As I write this concluding chapter, the K-CLASSIC is being translated and adapted in Germany and the United Kingdom. The United States plans to do the same, but nothing has happened yet. And conceivably other computerized tests are being developed all around the world. But I thought that was true 15 years ago.

WHAT DOES THE PAST SAY ABOUT THE FUTURE?

Sir Francis Galton reigned for about 20 years until Binet's new, more complex, approach replaced Galton's more simplistic sensory-motor methodology in 1905. Binet took over for about 60 years, until the growing fields of neuropsychology and learning disabilities pushed him to the side sometime in the mid-1960s, because they demanded a profile of scores in addition to a single, global IQ. And it's been Wechsler time ever since, 45 years and counting, although there are a variety of other excellent IQ tests that are also on the psychologists' shelves.

Past Controversies

IQ tests have rolled with the punches over the years, and sometimes the punches have been potent. The 1970s witnessed an array of complaints about IQ tests, most on the topic of racial bias in favor of the White middle class and against African Americans. Cries of intellectual genocide and demands for a moratorium on IQ testing (e.g., Williams, 1974a, 1974b) appeared in journals, at psychological conventions, in the popular press, and in the courts. (See, e.g., *Larry P. v. Wilson Riles,* an influential 1979 California case that declared IQ tests to be biased against African Americans; and *PASE v. Hannon,* a 1980 Illinois case that came to the opposite conclusion. For an excellent, in-depth review of these cases and the controversy surrounding them, see R. Elliott, 1987.) The Wechsler tests, the main target of the criticisms because of their popularity and virtual monopoly, responded slightly. They showed African American and Hispanic faces on test items (and in their advertisements) and made sure arithmetic word problems included an occasional Jose or Maria, but nothing changed too much on the Wechsler scene. In the 1980s, the K-ABC reduced ethnic differences for African Americans and Hispanics, and two other innovative theory-based IQ tests were developed (Binet-IV, WJ-R), but Wechsler's scales withstood both the competition and the attacks of bias. Ethnic bias in IQ tests has remained a key issue to the present day, especially regarding the assessment of students from bilingual backgrounds, but today's complaints lack the virulence of the 1970s. IQ tests have survived these criticisms. Test publishers now conduct rigorous statistical analyses to weed out "biased" items, but they've done relatively little else to address the problem.

Other attacks on the IQ construct have come from neuropsychologists such as Muriel Lezak (1988), who suggested that IQ tests be buried and allowed to rest in peace. Her main complaints were that the IQs were a global hodge-podge that did not correspond to anything meaningful in a neurological sense, and that even the separate subtests were too complex to reflect the functioning of specific areas of the brain. Again, the IQ tests withstood the challenge. They retained their popularity, even among neuropsychologists. But this time, the IQ tests did respond to the criticisms. They became increasingly rooted in neuropsychological theory (notably Naglieri and Das's CAS in 1997), they developed new tasks based on neuropsychological research (KABC-II, WISC-IV, WAIS-IV, Binet-5, DAS-II), and they included tasks in the overall battery that measured very specific skills such as auditory processing (Woodcock-Johnson, DAS-II). Even the shift from a few large global scales in the early IQ tests to an array of 4 to 7 specific abilities in all modern IQ tests reflects the pervasive influence of neuropsychological research on IQ test development. And, although I know that David Wechsler is turning over in his grave, the WISC-IV and WAIS-IV offer only Full Scale IQ and the four indexes and have completely eliminated the traditional Verbal and Performance IQs.

And I made him see red by merely suggesting that he eliminate a single item from the WISC, as I explained in an address in Atlanta (Kaufman, 2005a, 2005b).

Dr. Wechsler was intractable about eliminating items from his tests. He felt an attachment to every item on the WISC, and any item that traced back to the original Form II of the Wechsler-Bellevue was an all-hallowed item. Once I had the audacity to say to Dr. Wechsler that there is this one item on Comprehension that I think we ought to get rid of. He asked calmly, "Which one?" I replied timidly, "Why should women and children be saved first in a shipwreck?" He turned red and this one little vein on his scalp turned blue and started throbbing. I knew I was in trouble when that happened—that I had crossed a big line that I didn't even know existed. I was asking to get rid of an item that in 1972—during the time of outspoken feminists—was practically crying out, "Delete me." Dr. Wechsler looked at me with that vein quivering and I was thinking, "I'll be known as the man who killed David Wechsler." He put both arms on the table and he said sternly, "Chivalry may be dying! Chivalry may be dead! But it will not die on the WISC!"[2]

---

2. Copyright 2005 by the National Association of School Psychologists. Bethesda, MD. Adapted with the permission of the publisher. www.naspo nline.org

CHAPTER 10

The Current Attack on IQ Tests From the RTI Movement

I call it a current attack, but the RTI movement began in the 1980s, perhaps when Witt and Gresham (1985) reviewed the WISC-III and referred to it as an albatross that lacked treatment validity. They were targeting all IQ tests, claiming that research did not exist to support the use of test scores to plan educational interventions. And the ravaging of IQ tests was just as relentless from the special educators who despised the IQ-achievement discrepancy as a necessary requirement for identifying children with SLD. Their logic, as I explained in chapter 9, was that the discrepancy formula was filled with holes and had to be eliminated—and without the formula, who needs IQ tests in the first place? During the 1990s, despite the spate of anti-IQ articles in the literature (e.g., Siegel, 1999; Stanovich, 1991), I did not take the threat to IQ tests seriously—or at least no more seriously than I had taken earlier attacks. I felt that there would always be controversy about IQ tests, and IQ tests would always survive.

IDEA 2004 changed all that. Now I am not so sure. The issue is far from resolved, but the RTI-only faction is strong, vocal, persistent, and politically savvy. How the role of cognitive assessment for SLD identification will be resolved remains a mystery, as most of the 50 states, and countless school districts throughout the country, continue to wrestle with the implementation of the law. In the states that have already adopted an RTI-only policy, IQ testing in the schools will be almost nonexistent, except when intellectual disability is suspected. In states such as Oregon, which are guided by the intelligent use of IQ tests (Hanson, Sharman, & Esparza Brown, 2008), measures of intelligence will continue to be administered in conjunction with RTI approaches (Willis & Dumont, 2006). If IQ tests virtually disappear from the school scene in many districts throughout the nation and in some states altogether, how big a dent will that make in IQ test use? Big, in terms of *quantity,* little in terms of *quality.*

In fact, the quality of test use will increase. The identification of children with SLD has provided a prominent role for IQ tests for more than 30 years. But because of the discrepancy formula that loomed over every child referred for possible SLD, IQ tests were often given for the wrong reasons (to plug a number into a formula) by the wrong people (those who found no use for IQ tests *except* to plug into a formula). That will stop. Some states may continue to use the discrepancy formula because it is familiar and permitted by law (although states can no longer require it). But most states, I believe, that opt to use IQ tests will do so to identify the child's pattern of strengths and weaknesses. That approach will help identify a processing disorder as well as cognitive strengths for the purpose of individualizing educational planning. And that is intelligent testing.

IQ TESTING IN 2030

Over most of the next decade, I see a continuation of today's practices. IQ tests have become sophisticated, theory based, and exceptional in many ways. They reflect a refinement and upgrade over IQ-tests-past and will continue to be used intelligently for clinical, psychoeducational, and neuropsychological evaluations of children and adults. The best tests will continue to be revised and restandardized in a timely fashion because most test users are aware of the Flynn Effect and don't want to use a test with outdated norms. But these updated and undoubtedly improved IQ tests will be used less and less.

Computerized IQ tests will proliferate by 2015 and will rival individually administered IQ tests. At first there will be resistance, and the computerized tests will be used as screening tests, to determine whether an individual test needs to be administered, or as supplements to the clinical tests. But the computerized tests will win out because they are cost-efficient, they are time-efficient, and they have untapped potential to measure abilities with a precision that cannot easily be matched by a clinician (for example, measuring reaction time to a complex set of directions in milliseconds). Computerized tests of the future will be even more comprehensive than current IQ tests because of the adaptive testing feature (which allows more abilities to be measured in less time). Individual tests will continue to be used for groups that are not easily tested by computer, such as preschool children and adults with dementia, and by devoted clinicians who refuse to abandon the value of individual assessment for observing the behaviors of anyone, regardless of age. With regard to preschool children, psychologists will quickly find out that even children as young as 2½ years are computer savvy, and the clinicians will figure out, to their chagrin, that the computer is far more successful at holding the young child's attention than they are.

As computerized IQ tests become more popular, their quality will zoom exponentially. The genius geeks who spin out intricate video games will find it profitable to raise IQ tests to the next level, making the new breed of IQ test as interesting and challenging and intricate as the latest video game. In the 2020s, there will be a shift in emphasis from measuring IQ to measuring learning ability. The new IQ tests will have built-in training exercises, game-like in format but incisively effective at teaching new material. Instead of being tested once, the child or adult will be tested twice. After the initial test, the person will be trained in all areas that are identified as weaknesses and then retested.

This test-teach-test paradigm was proposed years ago, most prominently by the Israeli psychologist Reuven Feuerstein (1979), as the true measure of intelligence—not how well people can perform, but how much they can improve their performance through learning (building on methods for teaching *Gf* and *Gv* skills to the elderly; Schaie, 1996). Clearly, reasoning and spatial ability in the elderly can be improved, as even minor interventions lead to significant improvement in test performance (Labouvie-Vief, 1985). But will it be possible to truly improve elderly people's genuine, overall problem-solving ability—and not just teach them to score higher on one or two specific tests? Research on this "new" approach to measuring intelligence will help answer the key question of whether the decline in *Gf* with age can be reversed permanently and will identify the best methods for doing so. It will also have reverberations for SLD diagnosis, as RTI will have merged completely with IQ testing. And if the extremists who insist that a little bit of blood lead causes dramatic IQ loss were correct, then the new IQ tests would be perfect for children who had been exposed to microscopic amounts of lead.

And by 2030, neuroimaging techniques will have been perfected to the point at which fMRIs and DTIs can be given easily and inexpensively in the psychologist's office, the classroom, or the local shopping mall. All children and adults who are evaluated on the new test-teach-test computerized IQ tests will be given an fMRI during the initial test and again when tested after the intervention, to determine whether the new learning is accompanied by a shift in brain functioning. Research will determine what areas of the brain need to be activated to reflect the optimal approach to solving particular problems, and what areas represent inefficient problem solving. Perhaps those who show a shift in brain functioning from bad to good will truly have increased their IQ, in a fashion similar to that reported by the studies on reading interventions that document normalized brain functioning when poor readers significantly improve their reading ability. Neuroimaging might ultimately provide evidence that the decline in *Gf* or *Gs* with increasing age is not so inevitable after all.

Is my optimistic, high-tech vision of the future of IQ testing even remotely accurate? I hope so, but we'll just have to sit back and see what happens.

ARE IQ TEST DEVELOPERS SMART?

I will end this book on the same note on which I began it. In chapter 1, I talked about how difficult it is to tell people that I develop IQ tests, in part because IQ is so controversial. But it is also hard to tell people what I do because then they will expect me to be really smart (although they may reconsider if they read about the decline of reasoning ability in the elderly—I will be 65 when this book is published). Here are the sentiments I expressed at the end of my address in Atlanta (Kaufman, 2005a, 2005b).

I am reminded of an invited address I gave for the German/Dutch Neuropsychological Society in Cologne, Germany, in 1999. Nadeen and I were getting on this huge escalator in the Frankfurt Airport, which led to the train depot. This escalator was large enough to accommodate a huge luggage cart with hand-brakes. While on the escalator I tried to read the three rules listed, but I don't read German and the English was very small, so I only read the first two rules. The rule I didn't read was not to pile too much luggage on the cart. So I had put every piece of luggage on the cart and could not even see above the top. When I got to the top of the escalator, I remembered the first rule, which was to release the hand-brakes, so the cart could roll smoothly off the escalator. But we had too much luggage, and, instead of going straight, the off-balance cart veered into the metal side-wall at the top of the escalator. The continuous movement of the escalator started lifting the cart with our luggage up against the side wall, and it became precarious. Nadeen had the presence of mind to squeeze past me, grab the top piece of luggage from the cart, and manage to get safely off the escalator. (Her first instinct was to try to run down the escalator until she realized there was no place to hide and that I needed help.) The reduced weight allowed me to steer the cart straight, and we were suddenly safe from a near calamity, walking off the escalator onto safe ground. I must admit that during the entire episode, I had two thoughts in my mind. The first one was that we were going to die, and the second was the headline of the following day's paper: "IQ Test Developers Killed by Their Own Luggage."[3]

3. Copyright 2005 by the National Association of School Psychologists. Bethesda, MD. Adapted with the permission of the publisher. www.nasponline.org

References

Ahuja, G. (2008, September 30). What's Diane's ultimate job match? Could you see Diane as a bartender? ABC News, *Good morning America.* Retrieved November 14, 2008, from http://abcnews.go.com/GMA/story?id = 5913439

Alfonso, V. C., Johnson, A., Patinella, L., & Rader, D. E. (1998). Common WISC-III examiner errors: Evidence from graduate students in training. *Psychology in the Schools, 35,* 119–125.

Allison, J., Blatt, S. J., & Zimet, C. N. (1968). *The interpretation of psychological tests.* New York: Harper & Row.

American Academy of Pediatrics (AAP), Committee on Environmental Health. (2005). Policy statement—Lead exposure in children: Prevention, detection, and management. *Pediatrics, 116,* 1036–1046.

Anastasi, A., & Urbina, S. (1997). *Psychological testing* (7th ed.). Upper Saddle River, NJ: Prentice-Hall.

Angoff, W. H. (1988). The nature-nurture debate, aptitudes, and group differences. *American Psychologist, 43,* 713–720.

Baltes, P. B., & Lindenberger, U. (1997). Emergence of a powerful connection between sensory and cognitive functions across the adult life span: A new window to the study of cognitive aging? *Psychology and Aging, 12,* 12–21.

Baltes, P. B., & Schaie, K. W. (1976). On the plasticity of adult and gerontological intelligence: Where Horn and Donaldson fail. *American Psychologist, 31,* 720–725.

Barnett, W. S. (1995). Long-term effects of early childhood programs on cognitive and school outcomes. *The Future of Children, 5*(3), 25–50.

Barnett, W. S. (2004). Does Head Start have lasting cognitive effects?: The myth of fade-out. In E. Zigler & S. Styfco (Eds.), *The Head Start debates* (pp. 221–249). Baltimore: Paul H. Brookes Publishing.

Barnett, W. S., & Husted, J. T. (2005). Head Start's lasting benefits. *Infants and Young Children, 18,* 16–24.

Bayley, N. (1933). *The California First-Year Mental Scale.* Berkeley: University of California Press.

Bayley, N. (1969). *Manual for the Bayley Scales of Infant Development.* New York: The Psychological Corporation.

Bayley, N. (1993). *Manual for the Bayley Scales of Infant Development* (2nd ed.). San Antonio, TX: The Psychological Corporation.

Bellinger, D. C., & Needleman, H. L. (1983). Lead and the relationship between maternal and child intelligence. *Pediatrics, 102,* 523–527.

Berkowitz, B., & Green, R. F. (1963). Changes in intellect with age: I. Longitudinal study of Wechsler-Bellevue scores. *Journal of Genetic Psychology, 103,* 3–21.

Berrueta-Clement, J. R., Schweinhart, L. J., Barnett, W. S., Epstein, A. S., & Weikart, D. P. (1984). *Changed lives: The effects of the Perry Preschool Program on youths through age 19.* Monographs of the High/Scope Educational Research Foundation, Number Eight. Ypsilanti, MI: High/Scope Press.

Best, D. (2007, November). Testimony of Dana Best, MD, MPH, FAAP, on behalf of the American Academy of Pediatrics Energy and Commerce Subcommittee on Commerce, Trade, and Consumer Protection, H. R. 4040, the Consumer Product Safety Modernization Act. Department of Federal Affairs, Washington, DC.

Bigler, E. D., Lajiness-O'Neill, R., & Howes, N-L. (1998). Technology in the assessment of learning disability. *Journal of Learning Disabilities, 31,* 67–82.

Binet, A. (1903). *L'étude éxperimentale de l'intelligence.* Paris: Schleicher.

Binet, A., & Henri, V. (1895). La psychologie individuelle. *L'Année Psychologique, 2,* 411–465.

Binet, A., & Simon, T. (1905). Méthodes nouvelles pour le diagnostic du niveau intellectual des anormaux. *L'Année Psychologique, 11,* 191–244.

Binet, A., & Simon, T. (1916/1973). *Classics in psychology: The development of intelligence in children.* New York: Arno Press. (Original work published in French 1916)

Birren, J. E., & Morrison, D. F. (1961). Analysis of the WAIS subtests in relation to age and education. *Journal of Gerontology, 16,* 363–369.

Block, N. J., & Dworkin, G. (1976). *The IQ controversy.* New York: Pantheon Books.

Boehm, A. E. (1967). *The development of comparative concepts in primary school children.* Unpublished doctoral dissertation, Columbia University, New York.

Bogen, J. E. (1969). The other side of the brain: Parts I, II, and III. *Bulletin of the Los Angeles Neurological Society, 34,* 73–105, 135–162, 191–203.

Boll, T. J. (1981). The Halstead-Reitan Neuropsychological Battery. In S. B. Filskov & T. J. Boll (Eds.), *Handbook of clinical neuropsychology* (Vol. 1, pp. 577–608). New York: Wiley.

Botwinick, J. (1977). Intellectual abilities. In J. E. Birren & K. W. Schaie (Eds.), *Handbook of the psychology of aging* (pp. 580–605). New York: Van Nostrand Reinhold.

Bouchard, T. J., Jr. (1996). Galton lecture—Behaviour genetic studies of intelligence, yesterday and today: The long journey from plausibility to proof. *Journal of Biosocial Science, 28,* 527–555.

Bouchard, T. J., Jr. (1998). Genetic and environmental influences on adult intelligence and special mental abilities. *Human Biology, 70,* 257–279.

Bouchard, T. J., Jr., & McGue, M. (1981). Familial studies of intelligence: A review. *Science, 212,* 1055–1059.

Bouchard, T. J., & Segal, N. L. (1985). Environment and IQ. In B. B. Wolman (Ed.), *Handbook of intelligence* (pp. 391–464). New York: Wiley.

Bowers, T. S., & Beck, B. D. (2006). What is the meaning of non-linear dose-response relationships between blood lead concentrations and IQ? *NeuroToxicology, 27,* 520–524.

Braun, J. M., Kahn, R. S., Froelich, T., Auinger, P., & Lanphear, B. P. (2006). Exposures to environmental toxicants and attention deficit hyperactivity disorder in U.S. children. *Environmental Health Perspectives, 114,* 1904–1909.

Brody, N. (1985). The validity of tests of intelligence. In B. B. Wolman (Ed.), *Handbook of intelligence* (pp. 353–389). New York: Wiley.

Bryant, D. M., & Maxwell, K. (1997). The effectiveness of early intervention for disadvantaged children. In M. J. Guralnick (Ed.), *The effectiveness of early intervention* (pp. 23–46). Baltimore: Paul H. Brookes.

Burks, B. S. (1928). The relative influence of nature and nurture upon mental development: A comparative study of foster parent-offspring child resemblance and true parent-true child resemblance. *Yearbook of the National Society for the Study of Education, 27,* 219–316.

Caldwell, B., & Bradley, R. (1984). *Administration manual: Home observation for measurement of the environment* (Rev. ed.). Little Rock: University of Arkansas at Little Rock.

Campbell, F. A., Pungello, E. P., Miller-Johnson, S., Burchinal, M., & Ramey, C. T. (2001). The development of cognitive and academic abilities: Growth curves from an early childhood educational experiment. *Developmental Psychology, 37,* 231–242.

Campbell, F. A., & Ramey, C. T. (1995). Cognitive and school outcomes for high-risk African American students in middle adolescence: Positive effects of early intervention. *American Educational Research Journal, 32,* 743–772.

Campbell, F. A., Ramey, C. T., Pungello, E. P., Sparling, J., & Miller-Johnson, S. (2002). Early childhood education: Young adult outcomes from the Abecedarian Project. *Applied Developmental Science, 6,* 42–57.

Canfield, R. L., Henderson, C. R., Jr., Cory-Slechta, D. A., Cox, C., Jusko, B. S., & Lanphear, B. P. (2003). Intellectual impairment in children with blood lead concentrations below 10 μg per deciliter. *New England Journal of Medicine, 348,* 1517–1526.

Carlisle, J., & Dowling, K. (2007, April). *Development of health criteria for school site risk assessment pursuant to health and safety code section 901 (g): Child-specific benchmark change in blood lead concentration for school site risk assessment.* Final Report. Sacramento: Integrated Risk Assessment Branch Office of Environmental Health Hazard Assessment California Environmental Protection Agency.

Carroll, J. B. (1968). Review of the nature of human intelligence by J. P. Guilford. *American Educational Research Journal, 73,* 105–112.

Carroll, J. B. (1993). *Human cognitive abilities: A survey of factor-analytic studies.* New York: Cambridge University Press.

Carroll, J. B. (1997). The three-stratum theory of cognitive abilities. In D. P. Flanagan, J. L. Genshaft, & P. L. Harrison (Eds.), *Contemporary intellectual assessment: Theories, tests, and issues* (pp. 122–130). New York: Guilford Press.

Cattell, J. McK. (1890). Mental tests and measurement. *Mind, 15,* 373–381.

Cattell, J. McK. (1915). Families of American men of science. *Popular Science Monthly, 86*, 504–515.

Cattell, R. B. (1941). Some theoretical issues in adult intelligence testing. *Psychological Bulletin, 38*, 592.

Cattell, R. B. (1963). Theory of fluid and crystallized intelligence: A critical experiment. *Journal of Educational Psychology, 54*, 1–22.

Cattell, R. B. (1971). *Abilities: Their structure, growth, and actions.* Boston: Houghton-Mifflin.

Centers for Disease Control and Prevention (CDC). (2002, March). *Managing elevated blood lead levels among young children: Recommendations from the Advisory Committee on Childhood Lead Poisoning Prevention.* Atlanta: Author.

Centers for Disease Control and Prevention (CDC). (2005). *Preventing lead poisoning in young children.* Atlanta: Author.

Centers for Disease Control and Prevention (CDC). (2007). *Interpreting and managing blood lead levels <10 µg/dL in children and reducing childhood exposures to lead* [56 (RR08); 1–14; 16]. Atlanta: Author.

Chen, J., & Gardner, H. (2005). Assessment based on multiple-intelligences theory. In D. P. Flanagan & P. L. Harrison (Eds.), *Contemporary intellectual assessment: Theories, tests, and issues* (2nd ed., pp. 77–102). New York: Guilford Press.

Christensen, H., Henderson, A. S., Griffiths, K., & Levings, C. (1997). Does ageing inevitably lead to declines in cognitive performance? A longitudinal study of elite academics. *Personality and Individual Differences, 23*, 67–78.

Cicchetti, D. V., Kaufman, A. S., & Sparrow, S. S. (2004a). PCB research results derive from a false belief system: You've come the wrong way, baby! *Psychology in the Schools, 41*, 715–723.

Cicchetti, D. V., Kaufman, A. S., & Sparrow, S. S. (2004b). The relationship between prenatal and postnatal exposure to polychlorinated biphenyls (PCBs) and cognitive, neuropsychological, and behavioral deficits: A critical appraisal. *Psychology in the Schools, 41*, 589–624.

Cohen, G. (1972). Hemispheric differences in a letter classification task. *Perception and Psychophysics, 11*, 139–142.

Cohen, R. J., & Swerdlik, M. E. (1999). *Psychological testing and assessment* (4th ed.). Mountain View, CA: Mayfield.

Cohen, S. A. (1971). Dyspedagogia as a cause of reading retardation: Definition and treatment. In B. Bateman (Ed.), *Learning disorders* (Vol. 4, pp. 269–291). Seattle, WA: Special Child Press.

Colom, R., Lluis-Font, J. M., Andres-Pueyo, A. (2005). The generational intelligence gains are caused by decreasing variance in the lower half of the distribution: Supporting evidence for the nutrition hypothesis. *Intelligence, 33,* 83–91.

Conley, J. J. (1984). The hierarchy of consistency: A review and model of longitudinal findings on adult individual differences in intelligence, personality and self-opinion. *Personality and Individual Differences, 5,* 11–26.

Cordes, C. (1986). Intelligence: New definition lies beyond classroom and within mind. *APA Monitor, 17*(1), 7–9.

Cronbach, L. J. (1970). *Essentials of psychological testing* (3rd ed.). New York: Harper & Row.

Cronbach, L. J. (1975). Five decades of public controversy over mental testing. *American Psychologist, 30,* 1–14.

Cruickshank, W. M., Bice, H. V., & Wallen, N. E. (1957). *Perception and cerebral palsy.* Syracuse, NY: Syracuse University Press.

Cunningham, W. R., & Owens, W. A. (1983). The Iowa State study of the adult development of intellectual abilities. In K. W. Schaie (Ed.), *Longitudinal studies of adult psychological development* (pp. 20–39). New York: Guilford Press.

Daniel, M. H. (1997). Intelligence testing: Status and trends. *American Psychologist, 52,* 1038–1045.

Dean, R. S. (1984). Functional lateralization of the brain. *Journal of Special Education, 18,* 239–256.

Deary, I. J., Whiteman, M. C., Starr, J. M., Whalley, L. J., & Fox, H. C. (2004). The impact of childhood intelligence on later life: Following up the Scottish Mental Surveys of 1932 and 1947. *Journal of Personality and Social Psychology, 86,* 130–147.

Dejerine, J. (1892). Contribution à l'étude anatomique-pathologique et clinique des différentes variétés de cécité verbale. *Comptes Rendus des Séances et Mémoires de la Société de Biologie et de Ses Filiales, 44,* 61.

Devlin, B., Daniels, M., & Roeder, K. (1997). The heritability of IQ. *Nature, 388,* 468–471.

Dickens, W. T., & Flynn, J. R. (2001). Heritability estimates versus large environmental effects: The IQ paradox resolved. *Psychological Bulletin, 108*(2), 346–369.

Dietrich, K. N., Ris, M. D., Succop, P. A., Berger, O. G., & Bornschein, R. L. (2001). Early exposure to lead and juvenile delinquency. *Neurotoxicology and Teratology, 23,* 511–518.

Doll, E. A. (1935). A genetic scale of social maturity. *American Journal of Orthopsychiatry, 5,* 180–188.

Doll, E. A. (1965). *Vineland Social Maturity Scale.* Circle Pines, MN: American Guidance Service.

Doppelt, J. E., & Wallace, W. L. (1955). Standardization of the Wechsler Adult Intelligence Scale for older persons. *Journal of Abnormal and Social Psychology, 51,* 312–330.

Dukois, P. H. (1970). *A history of psychological testing.* Boston, MA: Allyn & Bacon.

Dumont, R., Willis, J. O., & Elliott, C. D. (2009). *Essentials of DAS-II assessment.* Hoboken, NJ: Wiley.

Dumont, R. P., Willis, J. O., Farr, L. P., & McCarthy, T. (1997). Self-administered, computerized home IQ testing: There's less there than meets the eye. *NASP Communiqué, 26*(1), 28–30.

Dunn, L. (1965). *Manual for the Peabody Picture Vocabulary Test (PPVT).* Circle Pines, MN: American Guidance Service.

Dunn, L., & Dunn, L. (1981). *Manual for the Peabody Picture Vocabulary Test—Revised (PPVT-R).* Circle Pines, MN: American Guidance Service.

Ellenberger, H. F. (1970). *The discovery of the unconscious.* New York: Basic Books.

Elliott, C. D. (1990). *Differential Ability Scales (DAS).* San Antonio, TX: The Psychological Corporation.

Elliott, C. D. (2007). *Differential Ability Scales—Second Edition (DAS-II).* San Antonio, TX: The Psychological Corporation.

Elliott, R. (1987). *Litigating intelligence: IQ tests, special education, and social science in the courtroom.* Dover, MA: Auburn House Publishing.

Ernhart, C. B. (1996). Bone lead levels and delinquent behavior—To the editor. *Journal of the American Medical Association, 275,* 1726.

Ernhart, C. B., Morrow-Tlucak, M., Wolf, A. W., Super, D., & Drotar, D. (1989). Low level exposure in the prenatal and early preschool periods: Intelligence prior to school entry. *Neurotoxicology and Teratology, 11,* 161–170.

Esquirol, J. E. D. (1828). Observations pour servir à l'histoire de l'idiotie. *Les Maladies Mentales.*

Esquirol, J. E. D. (1838). *Des maladies mentales considérées sous les rapports médical, hygiénique, et médico-légal* (2 vols.). Paris: Baillière.

Esters, I. G., Ittenbach, R. F., & Han, K. (1997). Today's IQ tests: Are they really better than their historical predecessors? *School Psychology Review, 26,* 211–223.

Falconer, D. S. (1960). *Introduction to quantitative genetics.* London: Oliver and Boyd.

Federal Register. (1996, June 7). Vol. 61, No. 111.

Federal Register. (1998, June 3). Vol. 63, No. 106.

Fergusson, D. M., Horwood, L. J., Lynskey, M. T. (1997). Early dentine lead levels and educational outcomes at 18 years. *Journal of Child Psychology and Psychiatry, 38,* 471–478.

Feuerstein, R. (1979). *The dynamic assessment of retarded performers: The learning potential assessment device, theory, instruments, and techniques.* Baltimore, MD: University Park Press.

Fischbein, S. (1980). IQ and social class. *Intelligence, 4,* 51–63.

Flanagan, D. P., & Harrison, P. L. (Eds.). (2005). *Contemporary intellectual assessment: Theories, tests, and issues* (2nd ed.). New York: Guilford Press.

Flanagan, D. P., & Kaufman, A. S. (2004). *Essentials of WISC-IV assessment.* Hoboken, NJ: Wiley.

Flanagan, D. P., & Kaufman, A. S. (2009). *Essentials of WISC-IV assessment* (2nd ed.). Hoboken, NJ: Wiley.

Flanagan, D. P., Kaufman, A. S., Kaufman, N. L., & Lichtenberger, E. O. (2008). *Agora: The marketplace of ideas. Best practices: Applying response to intervention (RTI) and comprehensive assessment for the identification of specific learning disabilities.* [DVD]. (Available from NCS Pearson, Inc., PO Box 1416, Minneapolis, MN 55440 Pearson Assessments.com)

Flanagan, D. P., & McGrew, K. S., (1997). A cross-battery approach to assessing and interpreting cognitive abilities: Narrowing the gap between practice and cognitive science. In D. P. Flanagan & J. L Genshaft (Eds.), *Contemporary intellectual assessment: Theories, tests, and issues* (pp. 314–325). New York: Guilford Press.

Flanagan, D. P., McGrew, K. S., & Ortiz, S. O. (2000). *The Wechsler Intelligence Scales and Gf-Gc theory: A contemporary approach to interpretation.* Boston: Allyn & Bacon.

Flanagan, D. P., Ortiz, S. O., & Alfonso, V. C. (2007). *Essentials of cross-battery assessment* (2nd ed.). Hoboken, NJ: Wiley.

Flynn, J. R. (1984). The mean IQ of Americans: Massive gains 1932 to 1978. *Psychological Bulletin, 95,* 29–51.

Flynn, J. R. (1987). Massive IQ gains in 14 nations: What IQ tests really measure. *Psychological Bulletin, 101,* 171–191.

Flynn, J. R. (1998a). IQ gains over time: Toward finding the causes. In U. Neisser (Ed.), *The rising curve: Long-term gains in IQ and related measures* (pp. 25–66). Washington, DC: American Psychological Association.

Flynn, J. R. (1998b). Rising IQ scores: Implications for the elderly. *Australian Journal on Ageing, 17,* 106–107.

Flynn, J. R. (1998c). WAIS-III and WISC-III IQ gains in the United States from 1972 to 1995: How to compensate for obsolete norms. *Perceptual and Motor Skills, 86,* 1231–1239.

Flynn, J. R. (2006). Tethering the elephant capital cases, IQ and the Flynn Effect. *Psychology, Public Policy, and Law, 12*(2), 170–189.

Flynn, J. R. (2007). *What is intelligence?* New York: Cambridge University Press.

Friel-Patti, S., & Finitzo, T. (1990). Language learning in a prospective study of otitis media with effusion in the first two years of life. *Journal of Speech and Hearing Research, 33,* 188–194.

Galton, F. (1869). *Hereditary genius: An inquiry into its laws and consequences.* London: Macmillan.

Galton, F. (1883). *Inquiries into human faculty and its development.* London: Macmillan.

Gardner, H. (1988). Beyond the IQ: Education and human development. *National Forum, 68,* 4–7.

Gardner, H. (1993). *Multiple intelligences.* New York: Basic Books.

Garfinkle, A. S. (1982). Genetic and environmental influences on the development of Piagetian logico-mathematical concepts and other specific cognitive abilities: A twin study. *Acta Geneticae Medicae et Gemeltologiae, 31,* 10–61.

Georgas, J., Weiss, L. G., van de Vijver, F. J. R., & Saklofske, D. H. (Eds.). (2003). *Culture and children's intelligence: Cross-cultural analysis of the WISC-III.* San Diego, CA: Academic Press.

Ghiselli, E. E. (1966). *The validity of occupational aptitude tests.* New York: Wiley.

Ghiselli, E. E. (1973). The validity of aptitude tests in personnel selection. *Personnel Psychology, 26,* 461–477.

Goddard, H. H. (1908). The Binet and Simon tests of intellectual capacity, *Training School,* 3–9.

Golden, C. J. (1981). The Luria-Nebraska Children's Battery: Theory and formulation. In G. W. Hynd & J. E. Obrzut (Eds.), *Neuropsychological assessment and the school-age child: Issues and procedures.* New York: Grune & Stratton.

Goldstein, G. (1984). Brain capillaries: A target for inorganic lead poisoning. *Neurotoxicology, 5,* 167–176.

Goldstein, K. (1942). *After-effects of brain injuries in war.* New York: Grune & Stratton.

Gordon, H. W., & Bogen, J. E. (1974). Hemispheric lateralization of singing after intracarotid sodium amylobarbitone. *Journal of Neurology, Neurosurgery, and Psychiatry, 37,* 727–738.

Gray, S. W., Ramsey, B. K., & Klaus, R. A. (1982). *From 3 to 20: The Early Training Project.* Baltimore, MD: University Park Press.

Gregory, R. J. (1999). *Foundations of intellectual assessment: The WAIS-III and other tests in clinical practice.* Boston: Allyn & Bacon.

Gregory, R. J., Lehman, R. E., & Mohan, P. J. (1976). Intelligence scores for children with and without undue lead absorption. In G. Wegner (Ed.), *Shoshone lead health project* (pp. 120–150). Boise: Idaho Department of Health and Welfare.

Gregson, D. (1989, June). Program Notes, The Westgate-Mainly Mozart Festival, Under the Stars at the Old Globe, San Diego, CA, p. 24.

Gresham, F. M. (2002). Responsiveness to intervention: An alternative approach to the identification of learning disabilities. In R. Bradley, L. Danielson, & D. Hallahan (Eds.), *Identification of learning disabilities: Research to practice* (pp. 467–519). Mahwah, NJ: Erlbaum.

Gresham, F. M., Reschly, D. J., Tilly, W. D., Fletcher, J., Burns, M., Prasse, D., et al. (2004). Comprehensive evaluation of learning disabilities: The danger of perpetuating old ideas. *School Psychologist, 59*(1), 26–29.

Gresham, F. M., Restori, A. F., & Cook, C. R. (2008, September). To test or not to test: Issues pertaining to response to intervention and cognitive testing. *NASP Communiqué, 37*(1), 5–7.

Grigorenko, E. L., & Carter, A. S. (1996). Co-twin, peer and mother-child relationships and I.Q. in a Russian adolescent twin sample. *Journal of Russian and East European Psychology, 34,* 59–87.

Guilford, J. P. (1967). *The nature of human intelligence.* New York: McGraw-Hill.

Guilford, J. P. (1975). Varieties of creative giftedness, their measurement and development. *Gifted Child Quarterly,* 107–121.

Guilford, J. P. (1988). Some changes in the structure-of-intellect model. *Educational and Psychological Measurement, 48,* 1–4.

Hale, J. B., Naglieri, J. A., Kaufman, A. S., & Kavale, K. A. (2004). Specific learning disability classification in the new Individuals with Disabilities Education Act: The danger of good ideas. *School Psychologist, 58*(1), 6–13, 29.

Hammill, D. D., & Bartel, N. R. (1978). *Teaching children with learning and behavior problems* (2nd ed.). Boston: Houghton-Mifflin.

Hanson, J., Sharman, L. A., & Esparza Brown, J. (2008, October). *Pattern of strengths and weaknesses in specific learning disability evaluation: What's it all about?* Draft Technical Assistance Paper to the Oregon Department of Education. Portland, OR: Oregon School Psychologists Association Pattern of Strengths and Weaknesses Committee (#419, 25 NW 23rd Place, Suite 6, Portland, Oregon 97210–5599).

Hanson, R. A. (1975). Consistency and stability of home environmental measures related to IQ. *Child Development, 46*, 470–480.

Hatzakis, A., Kokkevi, A., Maravelias, C., Katsouyanni, K., Salaminios, F., Kalandidi, A., et al. (1989). Psychometric intelligence deficits in lead-exposed children. In M. A. Smith, L. D. Grant, & A. L. Sora (Eds.), *Lead exposure and child development* (pp. 211–223). London: Kluwer.

Hebben, N. (2001). Low lead levels and neuropsychological assessment: Let's not be mislead. *Archives of Clinical Neuropsychology, 16*, 353–357.

Hebben, N. (2009). Review of special group studies and utility of the process approach with the WISC-IV. In D. P. Flanagan and A. S. Kaufman (Authors). *Essentials of WISC-IV assessment* (2nd ed., pp. 216–242). Hoboken, NJ: Wiley.

Herrnstein, R. J., & Murray, C. (1994). *The bell curve: Intelligence and class structure in American life.* New York: Free Press.

Hinshelwood, J. (1895). Word-blindness and visual memory. *Lancet, 2*, 1564–1570.

Hinshelwood, J. (1917). *Congenital word blindness.* London: H. K. Lewis.

Honzik, M. D., Macfarlane, J. W., & Allen, E. (1948). The stability of mental test performance between two and eighteen years. *Journal of Experimental Education, 17*, 309–324.

Horgan, J. (1993, June). Eugenics revisited. *Scientific American*, 122–132.

Horn, J. L. (1965). *Fluid and crystallized intelligence: A factor analytic and developmental study of the structure among primary mental abilities.* Unpublished doctoral dissertation, University of Illinois, Urbana-Champaign.

Horn, J. L. (1968). Organization of abilities and the development of intelligence. *Psychological Review, 75*, 242–259.

Horn, J. L. (1985). Remodeling old models of intelligence. In B. B. Wolman (Ed.), *Handbook of intelligence* (pp. 267–300). New York: Wiley.

Horn, J. L. (1989). Cognitive diversity: A framework of learning. In P. L. Ackerman, R. J. Sternberg, & R. Glaser (Eds.), *Learning and individual differences* (pp. 61–116). New York: Freeman.

Horn, J. L., & Blankson, N. (2005). Foundations for better understanding of cognitive abilities. In D. P. Flanagan & P. L. Harrison (Eds.), *Contemporary intellectual assessment: Theories, tests, and issues* (2nd ed., pp. 41–68). New York: Guilford Press.

Horn, J. L., & Cattell, R. B. (1966). Refinement and test of the theory of fluid and crystallized intelligence. *Journal of Educational Psychology, 57*, 253–270.

Horn, J. L., & Cattell, R. B. (1967). Age differences in fluid and crystallized intelligence. *Acta Psychologica, 26*, 107–129.

Horn, J. L., & Donaldson, G. (1976). On the myth of intellectual decline in adulthood. *American Psychologist, 31*, 701–719.

Horn, J. L., & Donaldson, G. (1977). Faith is not enough: A response to the Baltes-Schaie claim that intelligence will not wane. *American Psychologist, 32*, 369–373.

Horn, J. L. & Knapp, J. R. (1973). On the subjective character of the empirical base of Guilford's structure of intellect model. *Psychological Bulletin, 80*, 33–43.

Horn, J. L., & Knapp, J. R. (1974). Thirty wrongs do not make a right. *Psychological Bulletin, 81*, 502–504.

Horn, J. L., & Noll, J. (1997). Human cognitive capabilities: *Gf-Gc* theory. In D. P. Flanagan, J. L. Genshaft, & P. L.Harrison (Eds.), *Contemporary intellectual assessment: Theories, tests and issues* (pp. 53–91). New York: Guilford Press.

Horn, J. M., Loehlin, J. C., & Willerman, L. (1979). Intellectual resemblance among adoptive and biological relatives: The Texas adoption project. *Behavior Genetics, 9*, 177–207.

Hull, C. L. (1928). *Aptitude testing.* Yonkers-on-Hudson, NY: World Book.

Hultsch, D. F., Hertzog, C., Small, B. J., & Dixon, R. A. (1999). Use it or lose it: Engaged lifestyle as a buffer of cognitive decline in aging? *Psychology and Aging, 14*, 245–263.

Humphreys, L. G. (1962). The organization of human abilities. *American Psychologist, 17*, 475–483.

Hunt, J. McV. (1961). *Intelligence and experience.* New York: Ronald Press.

Hunt, J. McV. (1964). Introduction. In M. Montessori (Author), *The Montessori method* (pp. xi-xxxix). New York: Schocken Books.

Hunter, J. E. (1986). Cognitive ability, cognitive aptitudes, job knowledge, and job performance. *Journal of Vocational Behavior, 29,* 340–362.

Hunter, J. E., Schmidt, F. L., & Jackson, G. B. (1982). *Meta-analysis: Cumulating research findings across studies.* Beverly Hills, CA: Sage Publications.

Inhelder, B., & Piaget, J. (1958). *The growth of logical thinking from childhood to adolescence.* New York: Basic Books.

Jacobson, J. L., & Jacobson, S. W. (1996). Intellectual impairment in children exposed to polychlorinated biphenyls *in utero. New England Journal of Medicine, 335,* 783–789.

Jensen, A. R. (1969). How much can we boost IQ and scholastic achievement? *Harvard Educational Review, 39,* 1–123.

Jensen, A. R. (1980). *Bias in mental testing.* New York: Free Press.

Jensen, A. R. (1998). *The* g *factor: The science of mental ability.* Westport, CT: Praeger.

Johnson, D. L., & Walker, T. (1991). A follow-up evaluation of the Houston Parent-Child Development Center: School performance. *Journal of Early Intervention, 15,* 226–236.

Kamin, L. (1974). *The science and politics of IQ.* Hillsdale, NJ: Erlbaum.

Kamphaus, R. W., Winsor, A. P., Rowe, E. W., & Kim, S. (2005). A history of intelligence test interpretation. In D. P. Flanagan & P. L. Harrison (Eds.), *Contemporary intellectual assessment: Theories, tests, and issues* (2nd ed., pp. 23–38). New York: Guilford Press.

Kaplan, E. (1988). A process approach to neuropsychological assessment. In T. Boll and B. K. Bryant (Eds.), *Clinical neuropsychology and brain function: Research, measurement, and practice* (pp. 125–167). Washington, DC: American Psychological Association.

Kaplan, E., Fein, D., Morris, R., Kramer, J. H., & Delis, D. C. (1991). *The WAIS-R as a neuropsychological instrument.* San Antonio, TX: The Psychological Corporation.

Kaufman, A. S. (1976). A new approach to the interpretation of test scatter on the WISC-R. *Journal of Learning Disabilities, 9,* 160–168.

Kaufman, A. S. (1978). The importance of basic concepts in the individual assessment of preschool children. *Journal of School Psychology, 16,* 207–211.

Kaufman, A. S. (1979a). Cerebral specialization and intelligence testing. *Journal of Research and Development in Education, 12,* 96–107.

Kaufman, A. S. (1979b). *Intelligent testing with the WISC-R.* New York: Wiley.

Kaufman, A. S. (1983). Intelligence: Old concepts—new perspectives. In G. Hynd (Ed.), *The school psychologist* (pp. 95–117). Syracuse, NY: Syracuse University Press.

Kaufman, A. S. (1985). Review of Woodcock-Johnson Psycho-Educational Battery. In J. Mitchell (Ed.), *Buros' ninth mental measurements yearbook* (pp. 1762-1765). Lincoln, NE: Buros Institute, University of Nebraska.

Kaufman, A. S. (1990). *Assessing adolescent and adult intelligence.* Boston: Allyn & Bacon.

Kaufman, A. S. (1994). *Intelligent testing with the WISC-III.* New York: Wiley.

Kaufman, A. S. (1997, April). Intelligence testing and the measurement of IQ. Testimony before the California Air Resources Board in relation to declaring lead a Toxic Air Contaminant (TAC), Sacramento, CA.

Kaufman, A. S. (1999). Genetics of childhood disorders: Genetics and intelligence II. *Journal of the American Academy of Child and Adolescent Psychiatry, 38,* 626–628.

Kaufman, A. S. (2000a). Seven questions about the WAIS-III regarding differences in abilities across the 16- to 89-year life span. *School Psychology Quarterly, 15,* 3–29.

Kaufman, A. S. (2000b). Tests of intelligence. In R. J. Sternberg (Ed.), *Handbook of intelligence* (pp. 445–476). New York: Cambridge University Press.

Kaufman, A. S. (2001a). Do low levels of lead produce IQ loss in children?: A careful examination of the literature. *Archives of Clinical Neuropsychology, 16,* 303–341.

Kaufman, A. S. (2001b). How dangerous are low (*not* moderate or high) doses of lead for children's intellectual development? *Archives of Clinical Neuropsychology, 16,* 403–431.

Kaufman, A. S. (2001c). WAIS-III IQs, Horn's theory, and generational changes from young adulthood to old age. *Intelligence, 29,* 131–167.

Kaufman, A. S. (2005a, April). From David Wechsler to the new IDEA guidelines: 35 years in the eye of the IQ storm. Invited Legends Address presented at the meeting of the National Association of School Psychologists, Atlanta, GA.

Kaufman, A. S. (2005b, October and November). 2005 Legends of School Psychology Address: From David Wechsler to the new IDEA guidelines: 35 years in the eye of the IQ storm. *NASP Communiqué, 34*(2), 33–35, 37; and *34*(3), 31–34.

Kaufman, A. S. (2008). Neuropsychology and specific learning disabilities: Lessons from the past as a guide to present controversies and future clinical practice. In E. Fletcher-Janzen & C. R. Reynolds (Eds.), *Neuropsychological perspectives on learning disabilities in the era of RTI: Recommendations for diagnosis and intervention* (pp. 1–13). Hoboken, NJ: Wiley.

Kaufman, A. S. (2009). In what way are apples and oranges alike? A critique of Flynn's explanation of the Flynn Effect. Manuscript in preparation.

Kaufman, A. S., & Doppelt, J. E. (1976). Analysis of WISC-R standardization data in terms of the stratification variables. *Child Development, 47*, 165–171.

Kaufman, A. S., & Horn, J. L. (1996). Age changes on tests of fluid and crystallized intelligence for women and men on the Kaufman Adolescent and Adult Intelligence Test (KAIT) at ages 17–94 years. *Archives of Clinical Neuropsychology, 11*, 97–121.

Kaufman, A. S., Johnson, C. K., & Liu, X. (2008). A CHC theory-based analysis of age differences on cognitive abilities and academic skills at ages 22 to 90 years. *Journal of Psychoeducational Assessment, 26*, 350–381.

Kaufman, A. S., Kaufman, J. C., Chen, T., & Kaufman, N. L. (1996). Differences on six Horn abilities for fourteen age groups between 15–16 and 75–94 years. *Psychological Assessment, 8*, 161–171.

Kaufman, A. S., Kaufman, J. C., Liu, X., & Johnson, C. K. (in press). How do educational attainment and gender relate to Gf, Gc, and academic skills at ages 22 to 90 years? *Archives of Clinical Neuropsychology.*

Kaufman, A. S., & Kaufman, N. L. (1977). *Clinical evaluation of young children with the McCarthy Scales.* New York: Grune & Stratton.

Kaufman, A. S., & Kaufman, N. L. (1983). *K-ABC interpretive manual.* Circle Pines, MN: American Guidance Service.

Kaufman, A. S., & Kaufman, N. L. (1990). *Kaufman Brief Intelligence Test (K-BIT) manual.* Circle Pines, MN: American Guidance Service.

Kaufman, A. S. & Kaufman, N. L. (1993). *Kaufman Adolescent and Adult Intelligence Test (KAIT)*. Circle Pines, MN: American Guidance Service.

Kaufman, A. S., & Kaufman, N. L. (Eds.). (2001). *Specific learning disabilities and difficulties in children and adolescents: Psychological assessment and evaluation.* Cambridge, England: Cambridge University Press.

Kaufman, A. S., & Kaufman, N. L. (2004a). *Kaufman Assessment Battery for Children—Second Edition (KABC-II).* Circle Pines, MN: American Guidance Service.

Kaufman, A. S., & Kaufman, N. L. (2004b). *Kaufman Brief Intelligence Test—Second Edition (KBIT-2).* Circle Pines, MN: American Guidance Service.

Kaufman, A. S., & Kaufman, N. L. (2004c). *Kaufman Test of Educational Achievement—Second Edition (KTEA-II): Comprehensive Form.* Circle Pines, MN: American Guidance Service.

Kaufman, A. S., & Kaufman, N. L. (2005). *Kaufman Test of Educational Achievement—Second Edition (KTEA-II): Brief Form.* Circle Pines, MN: American Guidance Service.

Kaufman, A. S., & Kaufman, N. L. (2007). *Kaufman—Concepts-Lexique Attention-Séquentials-Simultanés-Informatisés sur CD-Rom* (K-CLASSIC). Paris: Les Editions du Centre de Psychologie Appliqué.

Kaufman, A. S., & Lichtenberger, E. O. (1999). *Essentials of WAIS-III assessment.* New York: Wiley.

Kaufman, A. S., & Lichtenberger, E. O. (2006). *Assessing adolescent and adult intelligence* (3rd ed.). Hoboken, NJ: Wiley.

Kaufman, A. S., Lichtenberger, E. O., Fletcher-Janzen, E., & Kaufman, N. L. (2005). *Essentials of KABC-II assessment.* Hoboken, NJ: Wiley.

Kaufman, A. S., Reynolds, C. R., & McLean, J. E. (1989). Age and WAIS-R intelligence in a national sample of adults in the 20 to 74 year age range: A cross-sectional analysis with education-level controlled. *Intelligence, 13,* 235–253.

Kaufman, A. S., & Wang, J. (1992). Gender, race, and education differences on the K-BIT at ages 4 to 90 years. *Journal of Psychoeducational Assessment, 10,* 219-229.

Kaufman, J. C. (2009). *Creativity 101.* New York: Springer Publishing.

Kaufman, J. C., Chen, T., & Kaufman, A. S. (1995). Ethnic group, education, and gender differences on six Horn abilities for adolescents and adults. *Journal of Psychoeducational Assessment, 13,* 49–65.

Kaufman, J. C., Plucker, J. A., & Baer, J. (2008). *Essentials of creativity assessment.* Hoboken, NJ: Wiley.

Kausler, D. H. (1991). *Experimental psychology, cognition, and human aging.* New York: Springer-Verlag.

Kavale, K. A., Kaufman, A. S., Naglieri, J. A., & Hale, J. B. (2005). Changing procedures for identifying learning disabilities: The danger of poorly supported ideas. *School Psychologist, 59*(1), 16–25.

Kavale, K. A., Kauffman, J. M., Bachmeier, R. J., & LeFever, G. B. (2008). Response-to-intervention: Separating the rhetoric of self-congratulation from the reality of specific learning disability identification. *Learning Disabilities Quarterly, 31*, 135–150.

Keeping score. (1988, February 1). *The Sporting News, 102*, p. 2.

Keith, T. Z. (1985). Questioning the K-ABC: What does it measure? *School Psychology Review, 14*, 9–20.

Keith, T. Z., Fine, J. G., Taub, G. E., Reynolds, M. R., & Kranzler, J. H. (2006). Higher order, multisample, confirmatory factor analysis of the Wechsler Intelligence Scale for Children-Fourth Edition: What does it measure? *School Psychology Review, 35*, 108–127.

Kerr, J. (1897). School hygiene in its mental, moral and physical aspects. *Journal of the Royal Statistical Society, 60*, 613–680.

Kirk, S. A. (1963). Behavioral diagnosis and remediation of learning disabilities. In *Proceedings of the Annual Meeting of the Conference on Exploration into the Problems of the Perceptually Handicapped Child* (Chicago), *1*, 3–7.

Kirk, S. A., McCarthy, J. J., & Kirk, W. D. (1968). *Examiner's manual: Illinois Test of Psycholinguistic Abilities* (Rev. ed.). Urbana: Illinois University Press.

Klassen, R. M., & Kishor, N. (1996). A comparative analysis of practitioners' errors on WISC-R and WISC-III. *Canadian Journal of School Psychology, 12*, 35–43.

Kohs, S. C. (1923). *Intelligence measurement.* New York: Macmillan.

Kordas, K., Canfield, R. L., Lopez, P., Rosado, J. L., Garcia Vargas, G., Cebrian, M. E., et al. (2006). Deficits in cognitive function and achievement in Mexican first-graders with low blood lead concentrations. *Environmental Research, 100*, 371–386.

Kotok, D. (1972). Development of children with elevated blood levels: A controlled study. *Journal of Pediatrics, 80*, 57–61.

Kyllonen, P. C., & Cristal, R. E. (1990). Reasoning ability is (little more than) working memory capacity?! *Intelligence, 14*, 389–433.

Labouvie-Vief, G. (1985). Intelligence and cognition. In J. E. Birren & K. W. Schaie (Eds.), *Handbook of the psychology of aging* (2nd ed., pp. 500–530). New York: Van Nostrand Reinhold.

Lally, J. R., Mangione, P. L., & Honig, A. S. (1988). The Syracuse University Family Development Research Program: Long-range impact on an early intervention with low-income children and their families. In I. E. Sigel (Series Ed.) & D. R. Powell (Vol. Ed.), *Annual advances in applied developmental psychology, Vol. 3. Parent education as early childhood intervention: Emerging directions in theory, research, and practice* (pp. 79–104). Norwood, NJ: Ablex Publishing.

Lamp, R. E., & Krohn, E. J. (1990). Stability of the Stanford-Binet Fourth Edition and K-ABC for young Black and White children from low income families. *Journal of Psychoeducational Assessment, 8,* 139–149.

Landrigan, P., Balow, R., Whitworth, R., Staeling, N., & Rosenbloom, B. (1975). Neuropsychological dysfunction in children with chronic low level lead absorption. *Lancet, 1,* 708.

Lanphear, B. P., Hornung, R., Khoury, J., Yolton, K., Baghurst, P., Bellinger, D. C., et al. (2005). Low-level environmental lead exposure and children's intellectual function: An international pooled analysis. *Environmental Health Perspectives, 113,* 894–899.

Lansdown, R., Yule, W., Urbanowicz, M. A., & Hunter, J. (1986). The relationship between blood-lead concentrations, intelligence, attainment and behaviour in a school population: The second London study. *International Archives Occupational Environmental Health, 57,* 225–235.

Levy, J. (1972). Lateral specialization of the human brain: Behavioral manifestations and possible evolutionary basis. In J. A. Kiger (Ed.), *Biology of behavior.* Corvallis: Oregon State University Press.

Levy, J., & Trevarthen, C. (1976). Metacontrol of hemispheric function in human split-brain patients. *Journal of Experimental Psychology: Human Perception and Performance, 2,* 299–312.

Levy-Agresti, J., & Sperry, R. W. (1968). Differential perceptual capacities in major and minor hemispheres. *Proceedings of the National Academy of Science, U.S.A., 61,* 1151.

Lewontin, R. C., Rose, S., & Kamin, L. J. (1984). *Not in our genes: Biology, ideology, and human nature.* New York: Pantheon.

Lezak, M. D. (1988). IQ: R.I.P. *Journal of Clinical and Experimental Neuropsychology, 10,* 351–361.

Lezak, M. D. (1995). *Neuropsychological assessment* (3rd ed.). New York: Oxford University Press.

Lichtenberger, E. O., & Kaufman, A. S. (2009). *Essentials of WAIS-IV assessment.* Hoboken, NJ: Wiley.

Lidsky, T. I., & Schneider, J. S. (2006). Adverse effects of childhood lead poisoning: The clinical neuropsychological perspective. *Environmental Research, 100,* 284–293.

Loehlin, J. C., Horn, J. M., & Willerman, L. (1994). Differential inheritance of mental abilities in the Texas Adoption Project. *Intelligence, 19,* 325–336.

Loehlin, J. C., Horn, J. M., & Willerman, L. (1997). Heredity, environment, and IQ in the Texas Adoption Project. In R. J. Sternberg & E. Grigorenko (Eds.), *Intelligence, heredity, and environment* (pp. 105–125). New York: Cambridge University Press.

Lohman, D. F. (1994). Spatial ability. In R. J. Sternberg (Ed.), *Encyclopedia of human intelligence* (pp. 1000–1007). New York: Macmillan.

Luria, A. R. (1966). *Higher cortical functions in man.* New York: Basic Books.

Luria, A. R. (1970). The functional organization of the brain. *Scientific American, 222,* 66–78.

Luria, A. R. (1973). *The working brain: An introduction to neuropsychology.* London: Penguin Books.

Manly, J. J., Heaton, R. K., & Taylor, M. J. (2000, August). The effects of demographic variables and the development of demographically adjusted norms for the WAIS-III and WMS-III. In D. S. Tulsky & D. Saklofske (Chairs), *The clinical interpretation of the WAIS-III and WMS-III: New research findings.* Symposium presented at the meeting of the American Psychological Association, Washington, DC.

Marjoribanks, K. (1972). Environment, social class, and mental abilities. *Journal of Educational Psychology, 63,* 103–109.

Matarazzo, J. D. (1972). *Wechsler's measurement and appraisal of adult intelligence* (5th, enlarged ed.). New York: Oxford University Press.

Matarazzo, J. D., Carmody, T. D., & Jacobs, L. D. (1980). Test-retest reliability and stability of the WAIS: A literature review with implications for clinical practice. *Journal of Clinical Neuropsychology, 2,* 89–105.

Mather, N., & Jaffe, L. E. (2002). *Woodcock-Johnson III: Reports, recommendations, and strategies.* New York: Wiley.

Matsubara, T., Fujita, K., Maekawa, H., Ishikuma, T., Kaufman, A. S., & Kaufman, N. L. (1994). *Interpretive manual for the Japanese K-ABC.* Tokyo: Maruzen Mates.

Mayman, M., Schafer, R., & Rapaport, D. (1951). Interpretation of the WAIS in personality appraisal. In H. H. Anderson & G. L. Anderson (Eds.), *An introduction to projective techniques* (pp. 541–580). New York: Prentice Hall.

McArdle, J. J., Ferrer-Caja, E., Hamagami, F., & Woodcock, R. W. (2002). Comparative longitudinal structural analyses of the growth and decline of multiple intellectual abilities over the life span. *Developmental Psychology, 38,* 113–142.

McCall, R. B. (1977). Childhood IQ's as predictors of adult educational and occupational status. *Science, 197,* 482–483.

McCarthy, D. (1972). *Manual for the McCarthy Scales of Children's Abilities.* New York: The Psychological Corporation.

McDermott, P. A., Fantuzzo, J. W., Glutting, J. J., Watkins, M. W., & Baggaley, R. A. (1992). Illusions of meaning in the ipsative assessment of children's ability. *Journal of Special Education, 25,* 504–526.

McFarlan, D. (1989). *Guinness book of world records* (27th ed.). New York: Sterling Publishing.

McGrew, K. S. (1997). Analysis of the major intelligence batteries according to a proposed comprehensive *Gf-Gc* framework. In D. P. Flanagan, J. L. Genshaft, & P. L. Harrison (Eds.), *Contemporary intellectual assessment: Theories, tests, and issues* (pp. 151–179). New York: Guilford Press.

McGrew, K. S. (2005). The Cattell-Horn-Carroll theory of cognitive abilities: Past, present, and future. In D. P. Flanagan & P. L. Harrison (Eds.), *Contemporary intellectual assessment: Theories, tests, and issues* (2nd ed.; pp. 136–181). New York: Guilford Press.

McGrew, K. S., Woodcock, R., & Ford, L. (2006). The Woodcock-Johnson Battery, Third Edition. In A. S. Kaufman & E. O. Lichtenberger, *Assessing adolescent and adult intelligence* (3rd ed.; pp. 561–628). Hoboken, NJ: Wiley.

McGue, M., Bouchard, T. J., Jr., Iacono, W. G., & Lykken, D. T. (1993). Behavior genetics of cognitive ability: A life-span perspective. In R. Plomin & G. E. McClearn (Eds.), *Nature, nurture and psychology* (pp. 59–76). Washington, DC: American Psychological Association.

McLaughlin, A. E., Campbell, F. C., Pungello, E. P., & Skinner, M. (2007). Depressive symptoms in young adults: The influences of the early home environment and early educational childcare. *Child Development, 78,* 746–756.

McNemar, Q. (1942). *The revision of the Stanford-Binet Scale.* Boston: Houghton Mifflin.

Meeker, M. N. (1969). *The structure of intellect.* Columbus, OH: Charles E. Merrill.

Meeker, M. N. (1975). *Glossary for SOI definitions.* El Segundo, CA: SOI Institute.

Meeker, M. N., Mestyanek, L., Shadduck, R. D., & Meeker, R. (1975). *SOI Learning Abilities Test.* El Segundo, CA: SOI Institute.

Meeker, M. N., & Shadduck, R. D. (1973). *Evaluation: SOI abilities workbook.* El Segundo, CA: SOI Institute.

Melchers, P., & Preuß, U. (1991). *Kaufman-Assessment Battery for Children (K-ABC). Deutschsprachige Fassung.* Lisse, Germany: Swets & Zeitlinger.

Melchers, P., Schürmann, S., & Scholten, S. (2006). *Kaufman—Test zur Intelligenzmessung für Jugendliche und Erwachsene handbuch* [German KAIT manual]. Leiden, The Netherlands: PITS.

Mercer, J. R. (1973). *Labeling the mentally retarded.* Berkeley, CA: University of California Press.

Mercer, J. R. (1977). The struggle for children's rights: Critical juncture for school psychology. *School Psychology Digest, 6,* 4–19.

Mercer, J. R., & Lewis, J. F. (1978). *System of Multicultural Pluralistic Assessment (SOMPA).* New York: The Psychological Corporation.

Michael, W. B. (1977). Cognitive and affective components of creativity and physical sciences. In J. C. Stanley, W. C. George, & C. H. Solano (Eds.), *The gifted and the creative: A fifty-year perspective* (pp. 141–172). Baltimore: Johns Hopkins Press.

Mill, J. S. (1875). *A system of logic ratiocinative and inductive, being a connected view of the vincioles of evidence and the methods of scientific investigation* (2 vols., 9th ed.) London: Longmans, Green, Reader and Dyer.

Miller, G. A. (1962). *Psychology: The science of mental life.* New York: Harper & Row.

Miller, T. L., & Reynolds, C. R. (1984). The Kaufman Assessment Battery for Children [Special issue]. *Journal of Special Education, 18*(3).

Montessori, M. (1964). *The Montessori method.* New York: Schocken. (First published in English 1912)

Morgan, A. E., & Hynd, G. W. (1998). Dyslexia, neurolinguistic ability, and anatomical variations on the planum temporal. *Neuropsychology Review, 8,* 79–93.

Morgan, W. P. (1896). A case of congenital wordblindness. *British Medical Journal, 2,* 1378.

Mulder, J. L., Dekker, R., & Dekker, P. H. (2004). *Kaufman Intelligentietest voor Adolescenten en Volwassenen* [Dutch KAIT manual]. Leiden, The Netherlands: PITS.

Naglieri, J. A. (1999). *Essentials of CAS assessment.* New York: Wiley.

Naglieri, J. A., & Bornstein, B. T. (2003). Intelligence and achievement: Just how correlated are they? *Journal of Psychoeducational Assessment, 21*, 244–260.

Naglieri, J. A., & Das, J. P. (1997). *Cognitive Assessment System.* Itasca, IL: Riverside Publishing.

Naglieri, J. A., & Gottling, S. H. (1997). Mathematics instruction and PASS cognitive processes: An intervention study. *Journal of Learning Disabilities, 33*, 591–597.

Naglieri, J. A., & Johnson, D. (2000). Effectiveness of a cognitive strategy intervention in improving arithmetic computation based on the PASS theory. *Journal of Learning Disabilities, 30*, 513–520.

Naglieri, J. A., & Kaufman, A. S. (2008). IDEIA 2004 and specific learning disabilities: What role does intelligence play? In E. L. Grigorenko (Ed.), *Educating individuals with disabilities: IDEIA 2004 and beyond* (pp. 165–195). New York: Springer Publishing.

Nation, J. R., & Gleaves, D. H. (2001). Low level lead exposure and intelligence in children. *Archives of Clinical Neuropsychology, 16*, 375–388.

National Association of School Psychologists (NASP). (2007). *NASP position statement on identification of students with specific learning disabilities.* Bethesda, MD: Author.

Needleman, H. L. (1989). The persistent threat of lead: A singular opportunity. *American Journal of Public Health, 79*, 643–645.

Needleman, H. L., & Bellinger, D. (2001). Studies of lead exposure and the developing central nervous system: A reply to Kaufman. *Archives of Clinical Neuropsychology, 16*, 359–374.

Needleman, H. L., & Gatsonis, C. A. (1990). Low-level lead exposure and the IQ of children, meta-analysis of modern studies. *Journal of the American Medical Association, 263*, 673–678.

Needleman, H. L, Riess, J. A., Tobin, M. J., Biesecker, G. E., & Greenhouse, J. B. (1996). Bone lead levels and delinquent behavior. *Journal of the American Medical Association, 275*, 363–369.

Neisser, U. (1967). *Cognitive psychology.* New York: Appleton-Century-Crofts.

Neisser, U. (Ed.). (1998). *The rising curve: Long-term gains in IQ and related measures.* Washington, DC: American Psychological Association.

Neisser, U., Boodoo, G., Bouchard, T. J., Jr., Boykin, A. W., Brody, N., Ceci, S. J., et al. (1996). Intelligence: Knowns and unknowns. *American Psychologist, 51*, 77–101.

Nisbett, R. E. (2009). *Intelligence and how to get it: Why schools and cultures count.* New York: W. W. Norton.

Orem, R. C. (Ed.). (1966). *A Montessori handbook.* New York: Capricorn Books, G. P. Putnam's Sons.

Orton, S. T. (1937). *Reading, writing and speech problems in children.* New York: Norton.

Otis, A. S. (1919). *The Otis Group Intelligence Scale.* New York: World Book.

Otis, A. S., & Lennon, R. T. (2006). *Otis-Lennon School Ability Test* (8th ed.; OLSAT 8). San Antonio, TX: The Psychological Corporation.

Owens, W. A. (1953). Age and mental abilities: A longitudinal study. *Genetic Psychology Monographs, 48,* 3–54.

Owens, W. A. (1966). Age and mental ability: A second adult follow-up. *Journal of Educational Psychology, 57,* 311–325.

Pearson, R. (Ed.). (1992). *Shockley on eugenics and race.* Washington, DC: Scott-Townsend.

Pederson, N. E., McGlearn, C. E., & Friberg, I. (1985). Separated fraternal twins: Resemblance for cognitive authorities. *Behavior Genetics, 15,* 407–419.

Pederson, N. E., Plomin, R., Nesselroade, J. R., & McClearn, C. E. (1992). A quantitative genetic analysis of cognitive abilities during the second half of the life span. *Psychological Science, 3,* 346–353.

Phelps, L. (1999). Low-level lead exposure: Implications for research and practice. *School Psychology Review, 28,* 477–492.

Pinneau, S. R. (1961). *Changes in intelligence quotient: Infancy to maturity.* Boston: Houghton-Mifflin.

Plomin, R. (1983). Developmental behavioral genetics. *Child Development, 54,* 253–259.

Plomin, R. (1989). Environment and genes: Determinants of behavior. *American Psychologist, 43,* 105–111.

Plomin, R., & Petrill, S. A. (1997). Genetics and intelligence: What's new? *Intelligence, 24,* 53–77.

Plucker, J. A. (in press). *Intelligence 101.* New York: Springer Publishing.

Pocock, S. J., Smith, M., & Baghurst, P. (1994). Environmental lead and children's intelligence: A systematic review of the epidemiological evidence. *British Medical Journal, 309,* 1189–1197.

Prifitera, A., Saklofske, D. H., Weiss, L. G., Rolfhus, E., & Holdnack, J. A. (2005). The WISC-IV in the clinical assessment context. In

A. Prifitera, D. H. Saklofske, & L. G. Weiss (Eds.), *WISC-IV: Clinical use and interpretation* (pp. 3–32). San Diego, CA: Elsevier Science.

Psychological Corporation, The. (1997). *WAIS-III/WMS-III technical and interpretive manual.* San Antonio, TX: Author.

Psychological Corporation, The. (2002). *WPPSI-III technical and interpretive manual.* San Antonio, TX: Author.

Psychological Corporation, The. (2003). *WISC-IV technical and interpretive manual.* San Antonio, TX: Author.

Psychological Corporation, The. (2004). *WISC-IV Integrated technical and interpretive manual.* San Antonio, TX: Author.

Psychological Corporation, The. (2008). *WAIS-IV/WMS-IV technical and interpretive manual.* San Antonio, TX: Author.

Rabbitt, P. (1993). Baseline changes in cognitive performance with age. In R. Levy & R. Howard (Eds.), *Treatment and care in old age psychiatry* (pp. 11–30). Petersfield, England: Wrightson Biomedical Publishing.

Ramey, C. T., & Campbell, F. A. (1984). Preventive education for high-risk children: Cognitive consequences of the Carolina Abecedarian Project. *American Journal of Mental Deficiency, 88,* 515–523.

Rapaport, D., Gill, M., & Schafer, R. (1945–1946). *Diagnostic psychological testing* (2 vols.). Chicago: Year Book.

Raven, J., Raven, J. C., & Court, J. H. (1993). *Manual for Raven's Progressive Matrices and Vocabulary Scales* (Section 1). Oxford, England: Oxford Psychologists Press.

Raven, J. C. (1938). *Progressive Matrices.* London: H. K. Lewis.

Reitan, R. M. (1955). Certain differential effects of left and right cerebral lesions in human adults. *Journal of Comparative and Physiological Psychology, 48,* 474–477.

Reitan, R. M. (1988). Integration of neuropsychological theory, assessment, and application. *Clinical Neuropsychologist, 2,* 331–349.

Reynolds, C. R. (1987). Playing IQ roulette with the Stanford-Binet, 4th edition. *Measurement and Evaluation in Counseling and Development, 20,* 139–141.

Reynolds, C. R., Chastain, R. L., Kaufman, A. S., & McLean, J. E. (1987). Demographic characteristics and IQ among adults: Analysis of the WAIS-R standardization sample as a function of the stratification variables. *Journal of School Psychology, 25,* 323–342.

Reynolds, C. R., & Kamphaus, R. W. (2003). *Reynolds Intellectual Assessment Scales.* Lutz, FL: Psychological Assessment Resources.

Reynolds, C. R., Kamphaus, R. W., & Rosenthal, B. L. (1988). Factor analysis of the Stanford-Binet: Fourth edition for ages 2 through 23 years. *Measurement and Evaluation in Counseling and Development, 21*, 52–63.

Reynolds, C. R., & Shaywitz, S. E. (2009). Response to intervention: Prevention and remediation, perhaps. Diagnosis, no. *Child Development Perspectives, 3*(1), 44–47.

Roback, A. A. (1961). *History of psychology and psychiatry.* New York: Philosophical Library.

Rodgers, J. L. (1998). A critique of the Flynn Effect: Massive IQ gains, methodological artifacts, or both? *Intelligence, 26*, 337–356.

Rodgers, J. L., & Wanstrom, L. (2007). Identification of a Flynn Effect in the NLSY: Moving from the center to the boundaries. *Intelligence, 35*, 187–196.

Roid, G. (2003). *Stanford-Binet Intelligence Scales, Fifth Edition.* Itasca, IL: Riverside Publishing.

Rose, R. J., Uchida, I. A., & Christian, J. C. (1981). Placentation effects on cognitive resemblance of adult monozygotes. *Twin Research 3: Intelligence, Personality, and Development*, 35–41.

Roszkowski, M. J. (2001). Review of the Revised Minnesota Paper Form Board Test, Second Edition. In J. C. Impara & B. S. Plake (Eds.), *Buros' fourteenth mental measurements yearbook* (pp. 1012–1015). Lincoln: Buros Institute, University of Nebraska.

Rowe, D. C., Jacobson, K. C., & Van den Oord, E. J. C. G. (1999). Genetic and environmental influences on vocabulary IQ: Parental education level as moderator. *Child Development, 70*, 1151–1162.

Ruff, H. A. (1999). Population-based data and the development of individual children: The case of low to moderate lead levels and intelligence. *Developmental and Behavioral Pediatrics, 20*, 42–49.

Ryan, J. J., Prifitera, A., & Powers, L. (1983). Scoring reliability on the WAIS-R. *Journal of Consulting and Clinical Psychology, 51*, 149–150.

Salthouse, T. A. (1985). Speed of behavior and its implications for cognition. In J. E. Birren and K. W. Schaie (Eds.), *Handbook of the psychology of aging* (2nd ed., pp. 61–92). New York: Van Nostrand Reinhold.

Salthouse, T. A. (1996). The processing speed theory of adult age differences in cognition. *Psychological Review, 103*, 403–428.

Salthouse, T. A. (2004). Localizing age-related individual differences in a hierarchical structure. *Intelligence, 32*, 541–561.

Sattler, J. M. (2008). *Assessment of children: Cognitive foundations* (5th ed.). San Diego, CA: Jerome M. Sattler.

Scarr, S., & Carter-Saltzman, I. (1982). Genetics and intelligence. In R. J. Sternberg (Ed.), *Handbook of human intelligence* (pp. 792–896). Cambridge, England: Cambridge University Press.

Scarr, S., & Weinberg, R. A. (1976). IQ test performance of Black children adopted by White families. *American Psychologist, 31*, 726–739.

Scarr, S., & Weinberg, R. A. (1978). The influence of "family background" on intellectual attainment. *American Sociological Review, 43*, 674–692.

Schaie, K. W. (Ed.). (1983a). *Longitudinal studies of adult psychological development*. New York: Guilford Press.

Schaie, K. W. (1983b). The Seattle Longitudinal Study: A 21-year exploration of psychometric intelligence in adulthood. In K. W. Schaie (Ed.), *Longitudinal studies of adult psychological development* (pp. 64–135). New York: Guilford Press.

Schaie, K. W. (1983c). What can we learn from the longitudinal study of adult psychological development? In K. W. Schaie (Ed.), *Longitudinal studies of adult psychological development* (pp. 1–19). New York: Guilford Press.

Schaie, K. W. (1984). Midlife influences upon intellectual functioning in old age. *International Journal of Behavior Development, 7*, 463–478.

Schaie, K. W. (1996). *Intellectual development in adulthood: The Seattle Longitudinal Study*. New York: Cambridge University Press.

Schaie, K. W., & Hertzog, C. (1983). Fourteen-year cohort-sequential analyses of adult intellectual development. *Developmental Psychology, 19*, 531–543.

Schaie, K. W., & Labouvie-Vief, G. (1974). Generational vs. ontogenetic components of change in adult cognitive behavior: A fourteen-year cross-sequential study. *Developmental Psychology, 10*, 305–320.

Schaie, K. W., & Strother, C. R. (1968). The cross-sequential study of age changes in cognitive behavior. *Psychological Bulletin, 70*, 671–680.

Schmitt, C. (1921). Extreme retardation in arithmetic. *Elementary School Journal, 21*, 529–547.

Schmitz-Sherzer, R., & Thomae, H. (1983). Constancy and change of behavior in old age: Findings from the Bonn Longitudinal Study on Aging. In K. W. Schaie (Ed.), *Longitudinal studies of adult psychological development* (pp. 191–221). New York: Guilford Press.

Schwartz, J. (1994). Low level lead exposure and children's IQ: A meta-analysis and search for a threshold. *Environmental Research, 65*, 42–55.

Segal, N. L. (1997). Same-age unrelated siblings: A unique test of within-family environmental influences on IQ similarity. *Journal of Educational Psychology, 89,* 381–390.

Segal, N. L. (1999). *Entwined lives: Twins and what they tell us about human behavior.* New York: Dutton.

Segal, N. L. (2000). Virtual twins: New findings on within-family environmental influences on intelligence. *Journal of Educational Psychology, 92,* 442–448.

Seguin, E. (1866/1907). *Idiocy: Its treatment by the physiological method.* New York: Bureau of Publications, Teachers College, Columbia University. (Reprinted from original edition 1866)

Seller, H. K. (1970). Parallel and serial stages in matching. *Journal of Experimental Psychology, 84,* 213–219.

Sharp, S. E. (1898–1899). Individual psychology: A study in psychological method. *American Journal of Psychology, 10,* 329–391.

Shaywitz, S. (2003). *Overcoming dyslexia: A new and complete science-based program for reading problems at any level.* New York: Alfred A. Knopf.

Shaywitz, B. A., Shaywitz, S. E., Blachman, B. A., Pugh, K. R., Fulbright, R. K., Skudlarski, P., et al. (2004). Development of left occipitotemporal systems for skilled reading in children after a phonologically-based intervention. *Biological Psychiatry, 55,* 926–933.

Shepherd, M. J. (2001). History lessons. In A. S. Kaufman & N. L. Kaufman (Eds.), *Specific learning disabilities and difficulties in children and adolescents: Psychological assessment and evaluation* (pp. 3–28). Cambridge, England: Cambridge University Press.

Shimamura, A. P., Berry, J. M., Mangels, J. A., Rusting, C. L., & Jurica, P. J. (1995). Memory and cognitive abilities in university professors: Evidence for successful aging. *Psychological Science, 6,* 271–277.

Shockley, W. (1987). Jensen's data on Spearman's hypothesis: No artifact. *Behavioral and Brain Sciences, 10,* 512.

Siegel, L. S. (1999). Issues in the definition and diagnosis of learning disabilities: A perspective on *Guckenberger v. Boston University. Journal of Learning Disabilities, 32,* 304–319.

Siegler, I., & Botwinick, J. (1979). A long-term longitudinal study of intellectual ability of older adults: The matter of selective subject attrition. *Journal of Gerontology, 34,* 242–245.

Silverman, L. K. (2009). The measurement of giftedness. In L. Shavinina (Ed.), *The international handbook on giftedness* (pp. 957–970). Amsterdam: Springer Science.

Silverstein, A. B. (1982). Note on the constancy of the IQ. *American Journal of Mental Deficiency, 87,* 227–228.

Simkin, B. (1992). Mozart's scatological disorder. *British Medical Journal, 305,* 1563–1567.

Skeels, H. M., & Dye, H. B. (1939). A study of the effects of differential stimulation of mentally retarded children. *Proceedings of the American Association on Mental Deficiency, 44,* 114–136.

Sparrow, S. S., Balla, D. A., & Cicchetti, D. V. (1984). *Vineland Adaptive Behavior Scales.* Circle Pines, MN: American Guidance Service.

Sparrow, S. S., Balla, D. A., & Cicchetti, D. V. (2005). *Vineland Adaptive Behavior Scales—Second Edition.* Bloomington, MN: Pearson Assessments.

Spearman, C. E. (1904). "General intelligence," objectively determined and measured. *American Journal of Psychiatry, 15,* 201–293.

Spearman, C. E. (1927). *The abilities of man.* London: Macmillan.

Sperry, R. W. (1968). Hemisphere deconnection and unity in conscious awareness. *American Psychologist, 23,* 723–733.

Spitz, E., Carlier, M., Vacher-Lavenu, M., Reed, T., Moutier, R., Busnel, M., et al. (1996). Long-term effect of prenatal heterogeneity among monozygotes. *Cahiers de Psychologie Cognitive* [Current Psychology of Cognition], *15,* 283–308.

Spitz, H. H. (1986). *The raising of intelligence: A selected history of attempts to raise retarded intelligence.* Hillsdale, NJ: Erlbaum.

Spitz, H. H. (1989). Variations in Wechsler interscale IQ disparities at different levels of IQ. *Intelligence, 13,* 157–167.

Spreen, O. (2001). Learning disabilities and their neurological foundations, theories, and subtypes. In A. S. Kaufman & N. L. Kaufman (Eds.), *Specific learning disabilities and difficulties in children and adolescents: Psychological assessment and evaluation* (pp. 283–308). Cambridge, England: Cambridge University Press.

Stanovich, K. E. (1991). Discrepancy definitions of reading disability: Has intelligence led us astray? *Reading Research Quarterly, 26,* 7–29.

Stern, W. (1914). *The psychological method of measuring intelligence.* Baltimore: Warwick & York.

Sternberg, R. J. (1984). Evaluation of the Kaufman Assessment Battery for Children from an information-processing perspective. *Journal of Special Education, 18,* 269–279.

Sternberg, R. J. (1988a). Beyond IQ testing. *National Forum, 68,* 8–11.

Sternberg, R. J. (1988b). *The triarchic mind: A new theory of human intelligence.* New York: Viking.

Sternberg, R. J. (1999). The theory of successful intelligence. *Review of General Psychology, 3,* 292–316.

Sternberg, R. J., Kaufman, J. C., & Grigorenko, E. L. (2008). *Applied intelligence.* New York: Cambridge University Press.

Storandt, M. (1977). Age, ability level, and method of administering and scoring the WAIS. *Journal of Gerontology, 32,* 175–178.

Strauss, A. A., & Kephart, N. C. (1955). *Psychopathology and education of the brain-injured child.* New York: Grune & Stratton.

Strauss, A. A., & Lehtinen, L. E. (1947). *Psychopathology and education of the brain-injured child: Vol. 2. Progress in theory and clinic.* New York: Grune & Stratton.

Strauss, A. A., & Werner, H. (1943). Comparative psychopathology of the brain-injured child and the traumatic brain-injured adult. *American Journal of Psychiatry, 99,* 835–838.

Tambs, K., Sundet, J. M., & Magnus, D. (1984). Heritability analysis of the WAIS subtests: A study of twins. *Intelligence, 8,* 283–293.

Tanner, J. M. (1962). *Growth at adolescence* (2nd ed.). Oxford, England: Blackwell Press.

Teasdale, T. W., & Owen, D. R. (1989). Continuing secular increases in intelligence and a stable prevalence of high intelligence levels. *Intelligence, 13,* 255–262.

Teasdale, T. W., & Owen, D. R. (2005). A long-term rise and recent decline in intelligence test performance: The Flynn Effect in reverse. *Personality & Individual Differences, 39,* 837–843.

Teasdale, T. W., & Owen, D. R. (2008). Secular declines in cognitive test scores: A reversal of the Flynn Effect. *Intelligence, 36,* 121–126.

Teele, D. W., Klein, J. O., Chase, C., Menyuk, P., & Rosner, B. A. (1990). Otitis media in infancy and intellectual ability, school achievement, speech, and language at age 7 years. *The Journal of Infectious Diseases, 162,* 685–694.

Teele, D. W., Klein, J. O., & Rosner, B. A. (1984). Otitis media with effusion during the first three years of life and development of speech and language. *Pediatrics, 74,* 282–287.

Terman, L. M. (1916). *The measurement of intelligence.* Boston, MA: Houghton-Mifflin.

Terman, L. M., & Childs, H. G. (1912). A tentative revision and extension of the Binet-Simon Measuring Scale of Intelligence. *Journal of Educational Psychology, 3,* 61–74, 133–143, 198–208, 277–289.

Terman, L. M., & Merrill, M. A. (1937). *Measuring intelligence: A guide to the administration of the new revised Stanford-Binet Tests of Intelligence.* Boston: Houghton Mifflin.

Terman, L. M., & Merrill, M. A. (1960). *Stanford-Binet Intelligence Scale: Manual, Form L-M.* Boston: Houghton Mifflin.

Terman, L. M., & Merrill, M. A. (1973). *Stanford-Binet Intelligence Scale: 1972 Norms Edition.* Boston: Houghton Mifflin.

Thorndike, R. L. (1963). Some methodological issues in the study of creativity. In *Proceedings of the 1962 invitational conference on testing problems.* Princeton, NJ: Educational Testing Service.

Thorndike, R. L., Hagen, E. P. & Sattler, J. M. (1986). *Stanford-Binet Intelligence Scale: Fourth Edition.* Chicago: Riverside.

Thurstone, L. L. (1938). Primary mental abilities. *Psychometric Monographs* (1).

Thurstone, L. L., & Thurstone, T. G. (1949). *Examiner's manual for the SRA Primary Mental Abilities Test.* Chicago: Science Research Associates.

Torgesen, J. K. (1998). Learning disabilities: An historical and conceptual overview. In B. Wong (Ed.), *Learning about learning disabilities* (2nd ed., pp. 3–34). San Diego, CA: Academic Press.

Torrance, E. P. (1962). *Guiding creative talent.* Englewood Cliffs, NJ: Prentice-Hall.

Torrance, E. P. (1974). *The Torrance Tests of Creative Thinking: Norms—technical manual.* Bensenville, IL: Scholastic Testing Service.

Torrance, E. P. (2008). *The Torrance Tests of Creative Thinking: Norms—technical manual, figural (streamlined) Forms A and B.* Bensenville, IL: Scholastic Testing Service.

Tuddenham, R. (1948). Soldier intelligence in World Wars I and II. *American Psychologist, 5,* 54–56.

Updike, C., & Thornburg, J. D. (1992). Reading skills and auditory processing ability in children with chronic otitis media in early childhood. *Annals of Otology, Rhinology, and Laryngology, 101,* 530–537.

U.S. Department of Education, Office of Special Education and Rehabilitative Services (OSERS). (2006, August). *Twenty-sixth annual report to Congress on the implementation of the Individuals with Disabilities Education Act.* Washington, DC: Author.

Vandenberg, S. G., & Vogler, C. P. (1985). Genetic determinants of intelligence. In B. B. Wolman (Ed.), *Handbook of intelligence* (pp. 3–57). New York: Wiley.

Verhaeghen, P., & Salthouse, T. A. (1997). Meta-analyses of age-cognition relations in adulthood: Estimates of linear and nonlinear age effects and structural models. *Psychological Bulletin, 122,* 231–249.

Vernon, P. E. (1979). *Intelligence: Heredity and environment.* San Francisco: Freeman.

Voyazopolous, R. (Ed.). (1994). *K-ABC: Pratique et fondements théoriques.* Paris: La Pensée sauvage.

Vreugdenhil, H. J. I., Lanting, C. I., Mulder, P. G. H., Boersma, E. R., & Weisglas-Kuperus, N. (2002). Effects of prenatal PCB and dioxin exposure on cognitive and motor abilities in Dutch children at school age. *Journal of Pediatrics, 140,* 48–56.

Wainer, H. (1990). *Computerized adaptive testing: A primer.* Hillsdale, NJ: Erlbaum.

Wallace, A., Wallechinsky, D., & Wallace, I. (1983). *The book of lists #3.* New York: Bantam Books.

Wasserman, G. A., & Factor-Litvak, P. (2001). Methodology, inference and causation: Environmental lead exposure and childhood intelligence. *Archives of Clinical Neuropsychology, 16,* 343–351.

Watkins, M. W., & Canivez, G. (2004). Temporal stability of WISC-III subtest composite strengths and weaknesses. *Psychological Assessment, 16,* 133–138.

Wechsler, D. (1939). *Measurement of adult intelligence.* Baltimore: Williams & Wilkins.

Wechsler, D. (1949). *Manual for the Wechsler Intelligence Scale for Children (WISC).* New York: The Psychological Corporation.

Wechsler, D. (1950). Cognitive, conative and non-intellective intelligence. *American Psychologist, 5,* 78–83.

Wechsler, D. (1955). *Manual for the Wechsler Adult Intelligence Scale (WAIS).* San Antonio, TX: The Psychological Corporation.

Wechsler, D. (1958). *Measurement and appraisal of adult intelligence* (4th ed.). Baltimore, MD: Williams & Wilkins.

Wechsler, D. (1967). *Manual for the Wechsler Preschool and Primary Scale of Intelligence (WPPSI).* New York: The Psychological Corporation.

Wechsler, D. (1974). *Manual for the Wechsler Intelligence Scale for Children—Revised (WISC-R).* New York: The Psychological Corporation.

Wechsler, D. (1975). Intelligence defined and undefined: A relativistic approach. *American Psychologist, 30,* 135–139.

Wechsler, D. (1981). *Manual for the Wechsler Adult Intelligence Scale—Revised (WAIS-R).* San Antonio, TX: The Psychological Corporation.

Wechsler, D. (1989). *Manual for the Wechsler Preschool and Primary Scale of Intelligence—Revised (WPPSI-R)*. San Antonio, TX: Psychological Corporation.

Wechsler, D. (1991). *Manual for the Wechsler Intelligence Scale for Children—Third Edition (WISC-III)*. San Antonio, TX: The Psychological Corporation.

Wechsler, D. (1997). *Manual for the Wechsler Adult Intelligence Scale—Third Edition (WAIS-III)*. San Antonio, TX: The Psychological Corporation.

Wechsler, D. (2003). *Wechsler Intelligence Scale for Children—Fourth Edition (WISC-IV)*. San Antonio, TX: The Psychological Corporation.

Wechsler, D. (2005). *Wechsler Intelligence Scale for Children: Fourth edition—Spanish*. San Antonio, TX: Harcourt Assessment.

Wechsler, D. (2008). *Wechsler Adult Intelligence Scale—Fourth Edition (WAIS-IV)*. San Antonio, TX: The Psychological Corporation.

Weinberg, R. A. (1989). Intelligence and IQ: Landmark issues and great debates. *American Psychologist, 43*, 98–104.

Weiss, L. G., Harris, J. G., Prifitera, A., Courville, T., Rolfhus, E., Saklofske, D. H., et al. (2006). WISC-IV interpretation in societal context. In L. G. Weiss, D. H. Saklofske, A. Prifitera, & J. A. Holdnack (Eds.), *WISC-IV: Advanced clinical interpretation* (pp. 1–57). San Diego, CA: Elsevier Science.

Wesman, A. G. (1968). Intelligent testing. *American Psychologist, 23*, 267–274.

Williams, R. L. (1974a). From dehumanization to Black intellectual genocide: A rejoinder. In G. J. Williams and S. Gordon (Eds.), *Clinical child psychology* (pp. 320–323). New York: Behavioral Publications.

Williams, R. L. (1974b). Scientific racism and IQ: The silent mugging of the Black community. *Psychology Today, 7*, 32ff.

Willis, J. O., & Dumont, R. (2006). And never the twain shall meet: Can response to intervention and cognitive assessment be reconciled? *Psychology in the Schools, 43*, 901–908.

Winneke, G., Brockhaus, A., Ewers, U., Kramer, U., & Neuf, M. (1990). Results from the European multicenter study on lead neurotoxicity in children: Implications for risk assessment. *Neurotoxicology and Teratology, 12*, 553–559.

Wissler, C. (1901). The correlation of mental and physical tests [Monograph supplement]. *Psychological Review, 3*.

Witt, J. C., & Gresham, F. M. (1985). Review of the Wechsler Intelligence Scale for Children—Revised. In J. Mitchell (Ed.), *Buros' ninth mental measurements yearbook* (pp. 1716-1719). Lincoln: Buros Institute, University of Nebraska.

Wolf, R. (1966). The measurement of environments. In A. Anastasi (Ed.), *Testing problems in perspective* (pp. 491–503). Washington, DC: American Council on Education.

Woodcock, R. W. (1978). *Development and standardization of the Woodcock-Johnson Psycho-Educational Battery.* Allen, TX: DLM/Teaching Resources.

Woodcock, R. W. (1990). Theoretical foundations of the WJ-R measures of cognitive ability. *Journal of Psychoeducational Assessment, 8,* 231–258.

Woodcock, R. W., & Johnson, M. B. (1977). *Woodcock-Johnson Psychoeducational Battery.* Itasca, IL: Riverside.

Woodcock, R. W., & Johnson, M. B. (1989). *Woodcock-Johnson Psychoeducational Battery, Revised Edition.* Itasca, IL: Riverside.

Woodcock, R. W., McGrew, K. S., & Mather, N. (2001). *Woodcock-Johnson III.* Itasca, IL: Riverside.

Yang, J., Zhu, J., & Pinon, M. (2006, August). Comparison of the Bayley-III and Bayley-II. Paper presented at the 114th annual convention of the American Psychological Association, New Orleans.

Yoakum, C. S., & Yerkes, R. M. (Eds.). (1920). *Army mental tests.* New York: Henry Holt.

Zhou, X. & Zhu, J. (2007, August). Peeking inside the "blackbox" of Flynn Effect: Evidence from three Wechsler instruments. Paper presented at the 115th annual convention of the American Psychological Association, San Francisco, CA.

Zimmerman, I. L., & Woo-Sam, J. M. (1973). *Clinical interpretation of the Wechsler Adult Intelligence Scale.* New York: Grune & Stratton.

Zimprich, D., & Martin, M. (2002). Can longitudinal changes in processing speed explain longitudinal age changes in fluid intelligence? *Psychology and Aging, 17,* 690–695.

Index

INDEX

Creativity 101
James C. Kaufman, PhD

Genius 101
Dean Keith Simonton, PhD

IQ Testing 101
Alan S. Kaufman, PhD

Leadership 101
Michael D. Mumford, PhD

Psycholinguistics 101
H. Wind Cowles, PhD

Intelligence 101
Jonathan Plucker, PhD

Anxiety 101
Moshe Zeidner, PhD
Gerald Matthews, PhD